More Praise for Galloway's Book on Running:

"I don't just endorse these thoughts and this book with my words. Jeff Galloway has led me to replot my own running course along the same lines as his. That's the highest compliment one running writer can pay another."

–Joe Henderson
West Coast Editor, *Runner's World*

"If there were a literary Olympics, Galloway's book would take the gold in the distance events – running away."

–Fred Hatfield
Editor-in-Chief
Sports Fitness Magazine

"Jeff Galloway is as dedicated a person as ever graced the running scene . . . . I'm sure this book will be of immense value to runners of all ages and both sexes, whether they are serious competitive runners, or in the sport for the fun and good health derived."

–Arthur Lydiard
Coach of New Zealand's Olympic running champions in 1960

"Galloway doesn't preach. He doesn't say this is the only way. He makes recommendations and gives you the facts to support the recommendations, enough facts to find your own way if that's more to your liking. In short, Galloway's book seems to be everything a running book ought to be."

–Eric Olsen
Women's Sports and Fitness Magazine

"Just when you thought that everything had been written about the simple act of running, along comes Jeff Galloway."

—**Bob Cooper**
City Sports Magazine

"Jeff Galloway has made an Olympic contribution to fitness and running with his new book . . . "

—**Bill Bowerman**
1972 USA Olympic Track Coach,
Coach Emeritus,
University of Oregon

"I am stimulated by everything Jeff Galloway writes about running. He understands the mind and heart of the runner . . ."

—**Richard G. Lugar**
United States Senator, Indiana

"Jeff Galloway, one of the authentic pioneers of the modern running movement, has given us a wise and welcome addition to the sport's literature."

—**James F. Fixx**
Author of *The Complete Book of Running*

"Jeff Galloway's experience as a nationally ranked distance runner and years of promoting running at all levels makes him the best possible source for the wealth of information contained in this book."

—**David L. Costill, Ph.D.**
Author of *A Scientific Approach to Distance Running*

GALLOWAY'S BOOK ON RUNNING

New and Revised

by Jeff Galloway

Illustrated by
Richard Golueke
Edna Indritz
David Wills

Shelter Publications, Inc.
Bolinas, California, USA

Distributed in the United States by Random House and in Canada by Random House of Canada Ltd.

Library of Congress Cataloging in Publication Data

Galloway, Jeff, 1945-
Galloway's Book on Running.

Bibliography: p.
Includes index.
1. Running. 2. Running-Training. I. Title.
GV1061. G34 1984 796.4'26 84-5585
ISBN 0-936070-03-X
ISBN 0-394-72709-6 (Random House)

We are grateful to the following publishers for permission to reprint portions of previously published material:

Runner's World for portions of the article *Road Racing in America* by Jeff Galloway that appeared in October, 1982, December, 1982 and March, 1983.

TAFNEWS PRESS for portions of *Computerized Running Training Programs* by James B. Gardner and J. Gerry Purdy. Copyright 1970 by TAFNEWS PRESS.

First printing: August, 1984
10 9
Printed in the United States of America

Shelter Publications, Inc.
P.O. Box 279
Bolinas, California 94924 USA

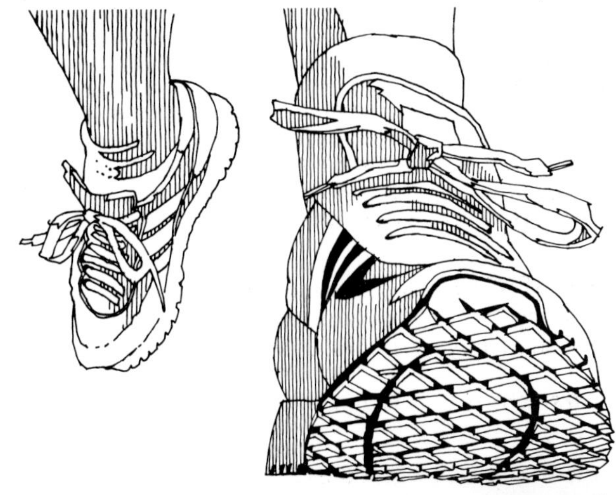

CONTENTS

STARTING

***STARTING** the right way is important. Here is a new type of running program, whether you are a brand new runner, or starting over. The five stages in the evolution of a runner—with the different physical and psychological characteristics of each stage and a simple program for getting started.*

1. *THE RUNNING REVOLUTION* 14

Running in New Zealand, 16
Jogging in America, 17
Aerobics for Fitness, 19
The Final Push by Runners, 20

2. *THE FIVE STAGES OF A RUNNER* 22
The Running Journey

The Beginner, 24
The Jogger, 25
The Competitor, 26
The Athlete, 28
The Runner, 30

3. *GETTING STARTED* 32

Monitor Your Pulse Rate, 33
Five Steps to Getting Started, 34

TRAINING

***TRAINING** is the heart of a sound running program. How the body works in relation to running, running "injury-free," why you should plan your running program in advance, the value of a runner's log and the concept of a training pyramid.*

4. *PHYSIOLOGY* 38
What Happens Inside When You Run

The Most Important Training Principle, 39
Aerobic/Anaerobic Exercise, 42
A Physiological Look at "The Wall," 44
Blood Chemistry, 47
Fast Twitch/Slow Twitch Muscles, 48

5. *PLANNING* 50
Where to Start

Running Slow in Order to Run Fast, 52
The Training Pyramid, 53
Base Training, 55
Hill Training, 57
Speed Training, 58

6. *YOUR RUNNING LOG* 60

Plan For Your Goal, 62
Monitor Your Morning Pulse and Weight, 65

7. *DAILY & WEEKLY MILEAGE PROGRAMS* 66
The Importance of Rest

Getting Stronger, 68
The Cause of Most Running Injuries, 68
Stress & Rest, 70
The Easy Day Rule, 72
Rest After Races, 72
The Easy Week Rule, 74
Cold Weather, 76
Hot Weather, 77

***RACING** gives you something to aim for. Speedwork, including interval training and "fartlek," how to judge your pace, and the art of racing 10K's or marathons. A special training program for running (and finishing) a marathon and racing tips for advanced competitors.*

8. ***SPEED*** 82
Top of the Pyramid

You Can Run Faster! 82
Fartlek, 84
Interval Training, 86
Warmup for Speedwork, 87
Most Frequent Cause of Speed Injuries, 90

9. ***PACING*** 92

Race Pace, 93
Adjusting Race Pace for Heat, 95

10. ***THE ART OF RACING*** 96
10K to Half Marathon

Riding the Peak, 99
Eating & Drinking Before the Race, 100
Hurting, 103
Tapping the Source, 104
The Countdown, 106
10K Training Charts, 108-114

11. ***RUNNING THE MARATHON*** 116
On as Little as 3 Miles a Day

A New Look at "The Wall," 118
Running Your First Marathon, 119
Improving Your Marathon Performance, 121
Recovery After the Marathon, 122
Marathon Training Charts, 123-131

12. ***THE ADVANCED COMPETITIVE RUNNER*** 132

Workouts, 133
Common Mistakes, 134
Weekly Hill Workouts, 135
Two Weekly Speed Sessions, 136
Advanced Fartlek, 136
Advanced Interval Training, 137
Barefoot Running, 138
Racing Strategy, 140
The Kick, 141
Bursting, 142

TUNING

complements a sound running program: form work, stretching and strengthening, running exercises and drills, and using will power to run faster. There is also a chapter on women's running, with emphasis on running during and after pregnancy.

13. FORM — 146
How to Run Stronger & Better

Erect Posture, 149
Armswing Tips, 150
Shorter Stride = Faster Running, 151
The CHP Rule, 152
Form Accelerations, 154
Running Form for Hills, 155

14. STRETCHING & STRENGTHENING — 158
Relaxing & Balancing

How Runners Should Stretch, 161
Three Runners' Stretches, 162
Strengthening Exercises, 166

15. RUNNING EXERCISES & DRILLS — 170
How to Strengthen & Improve Form

Knee Lifters, 172
Kick Outs, 173
Hill Springs, 174
Bounding, 175

16. WILL POWER — 176

17. WOMEN'S RUNNING — 182
By Barbara Galloway

Structural Differences in Women, 184
Menstrual Irregularities, 186
Running With a Passenger, 189
Getting Back in Shape After the Baby, 193

INJURIES

can be treated so as to speed recovery and get back on the roads soon. What to do right after an injury—before you see a doctor—and alternative exercises to stay in aerobic condition when you can't run. There are recommended lay-off times, starting-back workout routines and details on the four major runner's injuries: knees, Achilles tendons, heels and shins.

18. THE WALKING WOUNDED — 198

When Is It an Injury? 199
Before You See the Doctor, 200
Exercises to Do While Recovering, 202
If You Can't Exercise at All, 204
Getting Back on the Road, 206
What Went Wrong, 207

19. INJURY ANALYSIS & TREATMENT — 208

Knee Problems, 211
Achilles Tendon Problems, 216
Plantar Fascia & Other Heel Problems, 219
Shin Problems, 222

FOOD

is the runner's fuel. Since runners need and burn more energy than sedentary people, good nutrition and appropriate foods are important components of an endurance running program. Principles of eating for best performance, food and water tips for racing, and why running is such a good activity for shedding excess fat.

20. NUTRITION 228

Protein, 230
Fat, 231
Carbohydrates, 232

21. FUEL 236
Eating for Performance

Carbo Loading, 236
Fluids, 237
Pre-race Dietary Countdown, 239

22. RUNNING OFF FAT 240

Set Point, 241
Lose Fat, Not (Necessarily) Weight, 242
The 40-Minute Goal, 243
Coffee & Heavy Hands, 244

SHOES

are obviously the single most important part of a runner's gear. To choose the right ones, you must determine if your foot is "rigid" or "floppy", straight or curved. A shoe selection checklist for shoe shopping, advice on shoes appropriate for specific injuries, and different lacing techniques.

23. SHOE SECRETS 248

Breakfast at Bowermans, 249
The Rigid Foot, 251
The Floppy Foot, 252

24. SHOE SHOPPING 256

Shoe Selection Checklist, 258
Injuries That Influence Shoe Choice, 259

START TO FINISH

is a section on younger and older runners. Should kids run? Running programs for ages 5 to 18. What happens after 40? How increased concentration can get the over-40 runner into trouble and the value of running every other day.

25. SHOULD KIDS RUN? 262

26. RUNNING AFTER 40 264

APPENDIX

Predicting Your Race Performance, 271
Race Pace Chart, 274
Selected Reading List, 276
About the Author, 280
References, 282
Index, 283
Credits, 286

INTRODUCTION

IT WAS 1973. A beautiful September dawn was breaking over the Oregon Cascades as I headed east, racing through the early morning mist in an old Volvo sedan. My reliable car cruised along in fourth, but my mind shifted into neutral: it was time for reflection. What had I been doing for the past seven years?

I guess I was the running equivalent of a ski bum, working for college degrees in history and social studies during the school year, and following the racing circuit each summer. I'd had some wonderful times those summers–rich and varied experiences. I'd made lots of friends, shared the joys and agonies of racing with other competitors, traveled abroad and seen practically every state in the union.

One summer I'd been to Russia as a member of the U.S. National Track and Field team. At a track meet in Minsk, a crowd of 50,000 cheered only for their countrymen; victorious Americans were met with stony silence. No Holiday Inns awaited us in Dakar; we stayed in grass huts. Temperatures in this town on the west coast of Africa were so high that officials handed us water-filled sponges as we ran. In Morocco we ran a cross-country race on a horse track with a detour in the middle through a mud hole.

Another summer I bought a Eurail pass and traveled from one end of Europe to the other. I once ran an afternoon race in Luxembourg, then caught the midnight train to Torino, Italy, for a race the next day. Oh, for the resiliency of youth!

In 1972 I'd realized my life's dream: making the U.S. Olympic team. I'd also set an American record in the 10-mile. I felt happy about these achievements. But that was then. Now, though, rolling across Oklahoma, I realized I had to begin thinking about the future. I'd finished graduate school and had my teaching credentials, but after one year of teaching fourth grade in Raleigh, North Carolina, I missed the excitement of traveling and running. Yet I knew I couldn't keep driving around the country in an old car forever.

By the time I got to Nashville, I knew what I was going to do. With my eyes fixed on the road and a cup of coffee in hand, I dreamed of a running store stocked with the best gear, staffed by runners trained in the science of fitting shoes. Then I imagined a summer camp in the mountains where people could vacation and run with some of the world's best coaches. I could still be a teacher, I decided, but not one who would sit in front of a row of desks.

The idea seemed timely, for something new seemed to be

happening with running. New faces were starting to appear on the roads. The serious and often eccentric competitors were still out there of course, but now people of all ages, shapes and abilities seemed to be trickling out into the streets, sidewalks and parks. The vitality of regular endurance running was not only personally addictive, but socially contagious.

There was also a growing sense of communication among runners. People compared notes and traded tips. Runners began asking me questions and I enjoyed trying to work out creative solutions to their problems. It seemed that what I'd learned on the racing circuit could be helpful and instructive to everyday runners.

After arriving home, I found a store with the cheapest rent in Tallahassee—$125 a month. It was hardly in a prime location: a suburban neighborhood next to a beauty parlor, with no walk-by traffic. I withdrew my life's savings of $4000, borrowed $2000 from my grandmother and started learning the rudiments of running a retail business. At first we had no credit rating and very few equipment or clothing manufacturers would sell to us. The only shoe suppliers that would set up accounts for us were a warehouse operation with leftover Converse high-tops and a brand new unknown company called Nike. Since no one knew the store was there, and no one walked by, I printed up flyers and handed them out to students as I ran through nearby college campuses. Somehow we survived these growing pains, and after a year and a half, moved to Atlanta.

By 1976 the running boom was on, and business started picking up. By 1978 we were firmly established. There are now over 35 Phidippides stores nationwide and Vacation Fitness camps are in full swing. I've been able to make a career out of running—the dream has become a reality.

Business has its rewards, but it's the teaching that brings me the most satisfaction. I'm now back on the road (about a third of the time), conducting clinics and seminars, talking to beginners and veterans, to large groups and small.

This book was put together from hundreds of these experiences. I've learned firsthand about the problems of everyday runners, and the patterns of stress and rest that improve fitness while minimizing injury or fatigue.

There's much more to running than competition. Although a good deal of what follows will help runners go faster, the same principles—mileage programs, a running log, good form, hill training, stretching, strength exercises—apply to runners of all levels and with varying objectives. You may be just starting to run. If so, this book will help get you started comfortably and with confidence. If you've been running for a while, you'll learn how to make running more enjoyable, to better prepare for races and to avoid stress-related injuries. Veteran competitors will find new ideas on racing strategy and improving future performance. Whatever your level or goals, you want to run intelligently, stay healthy and strong, keep your weight down, run with good form, avoid injuries and have fun.

There's a great deal of information in this book, but only one message: *You can do it!* We find ourselves on this earth with a generous supply of hopes, abilities and expectations. Many people live out their lives without discovering how to rise above obstacles and enjoy the immense satisfaction and exhilaration of improving. With determination, patience and persistence, you can mold yourself into a runner and, in the process, have a more healthy and productive life.

STARTING

1 THE RUNNING REVOLUTION

RUNNING IS NOTHING NEW. The ancient Greeks had foot races at least as early as 776 B.C., the year of the first Olympics. The famous runner Phidippides, in 490 B.C., covered 300 miles in four days to solicit help from neighboring Sparta against the imminent invasion of Athens. In pre-industrial England, *footmen* were sent running ahead of horse-drawn carriages to warn their lords of danger. To this day, the Tarahumara Indians of northwestern Mexico compete in foot races and cover 150-200 miles a day—kicking a ball along the way. Running as a sport has existed for centuries, from informal tests

159
556
37

of ego and will, to high school track meets, to the Olympic games, but only recently have people from all walks of life taken to the roads en masse.

The reasons for running are diverse: to lose weight, become fit, feel good, reduce stress, compete, or share the experience with others. It may also have something to do with the advanced state of technology. Most work formerly done by hand is now done by machines. While our distant ancestors led physically active lives, covering long distances to gather roots, nuts and grains or to pursue game; while our grandparents or great-grandparents tilled the fields for food and handcrafted everyday necessities, we now find ourselves in a largely sedentary economy.

In increasing numbers, people are seeking to regain the health, fitness and leanness that was once natural to our physically active predecessors. A new spirit seems to have arisen. Perhaps when a society attains a high level of industrial and technological efficiency, those people who have long neglected their physical nature react and begin seeking ways to reestablish harmony between body, mind and spirit.

I was running before it caught on in America. Then in the late '60s I began to see a trickle of other runners out on the roads I once ran alone. By the early '70s, there were more and now, millions are out running regularly. It seemed to have been a natural evolution, but in retrospect I can pinpoint a few key people who helped propel running into the revolution we now see in our towns and cities: three teachers—Arthur Lydiard, Bill Bowerman and Dr. Kenneth Cooper; and three runners—Amby Burfoot, Frank Shorter and Bill Rodgers. There were many others of course, but these six were catalysts, reflecting and magnifying the spirit of the times. They were at the right places, at the right time, with the right inspiration for the new outlook that was crucial to the birth of fitness running.

Running in New Zealand. In the 1940s, Arthur Lydiard, a former rugby player, now overweight and working on the line at a New Zealand shoe factory, decided he had to make a change in his own life. Playing rugby weekends had done nothing to deflate the spare tire around his middle, so he decided he'd try to run off the excess weight. But watching the local runners of the day was discouraging. They sped around and around the track at full speed until they collapsed. "No pain, no gain" was the philosophy of the day.

Arthur wanted to get in shape, but not that way. Instead, he took to the open New Zealand roads and embarked on a conditioning program of long, slow runs. Over the months he lost weight. Over the years he became addicted to running and discovered a long-hidden competitive spirit. He began to wonder how he might fare in a marathon and soon Lydiard the jogger became Lydiard the racer. He eventually came to represent New Zealand in the 1951 Commonwealth Games.

A few local youngsters had begun running with Lydiard and eventually they asked if he'd be their coach. Lydiard agreed and developed his own program, emphasizing long slow runs, into a sequence of running workouts for his students. In the 1960 Rome Olympics, three of these neighborhood kids–Peter Snell, Murray Halberg and Barry Magee–won distance running medals. Lydiard became an acclaimed public figure and a national hero.

You might say Lydiard invented jogging. After the Olympics, he was frequently invited to speak to groups of sedentary men and women in their 30s, 40s and beyond. The people he talked to began to sense that they, like the formerly overweight rugby player, could run gently and improve their physical condition. Running not only could take off the weight, but could be fun. Lydiard transformed the public's image of running from an intense, tedious, painful activity into a social, civilized component of the active New Zealand lifestyle. The credibility of the Olympic medals gave Lydiard a platform from which to reach millions. He got them out of their chairs and onto the roads in the early '60s, and the underground running movement began.

Jogging in America. Bill Bowerman is one of the most successful track coaches in the United States, but his role in bringing jogging to America is of even greater importance. In the winter of 1962, shortly after his University of Oregon four-mile relay team broke the world record, an invitation came for a match race with the team from New

Zealand, the previous world recordholders. Bowerman and his team were the guests of Arthur Lydiard.

"The first Sunday I was down there," Bowerman recalled in Bill Dellenger's book, *The Running Experience,* "Lydiard asked me if I wanted to go out for a run with a local jogging club. I was used to going out and walking 55 yards, jogging 55 yards, going about a quarter of a mile and figuring I had done quite a bit.... We went out and met a couple hundred people in a park–men, women, children, all ages and sizes. I was still full of breakfast as Lydiard pointed toward a hill in the distance and said we were going to run to Two Pine Knoll. It looked about 1½ miles away. We took off and I wasn't too bad for about ½ mile, and then we started up this hill. God, the only thing that kept me alive was the hope that I'd die. I moved right to the back of the group and an old fellow, I suppose he was around 70 years old, moved back with me and said, 'I see you're having trouble.' I didn't say anything... because I couldn't. So we took off down the hill and got back about the same time the people did who had covered the whole distance."

Bowerman, then 50, spent six weeks in New Zealand and ran every day. He lost nearly ten pounds and reduced his waistline by four inches. By the time he returned to Oregon, he had learned to jog–slowly and comfortably. As soon as he arrived home, he got a call from Jerry Uhrhammer, a sportswriter from the *Eugene Register-Guard.* Uhrhammer wanted to know how the team had run, but Bowerman was much more excited about what he'd learned about jogging. Uhrhammer, who later became a jogger after open-heart surgery, published several articles based on Bowerman's revelations. Bowerman began staging Sunday morning runs and Uhrhammer publicized them.

Interest in the Sunday runs grew and Bowerman was asked to hold classes and clinics for neighborhood groups in Eugene. He did so, using some of his great Oregon distance runners as instructors. Before long Bowerman was overwhelmed with requests for information on this new phenomenon, so in 1966 he wrote a 20-page pamphlet–*Jogging*–with a Eugene cardiologist, Dr. Waldo Harris. The following year he published an expanded version of *Jogging*, which eventually sold over a million copies. The seeds of the jogging movement had been firmly planted in American soil.

Aerobics for Fitness. By 1960, more Americans were dying of heart disease than any other malady. A generation of Americans had leaped too quickly into the "good life."

People worked relatively hard until the mid-1940s. Finances kept meat consumption down and vegetable consumption up. Postwar prosperity, however, ushered in more leisure time, sedentary jobs and the funds to buy meat, cream, butter.... The rate of heart disease climbed rapidly.

The Air Force became concerned when its pilots started dying of heart failure, often bringing multi-million dollar planes down with them. Air Force officials showed great interest when one of its young doctors, Kenneth Cooper, suggested a study to see if exercise could influence the risk factor in heart disease.

Cooper had been doing his medical residency in Boston when Bill Bowerman returned from New Zealand. A high school and college track star (he ran a 4:18 mile), Cooper had high blood pressure and had gained 40 pounds after medical school and internship. One day, as he recalls in *The Aerobics Program for Total Well-Being*, he decided to go water skiing. Having been an expert skier in his youth, he "... put on a slalom ski, told the driver to accelerate immediately to almost 30 miles per hour, and prepared to have a great time, just like in the old days.

"But I was in for a surprise.

"Within three to four minutes I was totally exhausted, and I suddenly began to feel nauseated and weak. I told the boat driver to stop and get me back to land as quickly as possible. For the next 30 minutes, as I lay in nauseous agony on the shore, my head was spinning and I honestly couldn't put a series of logical thoughts together."

This experience had the same effect on Cooper that the Sunday New Zealand run had on Bill Bowerman. He embarked upon an exercise and diet program that brought his weight down from 210 to 170 and reduced his body fat from 30% to 14%. His enthusiasm about exercise and the heart disease factor in airplane crashes convinced the Air Force brass of the value of his proposed testing program. The results of his studies were published in the landmark book *Aerobics.*

Cooper's book was a popular explanation of the facts that were beginning to pile up—that the good life would be cut short by poor eating habits, and that exercise could overcome many of the risk factors. Americans were receptive to these ideas. What good was a fine home, family and income without the good health to enjoy them?

Cooper's aim was to counteract the great lethargy and inactivity of most Americans by demonstrating the benefits of regular exercise. Most important, he showed *how* to do it. His point system gave even out-of-shape beginners a guide to exercise. Millions of today's fit Americans owe their good health to *Aerobics.*

The Final Push by Runners. Just as the Olympic medals provided the fuel for Lydiard's fitness wildfire in New Zealand, Olympic success by Americans showed fellow countrymen that they, too, could be distance runners. Prior to the 1964 Tokyo Olympics, there had been only one gold medal won by an American distance runner since 1908–Horace Ashenfelter in the 1952 steeplechase.

All this changed in the Tokyo Olympics when Billy Mills, a complete unknown, upset Australian star Ron Clarke and Tunisian Mohamed Gammoudi to win the 10,000 meters. Four days later, American Bob Schul won the gold medal in the 5000 meters and one second back in third place was Bill Dellenger, a 30-year-old high school track coach from Springfield, Oregon.

After years of small fields, the number of entries in major U.S. road races began to increase. In 1964 the Boston Marathon, the country's oldest road race, topped 300 entries for the first time. In 1967, it went to 479; in 1970, 1150. San Francisco's Bay to Breakers showed a similar growth. From a field of 15 in 1963, there were 124 the following year, 1241 in 1969 and 75,000 in 1984!

Although there were more racers each year, Americans had still not won the country's most important marathon–Boston–since 1957, when a schoolteacher from Groton, Connecticut named John J. Kelley broke the course record. After Kelley's victory, the Finns and Japanese dominated the event until 1968 when another New Englander, also from Groton and coached by Kelley, won. The now-historic victory by my college roommate Amby Burfoot inspired thousands of recreational runners to take up the burgeoning sport.

Then, in the early 1970s, Frank Shorter, a Yale graduate and law student, developed into a national-class distance runner while a former track star in Oregon–Kenny Moore–moved off the track onto the roads and finished second in the 1970 Fukoka Marathon.

In 1971, both Shorter and Moore qualified for the Pan Am Games Marathon, which Shorter went on to win. Kenny Moore was a writer and went to work for *Sports Illustrated.* He wrote some inspiring accounts of world-class running that appealed to millions of readers.

The force of the American fitness revolution was magnified in 1972 at the Munich Olympics by ABC Sports, which selected the marathon as one of their feature events. That Shorter beat one of the greatest fields ever assembled by more than two minutes was final confirmation that Americans could indeed be successful distance athletes.

Further proof was provided a few years later when Bill Rodgers surprised everyone by winning the 1975 Boston Marathon. He went on to win it in 1978, 1979 and 1980. The likeable Rodgers had a young kid-like energy and openness so different from the cocky professional athletes of the day. He was accessible to the countless fans who lined up after the races to talk to him and he seldom refused an autograph.

Just as Lydiard, Bowerman and Cooper were teachers who awakened an interest in the benefits of regular exercise, so Burfoot, Shorter and Rodgers (all from the "baby boom" generation) provided inspiration at key times to the country's growing group of runners. Americans knew that physical activity was the secret to their future health, and that running, for many, was the common denominator.

2 THE FIVE STAGES OF A RUNNER
THE BEGINNER
THE JOGGER
THE COMPETIT

THE ATHLETE

THE RUNNER

I STARTED RUNNING when I was 13. I was immediately intoxicated with a beginner's enthusiasm: the very special thrill of exertion, and a feeling that my body had vast capabilities. Of course, I tried to maximize every jog and thrill on that first run and then had to hobble around for a week, almost too sore to move.

But once the soreness diminished I was back out there, running again. I was hooked. As in any skill or craft, there were various stages of involvement, competence and enjoyment. Now that I've been running for over 25 years, and have spent a great deal of time helping others weave running into their lives, I see a similar pattern of evolution in just about all runners.

Progress is a matter of learning, maturing and knowing yourself; one stage leads logically to the next. Not everyone has the same aspirations; all runners are not seeking Olympic gold. But understanding the experience common to most veteran runners—though you may not go through all five stages described here—will enable you to minimize the pitfalls and maximize the gains of your running future.

THE BEGINNER

Stage One—Making the Break

Every beginning is precarious. There you are, perched on the edge of starting something entirely new, yet there are distractions, even criticisms, that cause detours and dead ends. You want to be more healthy and fit, but you may not realize how secure you've become in an inactive world. Each time you go out for a run you encounter a new side of yourself—one that must somehow be integrated into your daily life.

There is usually a struggle within and without. The old lifestyle is there and offers security. When the energy of "beginning" wears off, it's harder to motivate yourself to go out for that daily run. You'll face a lot of obstacles at first. It's all too easy to stop when the weather turns cold, when it rains or snows, or when you feel the aches and pains of starting. You haven't had to deal with these things before and the temptation to quit is strong.

Your running may also be threatening to your less active friends. Eventually you—the beginner—and your non-running friends work it out. The transition period, however, can be unstable and uncomfortable for both. If you falter, the old world—comfortable in many ways—is waiting for you to slip back in. If you're lucky enough to make new friends who share similar fitness goals, you'll probably find refuge in the "fit" world while you gain your "running security."

Social reinforcement makes it easier to establish the fitness habit. One good approach is to find a group that meets regularly. Or you can make a pact with a friend who drags you out on bad days and vice versa. Races and fun runs are great opportunities to meet people.

At times, you may not progress as fast as you expected. We Americans are traditionally hyperactive and impatient. When we plant a seed, we not only want it to grow, we want it to become a tree by next week. We want *results.* When you start, you want to see physical and psychological benefits. But if you push too hard, you can tire yourself out and end up quitting in frustration.

The seed of exercise—if you don't crush it—will survive periods of moisture and drought. Just when it seems to be drying up, it will spring to life, rejuvenated, and propel you further down the road. Don't be discouraged, even if you've stopped. Tomorrow's another day. Many beginners stop and start again 10 or 15 times before they get the habit established.

Beginners who don't put pressure on themselves seem to have an easier time staying with it. If you simply walk/jog 30-40 minutes every other day, you'll find yourself gently swept along in a pattern of relaxation and good feeling. Your workout starts to become a special time for you.

As you make progress you find within yourself the strength and security to keep going. At first you're "just visiting" that special world when you go out for a run. But gradually you begin to change. You get used to the positive relaxed feeling. Your body starts cleaning itself up, establishing muscle tone, circulating blood and oxygen more vigorously. One day you find you're addicted, and the beginner becomes a jogger.

THE JOGGER

Stage Two—Entering the New World

The jogger feels secure with running. It may be hard to start each day's run but, unlike the beginner, you can identify with those who are addicted. You may be intimidated by the "high achievers" —competitors and marathoners—but you have begun to understand the benefits of fitness and made a significant break with the old, non-fit world. The jogger's runs are satisfying in themselves. There is almost always a "glow" at the end of the run, a reward for the effort. If you miss a run you may feel guilty—a rare experience for the beginner. Beginners often complain that they're bored while running, but joggers find this problem decreases and then disappears as their distances increase.

Rarely does a jogger have a plan or goal. Most run as a healthy diversion and don't feel the need to get anything more out of it. They just get out there when they can and do what they can. Those who *do* feel they need a plan often think they don't know enough to prepare one. They may pick up a few tips from a more experienced running friend or ideas from a running magazine. Unfortunately this often ends in frustration or injury because such plans are not based upon the jogger's own individual abilities and goals, but upon someone else's.

At first you probably needed a group or at least another

person for motivation and direction. As a jogger you are a bit more independent. You'll prefer company to running alone, but you'll pick and choose your group with care. Most beginners seek anonymity within a group while joggers often enjoy identification with a group.

As a beginner you may have attended a few fun runs or an occasional race. Joggers, however, mark the local 10K's on their calendars. These are motivational stepping stones to keep the daily runs on track. There will often be one major race in the jogger's schedule, like the Bay to Breakers, Peachtree Road Race or the Corporate Challenge. Although you're not running competitively or for time improvement, a sense of competition may begin to develop. By piecing together a growing series of successful and non-threatening running experiences, you begin the transition into a more fit lifestyle.

There are always conditions—injury, a long stretch of bad weather, a partner dropping out—that may stop your running and force you to start over again as a beginner. When the year's big race is over, you may lose the motivation to keep going. A jogger will sometimes give up running completely, but usually will start again after an extended layoff.

THE COMPETITOR

Stage Three—When Competition is the Main Driving Force

There is a competitive streak, sometimes hidden, in all of us. As we continue to run, it will most likely surface. If kept under control, the competitive urge can be a great motivator, stimulating you to train well and to push yourself further than you might have otherwise. But with many runners, competition, rather than the many other benefits of running, becomes the goal.

You become a competitor when you start to plan your running around racing goals. It all starts innocently enough. After a few races you begin to wonder how fast you might run if you really trained. Before you know it you're caught in a compulsive drive to run faster at the expense of running enjoyment.

Not all joggers enter this stage. Many simply remain joggers while a very few pass directly to the stage of "runner." If you do find yourself becoming obsessed with competition, however, here are some things you might expect:

Initially the competitive spirit is exciting and rewarding.

You're running faster because of increased training. You read everything you can on training, stretching, nutrition, etc., and become somewhat of an expert on each. There are always new training techniques to try out and you give them all a whirl. (Only later do you realize that many of them are contradictory.)

But as the competitive drive grows, you start feeling insecure. You no longer value your daily runs for their own worth, but think only of how well they prepare you for races and better times. Missing a run seems to spell racing doom. You can almost feel the fat being deposited on your body and see the seconds you fought hard to erase ticking back on the clock. When you hear of a workout a friend has performed before achieving a personal record, you have to match it or die trying.

Occasionally you'll run alone, but often you'll seek out small groups of better runners to train with and find you're making every workout a race; you'll push the pace to "victory" or make others earn theirs. In the same way, every race becomes a challenge to a new personal record. You may begin to choose races for the ease of terrain and lack of quality competition.

Once the competitive spirit has taken over you tend to lose sight of your limitations. If a small mileage increase brought about a small improvement, you'll try large mileage increases to gain a large improvement. Although you've read many times about the need for rest, you feel that yours is a special case—you don't need as much recovery time as other mortals. For weeks you may feel tired most of the time, yet have trouble sleeping at night. You become irritable and make life difficult for your family and friends. Finally you push too far and break down with injury, sickness or fatigue, and you either can't or don't want to run.

At this point you may feel betrayed by your body. Here you are trying to mold it into greatness and it won't respond. You fail to realize the improvements you've made during the past months or year and only visualize your fitness slipping away, your goals going down the drain. Thinking that your body is tricking you (or that an injury layoff is a sign of weakness) you get back into training too soon. Trying to run through the problems only makes them worse and leads to new injuries, and you miss the very races you've pushed yourself so hard for.

Still, when the frustration has passed (and the pounds have

settled back on) you'll probably start running again. Hopefully you'll have learned a lesson. You'll "recycle" and work your way up the ladder again. When you've put competition into perspective you'll pass into the stage of "athlete," or even "runner."

There are some very positive lessons to be learned from competition and fortunately not all competitors have to go to such extremes to learn them. Pushing through tiredness and discomfort in a race to a new personal record is not only rewarding in itself, but gives you an idea of what you can do in other areas of your life. Strengths we have never used lie buried in each of us. Being challenged to our limits through competition helps these surface. Competition can be the path-finding mission which allows us to map our inner resources. At the same time, experiencing some frustration and pain can help us realize our limitations. By struggling we discover a bit more about the person inside us; we can learn from our mistakes and move on to new heights.

THE ATHLETE
Stage Four—Being the Best You Can Be

As an athlete, you find more meaning in the drive to fulfill your potential than in compulsively collecting times and trophies. You've finally got a handle on competition, and it's not the only motivation. Being an athlete is a state of mind which is not bound by age, performance or place in the running pack.

For a competitor, victory and defeat are tied to performance. Times, flat courses, ideal conditions are all important. For the athlete, victory lies in the *quality* of effort. When you run close to your potential on a given day, it's a victory. You internalize competition and transcend it, knowing your limits and capabilities. You understand what's important and what you must do to accomplish it. As you compete, you breathe in the race, vaporize it, absorb what you need and exhale the rest. Running becomes your own work of art.

Competitors search for races they can win. Athletes look for competition, but are not intent on a higher ranking or better performance (from a flat, fast course, etc.). They thrive on a challenging competition that is run in the best way possible—from the inside out—and they are, not incidentally, rewarded in the long run by faster times. Nevertheless, athletes are also found in the back of the pack, or they may choose smaller races over the big media events because they don't want to feel lost in the sea of humanity.

Gradual progress is more important to the athlete than a fast time in a given race. You now have an internal concept of what you can do. When progress slows or is blocked, you revise. With every run, your internal training computer is fed with good data that gives you a new readout of possibilities. You know when to disregard a bad run and not get depressed.

Though you once may have been a competitor who read everything and tried most of it, as an athlete you now read only what has practical value. When problems arise you look for literature on the subject by authors you trust. Your reading ties into an overall plan. You're no longer sampling everyone's tips and tricks like treats out of the cookie jar.

Planning is important. Although you're flexible, you plot goals and races 6-9 months in advance. The athlete is capable of continuous re-evaluation, and may change goals from week to week. Plans are not always written; some athletes are so in tune with their bodies they can work from a mental notebook. Whether your plan is written or "programmed" you know where you're going. You may not know the exact vehicle you'll take, but you know you *will* arrive.

Like other humans, athletes are not perfectly consistent. Sometimes you'll slip back and become a competitor. After a series of successes, you may become dissatisfied with performances that fall short of your goals. Rather than evaluating, analyzing and re-adjusting, you may dwell upon the bad day, the slump, or the poor showing, and feel a sense of failure.

Great athletes at any level realize that "success" is in the eye of the performer. There can be success in every experience. If you can seize upon the positive aspect of each experience you can string together a series of successes that form a pattern of progress.

Some athletes reach a level of achievement or satisfaction and retire from competition; a few even quit running entirely. Many choose a reduced level of activity, others maintain a fairly high yet sensible level. Many continue to grow and move into the final and most rewarding stage, the runner.

THE RUNNER
Stage Five—The Best of All Stages

The final stage of the running journey blends the best elements of all the previous stages. The runner balances the elements of fitness, competition, training and social life and blends running with the rest of his or her life. There may be times when the runner reverts to earlier stages—mature people in any field have this problem—but these are only passing bouts that are assimilated into the overall harmony. The runner is a happy person.

As a runner, *the primary focus of your life is not running.* It may be family, friends, work, and is often a blend of many things. Running is now a natural part of your daily program—as is eating, sleeping or talking. You know you'll get in that daily run although you may not know when. When you *do* miss a run you aren't in agony. In fact, you don't miss many days over the span of a year.

If scientists announced tomorrow that running was harmful, you'd read the news with interest and go out on your daily run. You know about the positive effects of exercise, but that alone doesn't get you out on the roads. You get so much satisfaction from the experience itself that running has become a necessary and stable part of your active lifestyle.

As a runner, you'll enjoy the companionship of running with others, but most of your running will be done alone. You appreciate the peace and inner reflection provided by the solitary run more than you did in the earlier stages.

Great satisfaction comes from being able to mold your body into form, and there is an art in combining just the right amounts of strength, endurance, form and performance training. A race can be the opportunity to pull out deep hidden strengths. Once you've learned these things, the joy lies not in the race, but in the running.

Even though you may plan for occasional competition with the same care as a competitor, there is none of that fixated intensity. The race isn't sacred. If stresses or problems arise there are always other races.

Occasionally the runner is injured. This is usually due to reverting to one of the earlier stages in a workout or race. Now—through experience—you'll know the difference between a common ache and a problem and you'll back off at the first sign of the latter. You'll sacrifice workouts, races and time goals to heal an injury early and get back to 100% as soon as possible.

As a runner you experience the enjoyment of each stage and retain the best of each of them. You can relive the beginner's excitement in discovery, appreciate the jogger's balance of fitness and enthusiasm, share the competitor's ambition, and internalize the athlete's quest. Having consolidated and balanced all these stages, you appreciate the creative and positive aspects of each and let them enrich your running life.

3 GETTING STARTED

WE'VE ALL HEARD HORROR STORIES about the pain and agony of the first week of running. In fact, this is probably why so many people give it up soon after they start or say they're bored, or go on about how they hate running. They never get past that painful stage.

Starting any new activity takes courage and strength. To cross from the known to the unknown requires a leap of faith. Newton's law applies: a body at rest tends to stay at rest.

Once you overcome inertia and and get past the painful stage, the reverse law applies: a body in motion tends to stay in motion. If you start slowly, gradually increase the exertion through a series of small steps, and rest adequately throughout, you can improve your condition steadily with little risk of soreness or injury.

Set Aside 30 Minutes. The threshold to fitness is three 30-minute periods of endurance running each week. Make an appointment with yourself. This is the time for *you*, a sacred half hour. To take this time away from the rest of the world may seem difficult at first, but you can do it if you really want to. Once you habitually set this time aside, you're almost certain to gain fitness and lose weight. Effort, in a sense, is not as important as scheduling. If you get out there regularly, the results are practically guaranteed.

A Benign Addiction. By regularly exercising 30-40 minutes several times a week for about six months, runners (or walkers) seem to develop an addiction to the relaxed feeling that comes at the end of the run. It is suspected that this is caused by the beta endorphin hormones which lock into your mid-brain area and produce a subtle tranquilizing effect. The body and mind begin to anticipate this after-exercise effect and miss it when you don't exercise. The withdrawal symptoms vary: crankiness, tiredness, irritability, depression, etc. This natural reward will sustain you if you can just stick with your program for six months. It may not even take that long, but if it does, a half-year isn't a big investment for improved health and fitness the rest of your life.

Monitor Your Pulse Rate. The key to strengthening your heart is keeping your pulse rate high enough, but not too high. Research by Dr. Kenneth Cooper at the Aerobics Research Institute and by others has shown the threshold level to be 70-80% of your maximum heart rate. This isn't necessary in the beginning; but after you've established a program, maintaining this heart rate for 30 minutes, three times a week, will strengthen your lungs and heart, improve circulation of blood and oxygen and tone up your muscles.

Note: *Anyone with high blood pressure, who is overweight, or has had a heart problem or family history of heart disease, should consult a doctor before taking part in strenuous aerobic exercise.*

Two Methods of Calculating Maximum Heart Rate

1. Have a *maximum oxygen uptake* test performed. This is done on a treadmill and is very strenuous, but gives you the most accurate measure of your maximum.

2. Subtract your age from 220.

   Example: 220
- 35 years old
185 max. heart rate.

   Then take 70-80% of that as your target zone.

   Example: 185 x 70% = 129.5 threshold rate.

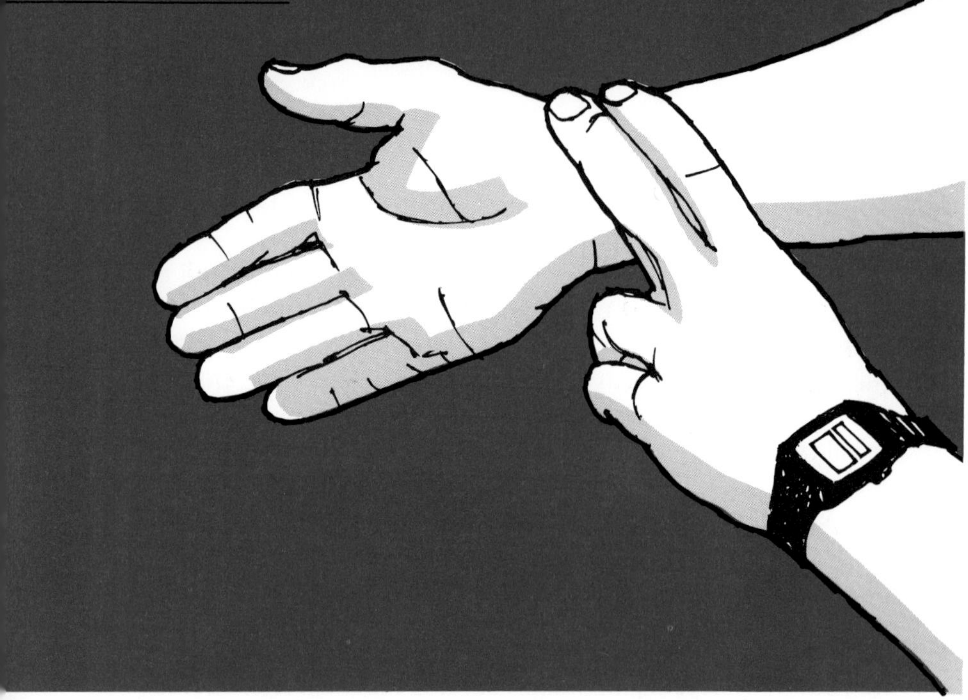

Most runs should show a heart rate of 70% or slightly higher. On speed days the heart rate will go up to 80% and even 90%, but too much exercise at these higher levels will lead to overstress. If you are running at 80% or higher on easy days or long days, you are probably going too fast.

Monitor your pulse rate while walking by finding an artery on your wrist with your finger. (Do not use your thumb because it also has a pulse.)

Count the beats for 15 seconds and multiply by four to get your pulse rate. Generally, when you're running you're already in the target zone, but when you're just starting you may want to check your heart rate this way. After a while you'll get to know when you're working hard enough, and if you go beyond 80% of your heart rate you'll feel uncomfortable. You'll soon learn to control this by taking walking breaks before getting uncomfortable.

Note: *This pulse rate data is provided primarily for beginners. I don't recommend using heart rate as a gauge of a sufficient workout for regular runners. First, it's too hard to get an accurate pulse count when exercising; if you miss just one count, you've lost accuracy. Second, the heart rate drops rapidly when you stop to check. Several studies have shown that practically everyone who runs (as opposed to "walks") has the heart operating in the target zone.*

FIVE STEPS TO GETTING STARTED

Start by Walking. Everyone needs to feel comfortable and successful right from the start. Begin by walking for 30 minutes. Keep doing this until it feels easy.

Walk Briskly. When normal walking becomes easy, walk briskly for 30 minutes and monitor your heart rate every 5-8 minutes. If it seems below the target zone, pick up the pace. Many people will never want or need to go beyond a brisk walk, provided they can maintain their target pulse rate.

Insert a Few "Jogs." When you are comfortable walking briskly and want to step up the pace, simply insert 3-4 "jogs" of 100 yards or so (about the length of one football field or a city block) into your 30-minute walk. Warm up by walking slowly, build into a brisk walk and then do the short jogs when you feel ready.

Increase the Running as Desired. Increase the running segments as you feel stronger, always avoiding discomfort. You may eventually fill in the 30 minutes with slow running—or you may keep your walking breaks. You're using the running to push the heart rate above the threshold and the walking to keep from getting uncomfortable.

Step It Up. Increase the time to 40 minutes three times a week. Work up to 60 minutes for one of these weekly sessions, which will increase the cardiovascular as well as mental benefits.

Don't underestimate the effect of rewards. Small regular rewards for specific accomplishments will often spark interest when motivation is down. Promise yourself something—a dinner out, a new pair of shoes, a good book—for finishing each of the five steps above, for when you finally put in your first hour-long session, etc. If you feel "down," find yourself a positive experience, or see someone who will bring you up. Look for something good in every run.

When you're in shape, you begin to think differently about yourself and your life. It's always hard to shake off the sedentary lifestyle, and the adjustment period—once you do—is difficult. But if you make it through this period, an addiction often occurs which makes the activity self-sustaining. So *have faith!* Better times are coming. Be patient and enjoy yourself.

HELPING SOMEONE ELSE GET STARTED

Don't preach. If you've made a recent and powerful change in your health and lifestyle it's all too easy to get up on the soap box—the born-again runner. When you do it's going to turn others off, even cause a "backlash" against running. Motivation must come from within. Your friends and people you meet will know when their time has come. Trying to turn a non-physical friend on to running is like preaching to a stone.

Some "Do's" and "Don't's" of Helping Someone Get Started

Do:

Wait until the person asks for help or advice.

Watch a fun run or race together. This is the best way to get a beginner excited.

Show personal interest and listen well to your friend. Then offer advice based on his or her goals—not yours.

Recommend some good reading material like—ahem!—this book.

Don't:

Don't promise running will improve everything from sex to falling hair (at least not falling hair).

Don't drag your prospect out on the roads like an animal with prey.

Don't threaten instant cardiovascular doom if your friend doesn't start training tomorrow.

Don't talk for more than four hours straight on the wonderful changes you've made through running.

The greatest problem for a beginner is "How do I get started and stick with it?" The answer must come from within, but you, as the advisor or coach, can help stage a series of successes to ensure continued progress.

TRAINING

4 PHYSIOLOGY

WHAT HAPPENS INSIDE WHEN YOU RUN

THE BEST WAY to start training is to understand the vital processes of the body—at least those that relate directly to running. If you understand some of your body's inner workings and are sensitive to its needs and states of tiredness, it can perform magnificently for you. Without such sensitivity you can too easily push yourself into pain or injury. It's often a series of small errors in training that leads to substantial injuries. With a little fine tuning, however, most of us can make our training safer and more productive.

Unity of Body and Mind. First, let's try to shed two or three thousand years of Western thinking—the idea that mind and body are separate entities, even adversaries. Westerners tend to think of the body as a slave, a chariot that can be driven and pushed at will. We often let our minds drive us toward goals, pushing to exhaustion or injury. Then we limp around in the aftermath, trying to re-establish communication.

In contrast, Eastern philosophy stresses unity of mind and body. Instead of a dichotomy, body and mind are a team communicating and working toward the same goal. Dr. E.C. Frederick, physiologist and author of *The Running Body*, illustrates the different approaches with a story about the first two people to climb Mt. Everest, Sir Edmund Hillary and his Sherpa guide, Tensing Norgay.

When reporters asked how they made the difficult climb, Hillary replied that they had ". . . conquered the mountain"–it was an obstacle they had attacked and overcome. The Sherpa, who had lived on and in the shadow of the mountain all his life, said that he and the mountain had worked together to attain the peak.

Mountains can be climbed, miles run and goals attained when the mind and body work together. When the mind coaxes adaptations out of the body, steady progress can result. But the "macho" mind that forces its intentions upon a slave-like body will only reduce it to an injured slave.

The Most Important Training Principle. Most of us know that we must stress ourselves in training sessions. Exercise stresses the muscles and stimulates them to grow stronger. Without enough rest after the stress, however, the muscles are driven to exhaustion or injury. Stress must be balanced by rest in sufficient quantity and quality for adequate growth.

Hard or long runs must *always* be followed by several easy days in which the pace or distance is reduced. In addition, you must build rest *weeks* into your program: every second or third week, you should automatically reduce total mileage. This gives your muscles the extra time to "catch up."

Improvement is based upon the quality of your speedwork and the length of your long run. By running easily in between these two "quality days" you will recover, rebuild stronger and chances of injury will be greatly reduced. Common mistakes that lead to injury are:

- Trying to attain a high mileage level week after week.
- Running daily runs too fast.
- Not enough rest.

What Goes On Inside the Muscle. When most people think of a cell, they generally picture a round basic cell, surrounded by a membrane, with a nucleus at the center. Like a bacteria or amoeba seen through a high school microscope. But there are hundreds of millions of cells in the human body, with a variety of functions and a diversity of shapes. The ones we are concerned with here—the skeletal muscle cells—are quite different from skin cells or those round single-celled organisms studied for their simplicity.

A muscle cell is a fiber, composed of smaller and smaller units of fibers, and can run the entire length of the muscle. Picture a length of electrical conduit with bundles of wires inside. The muscle cell is like this. There is an external membrane, the *sarcolemma,* inside of which there are bundles (*myofibrils*) of fibers. Also inside the muscle cell are the *mitochondria,* the "power plants" of the cell, which break down fuel (from food) into usable energy.

What Happens When the Muscle is Overstressed. Muscles are generally capable of performing the amount of work they have been accustomed to during the previous 7-14 days. Your recent training has developed them to a certain fitness level. If you push beyond this level, you strain the horses that do the actual work—the individual muscle cells.

Cells pushed beyond their capacity are damaged with tears in the membranes. The mitochondria within the cells become swollen and glycogen, the fuel stored within the mitochondria, is often almost depleted.

Following is a brief description of some of the physiological aspects of two important rest principles. Then in Chapter 8, *Daily and Weekly Mileage Programs,* we'll look at the practical aspects of these short-term and long-term considerations.

The Easy Day (Short Term). Research has shown it takes 48 hours to repair this stress-related damage. *With rest*, each overstressed cell is programmed to rebuild stronger when it is broken down, so it can handle a greater load next time. Cell walls become stronger as the membrane rebuilds a bit thicker. The mitochondria increase in size and number so they can process more energy. Vessels and arteries repair and strengthen, and over several months more capillaries are produced to better deliver nutrients and withdraw wastes. (See Changes Inside the Muscle Cells, p. 71.)

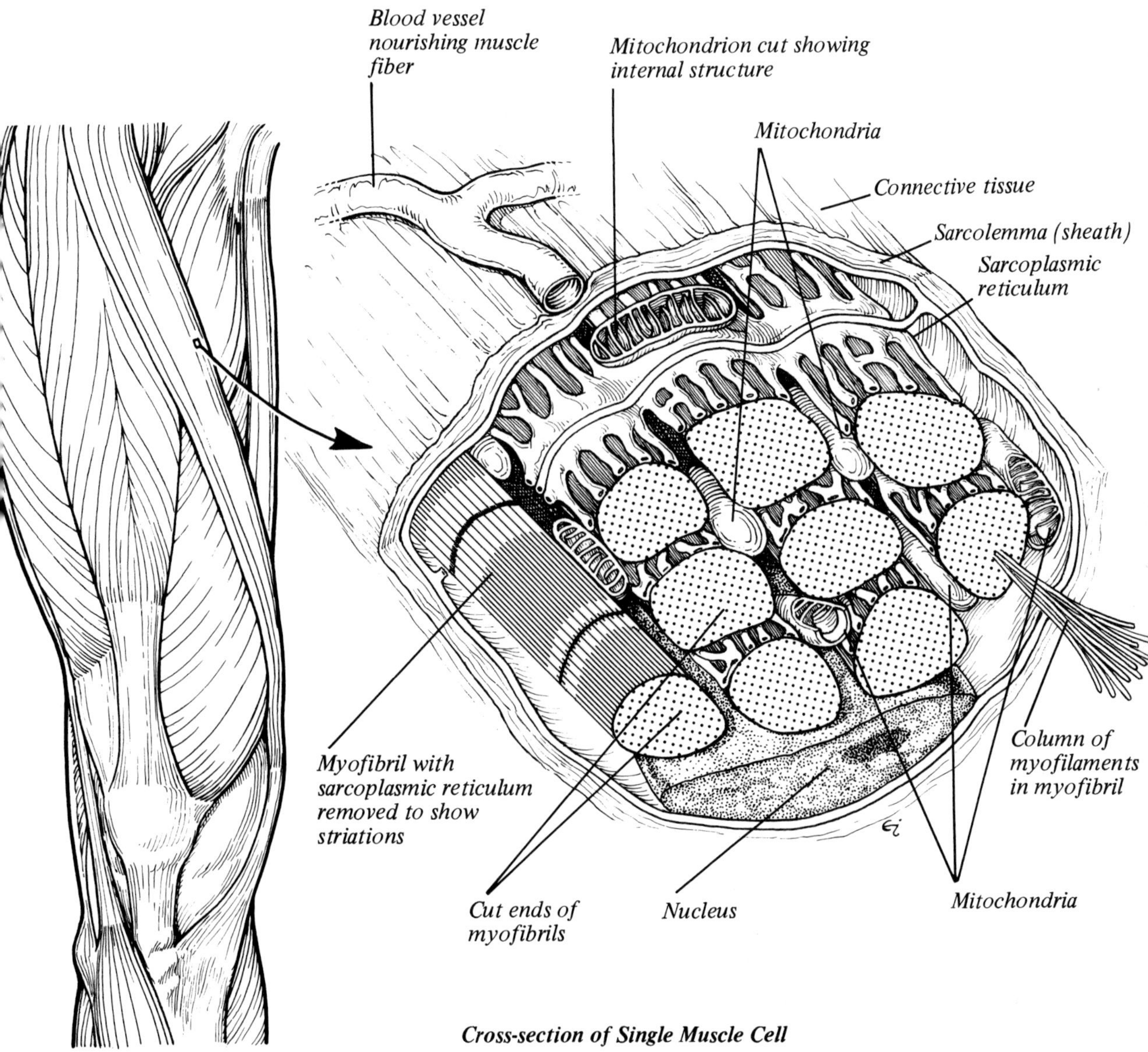

Cross-section of Single Muscle Cell

Magnified view of short segment of a single muscle fiber taken from the sartorius muscle of the leg. The sheath from the fiber has been cut away to show the internal structure. The mitochondria, the "power plants" of the cell, are shown in both intact and cut-away form.

You can see why it is important to give yourself 48-hours rest in between stressful runs. This doesn't mean you should stop running completely. I have found that easy running during the 48-hour period brings about a quicker recovery than complete rest. Even on slow runs, the blood vessels in the area dilate and allow more blood to flow into the stressed area—this is called reactive hyperemia. Slow, shorter runs in between hard ones will bring restorative blood with oxygen, training nutrients and more fuel to the battered area. You can't push your training ahead and avoid the 48-hour rule without paying dearly. Maybe it won't happen right away, but eventually injury will result.

The Easy Week (Long Term). The second important rest concept is that it takes about 21 days for muscles to adapt to the stress when you move into a new and more challenging training program. After about 11 days you'll feel stronger when the muscles have adapted to about half the stress. There is a strong temptation then to think you're ready to increase the stress again, but the body is not quite ready. After three weeks, the body has theoretically adapted and is ready for a new stress load.

I have found, however, that by *reducing* stress on the second or third week—cutting mileage by 30-50%, say—the body comes around quicker and is ready for new challenges. This allows for more of the ruptured fibers to be rebuilt and for the muscles to be rested and re-stocked for the next challenge. Again, as with the 48-hour rule, you may break this rule and get away with it for a while but you'll pay later in tiredness and injury. You can push yourself too far for some time, but your body will ultimately protect itself by breaking down.

A more detailed explanation of the Easy Day *and the* Easy Week *concepts follow on* *pp. 72-74**, along with guidelines for putting these principles to work in your daily and weekly mileage programs and examples of the concepts in practice.*

Aerobic/Anaerobic Exercise.

Aerobic means "in the presence of oxygen." You are running aerobically when you run slowly and comfortably and do not exceed the pace or distance for which you have recently trained. Here your muscles are strong enough to carry the load and there is enough oxygen available from the blood stream. The few waste products that are produced are easily whisked away in the blood before building up and obstructing muscle function.

Anaerobic running is when you exceed the speed and/or distance for which you have trained. The muscles are pushed beyond their capacity and need more oxygen than the body can supply. For a limited period of time, muscles continue to function by utilizing chemical processes that free oxygen from within the muscle itself. The amount of oxygen available this way is quite limited, large amounts of waste build up and the muscles get tight and sore. You find yourself huffing and puffing, and slowing down. After the exercise is over, this oxygen must be "paid back" to the muscle (the "oxygen debt"). One of the main purposes of speedwork is to give you anaerobic experience in measured doses; if you follow it with sufficient rest, you'll train your body to deal with oxygen debt.

The Food-Into-Energy Cycle. When you eat carbohydrates (bread, fruit, starches, sugars, etc.), they are broken down into simple sugars, some of which is then re-combined into glycogen and stored in the muscles as fuel. Glucose, lactose (milk sugar) and fructose (fruit sugar) are mono-saccharides and are converted into glycogen in one step. Sucrose (white sugar) is a di-saccharide and requires an additional step, using extra energy and slowing down the process.

After being absorbed through the walls of the stomach, glucose is transported by the blood throughout the system. Muscle cells absorb this energy source and store it as glycogen for use during exercise. Extra supplies are stored in the liver. When all storage areas are filled, glucose is converted to fat and stored as such.

For the first 10 minutes of aerobic exercise, the exercising muscles will use the most convenient energy source, the glycogen in the muscle cell, almost exclusively. Glycogen combines with oxygen from your blood to produce energy and several waste products, including lactic acid. As long as you are not exercising anaerobically (out of breath, etc.), the percentage of lactic acid will be relatively low and the blood can whisk it away.

After about 10 minutes of exercise, your body will start a transition to fat as a fuel source. It takes this long for the stored fat to release free fatty acids into the blood in sufficient numbers to satisfy the demands of so many hungry muscle cells. After about 30 minutes, fat becomes the primary fuel source, with a small "primer" of glycogen. (Just because you're burning fat doesn't mean you should be eating a lot of fat. Carbohydrates are the best source of energy; too much dietary fat can hamper your performance.)

A Physiological Look at "The Wall." Fat is a more abundant fuel than glycogen. Whereas glycogen stores are limited (normally about 20 miles worth), even a skinny person has enough fat for about 600 miles. The trade-off for this long-range fuel is that fat can only be burned aerobically (in the presence of oxygen). As long as you run within the pace and at the distance you've been training for—you will burn mostly fat. When you run faster than you've trained, or farther, you overwhelm the muscles. They are forced beyond their capacity and cannot get enough oxygen. In this anaerobic situation glycogen is burned, and large amounts of lactic acid and waste products pour into the muscles faster than they can be removed. This is what causes your muscles to get tight and *burn* and this is what causes you to slow down and hit "the wall." Once the muscles have shifted to glycogen, it's unlikely that they can shift back to fat. You'll be depleting your limited supply of glycogen very quickly.

One important objective of training is to teach the body to conserve glycogen and deal with lactic acid buildup. Your base period training (see pp. 55-56) will improve the blood's capacity to deliver oxygen and withdraw wastes. Speedwork and long runs gradually push back the point at which you start becoming anaerobic; they also teach you to deal with the discomfort and burden of lactic acid buildup without slowing down as much as before. When you have fine-tuned the muscles through speedwork, you will accumulate approximately the same amount of waste, but won't have to slow down as much because now you're used to the feeling.

By pushing too far beyond your current capabilities you can cause your body some serious damage. When you have run too far or too fast and have shifted to glycogen as a fuel source you're on unstable ground in a long race. Glycogen is the only fuel used by the brain and the supply of this energy source is greatly limited. At critically low levels of glycogen, your body's survival defenses take over and reserve what's left for the brain. When the brain senses a low supply, it protects itself by making it difficult for you to concentrate

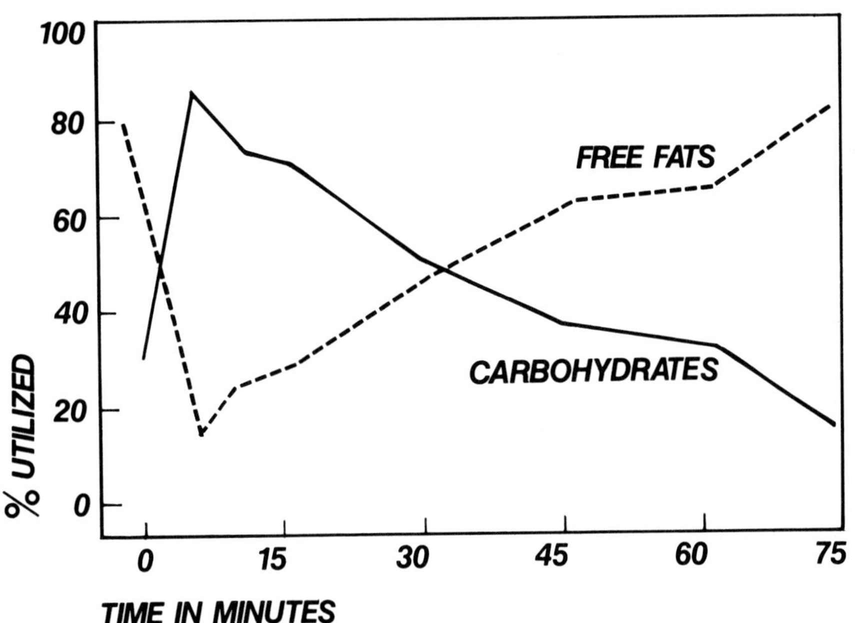

Estimate of energy derived from carbohydrates and fats in 75 minutes of running. Note that at 30 minutes you start burning more fats than carbohydrates. Adapted from A Scientific Approach to Distance Running *by David L. Costill. (See p. 271.)*

on finishing the long event—or even telling you to quit. These are warning signs that should put you on alert.

What's a working muscle to do? There's not enough oxygen to burn fat, and the glycogen supply has been stolen. Glycogen *can* be processed from fat, and from muscle protein. This is a very uncomfortable process and leaves much waste—but it is done. When nearby fat stores are used up and the exercising muscle absolutely demands glycogen, exercising muscle tissue may be broken down itself.

Remember to take care of your body. An injured body cannot perform. Damaged, overstressed muscles cause you to miss training and retard progress. Stay within the bounds of the training you have done in the recent past and push only slightly beyond this once a week to improve speed and endurance.

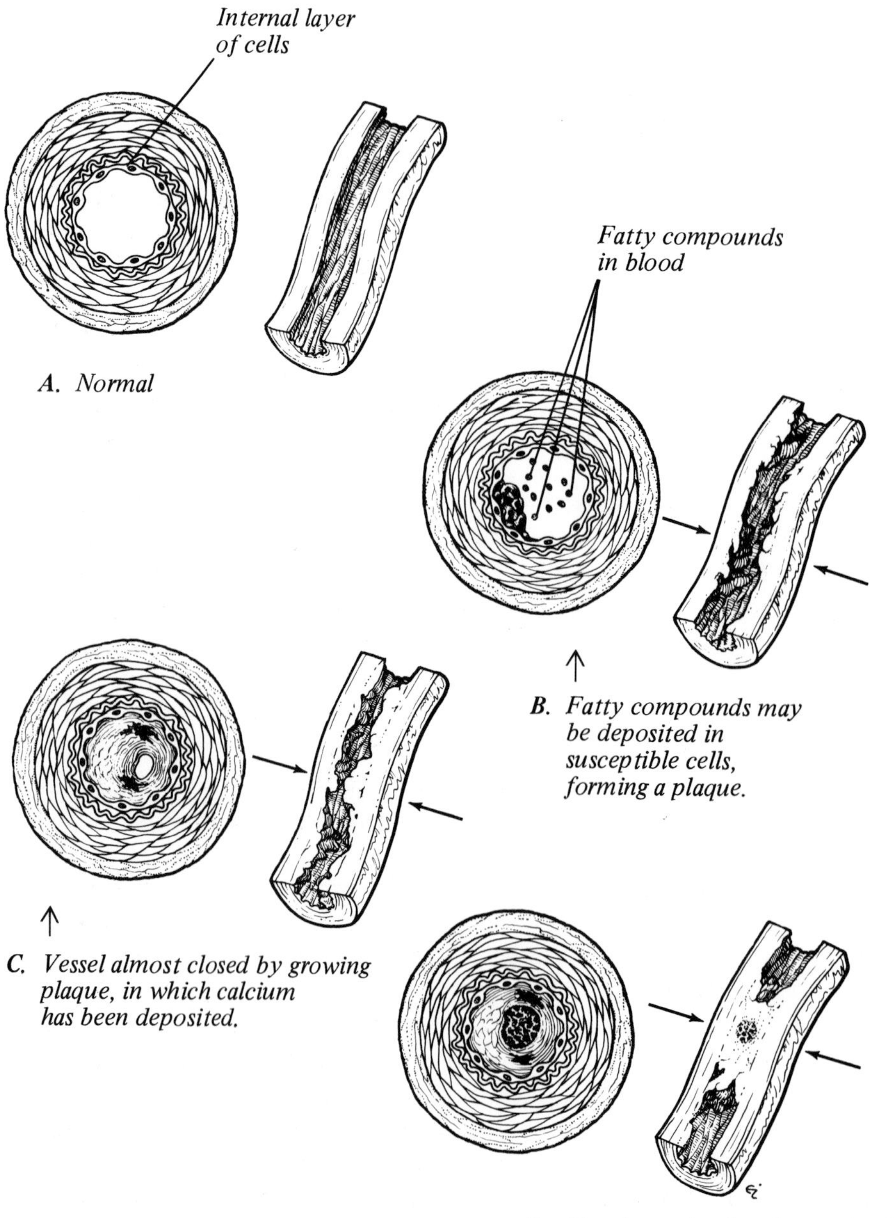

Inside look at heart disease. Shown here are a normal artery and three stages of progressive closure from an excess of fats in the diet.

Blood Chemistry. Our bodies were not intended to digest large amounts of fat. The marvelous instruments we've inherited from our ancient ancestors were designed for processing foods high in complex carbohydrates (grains, vegetables, fruits). Although small amounts of fat can be easily taken care of, the modern diet—rich in fried foods and red meat—overwhelms the body's processing capacities. The walls of our circulatory and organ systems become coated with the excess of these fats, particularly if the arteries or heart passages are naturally narrow through heredity. This can lead to a variety of serious circulation problems, especially in the vessels that supply blood to the heart. Fats have also been linked to other serious diseases, such as cancer of the colon.

Regular endurance athletes choose complex carbohydrates over fats for fuel. The myth of a high-protein, animal-source food diet for strength and endurance is fading fast. In fact, Rob De Castella, winner of the 1983 World Marathon Championships in Helsinki, adheres strictly to the Pritikin high-carbohydrate, low-fat diet. In the 1982 Ironman Triathlon, the grueling three-event distance race in Hawaii, Dave Scott, Scott Tinley and Scott Molina, who finished first, second and fourth respectively, all followed the Pritikin diet. Carbohydrates are easier to digest, leave one feeling "lighter" and provide the best fuel for endurance events. (See *Fuel,* p. 236.)

The Heart . . . and Its Supporting Cast. The heart is an endurance muscle, a pump that squeezes blood into the body every minute of every day. Like any muscle, it needs regular exercise or it will deteriorate. Working at a desk job, without any supplemental physical exercise, there is not enough exertion to maintain the heart in healthy condition. Over time, deposits may build up in lazy heart arteries. The small and crucial passageways in this vital organ must be kept clean and functioning. Regular endurance exercise will accomplish this.

Exercising muscles are in a real sense small pumps that pull blood in from the heart and then push it back. The heart is forced to increase its pumping speed to send needed blood to the exercising muscle. The sustained increase in heart rate will keep this important muscle fit and lean.

Endurance exercise also increases the number of capillaries and promotes a better flow of nutrients to the cells and a better withdrawal of wastes. When you exercise regularly, your body increases its output of blood and your blood volume increases, so more blood is available to the exercising cells. The sustained pressure during several months of long runs forces little tongues of capillaries into the muscle cells. The result is a greater flow of oxygen to a greater number of cells all over the body, helping them work to capacity. The heart muscle becomes stronger, is given an extra infusion of oxygen and is regularly cleaned.

As the heart gets stronger, it sends a greater flow of blood throughout the body with each stroke. With fewer squeezes, the "fit" heart will accomplish more work, and your resting pulse rate will go down.

See p. 34 for an explanation of monitoring your heart rate as a guide to workout performance.

Fast Twitch/Slow Twitch. Some people can run faster, and others farther. If you could look inside your muscle cells you could tell whether you were born to run sprints or distance events. If you have a high percentage of fast twitch muscle fibers you have a tendency to run fast. These sugar-burning muscle cells fire quickly, burn fuel quickly and are not resistant to fatigue. In contrast, slow twitch fibers burn fat, can be trained to fire repeatedly for a long time and resist fatigue.

Sports scientists can determine an individual's percentage of fast or slow twitch muscle fiber by injecting a needle into the muscle and withdrawing a small sample to examine under a microscope. It is a relatively simple procedure, but a bit painful and usually done only for research studies. Runners with a predominance of slow twitch muscles (I have 97%) must abandon hope for a fast finishing kick. Speedy runners, however, can train their fast twitch muscles to become fat burners and act as slow twitch fibers.

The Lungs. When you breathe, air enters through your mouth and/or nose and then travels through the back of your throat (the pharynx) and your windpipe (the trachea). At its lower end the trachea branches out to form the bronchi, one of which enters each lung. These then subdivide and eventually lead to several hundred million air sacs—the *alveoli*—that accomplish the exchange of gases: oxygen in, carbon dioxide out.

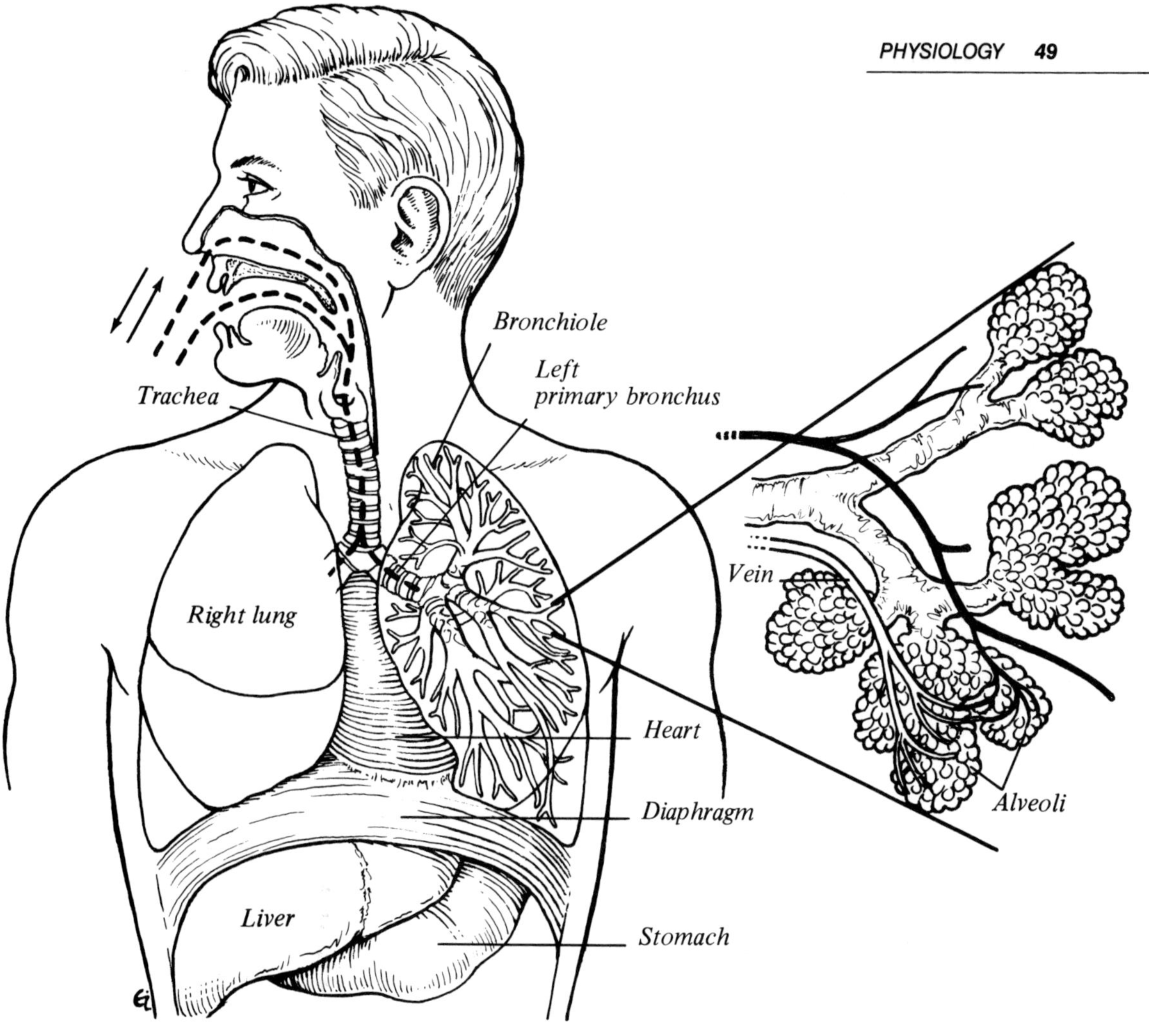

Air is exchanged through the nose and/or mouth. Air enters the lungs via the trachea, which branches to form the bronchi, which in turn branch, tree-like, to form smaller subdivisions, the bronchioles. Here a terminal bronchiole is enlarged to illustrate the air sacs (alveoli), in which exchange of gases takes place between air and blood.

Exercise puts the lungs under greater pressure to perform. More alveoli are involved in the process of gaseous exchange and their ability to perform this task rapidly and efficiently is improved. Continued smoking and prolonged exposure to air pollution can significantly reduce the ability of the alveoli to accomplish this exchange and diminish the capacity of whole sections of the lungs to function. Fortunately exercise, running in particular, can help reverse this process and over time enable the tissue to regain its functional ability (unless the smoking and air pollution have destroyed the walls of the alveoli themselves, as in emphysema).

5 PLANNING

WHERE TO START

IN SUMMER, 1983, I got a call from Marlene Cimons, a runner and a staff writer for the *Los Angeles Times.* I'd met Marlene earlier at the Boston Marathon and she'd been interested in my new approach to training. "Do you think I could improve my marathon time of 3:53?" she asked.

I asked a few questions about her background and then said I could practically guarantee better performance if she followed some different training principles. Marlene was eager to give it a try, so I set up a running program for her. We agreed we'd talk on the phone every few weeks so I could monitor how things were going and recommend any necessary adjustments.

As she got into her new routine, she decided it might make a good story for her paper. Would this new approach–planning her training in advance and emphasizing long, slow runs–lead to better performance? She sent away for an application to the Nike-Oregon Track Club Marathon in Eugene, Oregon, that fall and I agreed to run with her in the race, to keep her on pace and provide psychological support.

Marlene followed the major points of the marathon training program (see the chart on p. 126), but one thing she had trouble with, and that we argued over, was the long run. She got up to 20 miles and didn't want to run farther. (As you'll see in the following pages, the program recommends that you work your way up to running at least the race distance before the race, so your body is prepared for the strain.) She had a mental block, based on painful experiences "crashing" each time she'd gone 20 miles, either in practice or racing. She was afraid she'd hurt herself before the race.

I explained Arthur Lydiard's theory of long, relaxed running. I told her to go slow, to stop and walk when tired, but to be sure to go *farther* than the race *before* the race. This way she shouldn't hit "the wall" she so dreaded. I also pointed out how this principle of easy long runs had not only been used by Lydiard's Olympic champions, but now by neighborhood runners throughout the country to run (and finish) marathons.

I finally convinced Marlene to continue her long runs and to build up to 26 miles. We met in Eugene that September and Marlene ran 3:44:49, improving her previous best time by 8½ minutes–even on a very warm and humid day. She not only didn't "die" at the end, but managed a final sprint the last 200 yards. She was inspired and elated, and wrote an article on her experience.

Running Slow in Order to Run Fast. Marlene's experience is typical for runners at all levels. Steady, relaxed running over several months is not only enjoyable, but cuts down on injuries and is the best base for competitive running. Not only can you run slow in order to run fast, but by carefully organizing slow running into a planned schedule, you can probably run faster than ever before.

Lydiard's Strategy Applied to Everyday Runners. Over the past 12 years I've worked with runners at clinics, in running camps and in our running stores and I've developed a series of innovations and planning techniques that allow everyday runners to tap into the successful concepts developed by Lydiard. I've come to visualize this program as a pyramid with a strong foundation of easy running, a transition zone of hill training and finally a speed program that brings a runner to his or her peak for a race.

What's interesting is that these same principles used by world-class runners apply to runners of all levels. With these basic training concepts, not only do elite runners achieve world records, but beginners will get fit and have fun, joggers will be able to run their first marathons and experienced runners will improve their personal records.

Starting Your Program. Your training program has already started. Your past exercise activity will be the basis upon which you'll build your long-range program. Adults who were active as children have a headstart. So don't be surprised if a fellow sedentary office worker takes up running and improves faster than you. Start with what you're presently doing, so long as it's not already too much; then build in the specific workouts, rest and other adjustments described below.

Most of the runners I have counseled have initially *decreased* their mileage by adding strategic rest. This has allowed them to increase the quality of work on the hard days—and has invariably led to better performance. But even if you've been sedentary for many years, don't be discouraged; you can probably do things you never believed were possible.

Define Your Goals. First think about your goals. Why do you want to run? To lose weight, feel good, regain muscle tone, stay fit year-round? All of these plus enter some races? Or become a competitive runner and race frequently? Think about what you want out of your running. What do you want to achieve in the next six and 12 months? Asking these questions will help you organize a plan and make your pursuit more effective.

Don't Use Anyone's Program But Your Own. The best training program for you is the one that meets your particular needs. This applies to beginners as well as to world-class runners. Don't adopt the successful program of a friend. Although he is succeeding, he may be improving on inborn talent "in spite" of his program. All of us have strengths, weaknesses and limitations which need to be considered in customizing a program. It's fine to try new training ideas, but experiment with only one at a time. Then blend the successful ones into your program to fit your own demands, rest needs and current level of performance.

THE TRAINING PYRAMID

The training pyramid is normally a 4-6 month cycle with each stage building to the next. As I mentioned before, it is used by elite runners to improve endurance and speed, but in the following pages I'll show how *you* can use the pyramid concept to achieve your goals, whatever they may be. At the peak of the pyramid is the race the runner is aiming for. You can use the principles to achieve your race goal, or as a general guide to a balanced running program. Whether you race or not, these concepts will improve your running, make it more enjoyable and develop your overall cardiovascular capacity and fitness.

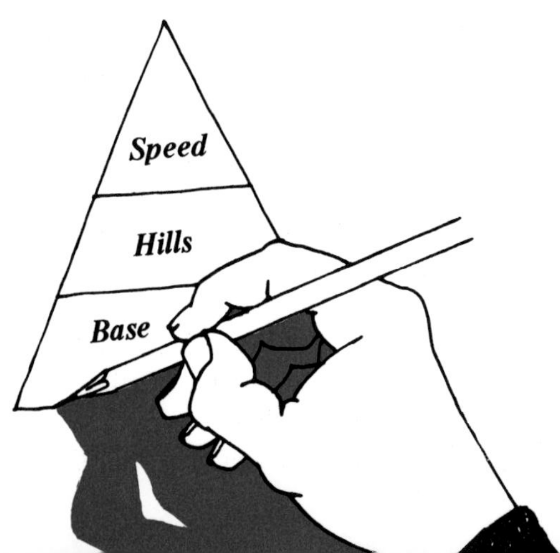

Speed: *35%*

Continue long runs.
Cut total mileage 10%.
Replace hills with speedwork, once a week.
Gradually build number of reps.
Rest between long runs, speedwork and races.
Do maximum eight weeks speedwork.

Hill Training: *15%*

Same as base period except for hill repeats.
Once a week, run hills (10-15% grade), 150-200 yards.
Run uphill at 80-85% effort (about 5K race pace).
Jog easy in between to recover.
Start with 4 hills, build up to 8-12.

Base Training: *50%*

Daily runs, which are relaxed, easy and comfortable.
Long runs every other week.
Pace: Run at comfortable speed; if in doubt, go slower.
Form work: 4-8 accelerations during daily run, twice a week.
Races: At most, every other week and alternating with long run.

BASE TRAINING

Daily Runs. Your ultimate performance is governed by your base work–aerobic training. You can only improve a certain amount by speedwork. But it's the sustained period of long, steady running that is the foundation for running faster.

The base part of the pyramid consists of several months of steady aerobic running. Aerobic running develops a better circulatory system by strengthening the heart and increasing the amount of blood pumped through the circulatory system. This means nutrients and oxygen can get to the muscle cells more efficiently and wastes are more easily removed. Your muscles can do more work with less effort. You are building up your *vital transport system* in preparation for the speedwork phase which will ultimately help you run faster.

Long Runs. Long runs develop cardiovascular efficiency to its maximum. *They are the single most important element in your program.* The sustained pumping of the heart helps the heart, arteries and veins become more efficient in transporting the blood and allows the lungs to absorb oxygen more efficiently. When the muscles are pushed to their limits (as in a race) they will respond better and work longer because of this strengthening of the circulation system.

How long? If you're interested in running faster or racing–no matter how far down the line–here is what you do: Start with the distance of your longest run in the last three weeks and increase by one mile a week until you have reached 12 miles. At that point, increase by two miles every two weeks. The intervening weeks will give your body a much-needed chance to recover and rebuild for the next long one. When you get up to 20 miles for a marathon, 16 for a 10K, go into a holding pattern. Don't go beyond these distances until your speed phase.

In the speed phase of your pyramid, you'll continue these long runs and for top performance, extend them to *beyond* the distance of the race you're aiming for. Ideally you should build up to a run of 16-18 miles for the 10K, 28-30 for the marathon.

The other runs in your program will not change very much, if at all. *You will be increasing distance primarily through the long run, not through more miles each day.* You can run races during the base period, but don't need to. If you do, they should not be run at top speed, and should be run on weeks when there is no long run.

Note for Non-Competitive Runners. Long runs are used by competitive endurance runners of all levels. World-class racers have been using the principle for years now, and more and more weekend 10K or marathon runners are recognizing its value in improving overall speed and race performance. But the principle of the long run can be used by all runners, even those who run only 2-3 miles a day, three times a week. If you are not interested in racing or competing, just scale down the length of the long run as described above. The idea is to run longer one day every two weeks. If you run three miles a day during the week, start going four miles one day, then two weeks later, five miles. If five miles feels long enough, hold it at that, and have a five-mile run every two weeks. But if you want to, keep increasing a mile every two weeks—make that be a special day. It will give you more endurance, help burn more fat, get you in better condition—and make you feel better, even if you never intend to race.

The long run is described in detail on pp. 119-120.

Pace. In both daily runs and long runs, go 1½-2 minutes slower than your current 10K race pace. I run 2 minutes slower. Even if you feel comfortable at a faster pace, slow down and learn to enjoy the slower running. This will give you the rest you need to run faster in races.

Form Work. Twice a week, on easy days, run 4-8 accelerations during the run with complete recovery in between. For 100-200 yards accelerate to a speed that is fast but not all-out (about current one-mile race pace). Keep it under control. Think about your form then, but don't worry about it at other times while running.

Form is described in detail on pp. 146-157.

Races. Races can be run for practice, as stepping stones to the big race you are aiming for—but no more often than every other week. One per month is a better policy. Don't run them all-out, but use them as harder-than-normal runs (no faster than half the time difference between your mile pace for a 10K and your relaxed training pace).

HILL TRAINING

Base period training gives you endurance and cardiovascular efficiency. Before jumping into speedwork, however, the body needs a period of transition to build strength. Hills prepare the muscles for faster running without going anaerobic.

Lydiard maintains that *hills are the only beneficial type of resistance training for runners,* and that hill training will enable you to run better on all types of terrain. I agree. Hills strengthen running muscles while they are running. This gives functional strength as opposed to the specific and limited strength of weight training.

Hills strengthen the main driving muscles–quadriceps, hamstrings and especially calf muscles. As the calf muscles get stronger, you can support your body weight farther forward on your feet and use the mechanical advantage of the ankle. This leads to more efficient running because the ankle is such an efficient mechanical lever.

As the base period develops the internal "plumbing," hill training develops *strength for running.* The legs get a taste of working hard without going into oxygen debt and without the hard impact/trauma of speedwork.

In the hill phase of the pyramid, the only real change from the base period is the hill workout one day a week. All other training remains the same. Most runners do hill work mid-week–on Tuesday or Wednesday.

Find a hill with a moderate grade, about 10-15%. If it's too steep you can't develop a good sustained drive and rhythm. Run at about 85% effort (slightly faster than 10K race pace) and jog slowly down to recover. If you need more rest in between, take it. This is not supposed to be an anaerobic workout. Start with about four hills and increase by one a week until you can run 8-12 hills. Give yourself at least two days rest between hill workouts and races or long runs.

Hill training usually lasts 4-6 weeks. Experienced, competitive runners can run two hill workouts a week, but be careful about this, because it's stressful and makes injury more likely.

Hill running form is described in detail on pp. 155-156.

SPEED TRAINING

Your *base period* gives you endurance, and that, along with strengthening *hill training* gets you ready for *speed.* So long as you continue the long runs, the speedwork will enable you to run faster for all distances. Each workout pushes the body farther than it went the week before. The working muscles thus gradually experience the increased workload. The rest period that follows allows rebuilding for the next test. The final workouts in the speed phase will gradually build until they simulate race conditions.

In the early part of this century, speedwork consisted of running time trials and races. Athletes ran races without training in between. In between races the more ambitious ran time trials at their race distance. Training this way, they rarely increased their speed.

Interval training and *fartlek* ("speed play," see pp. 84-87) were introduced in Europe about 1920. These methods divided the race distance into several parts. Runners ran faster than race pace for a set distance, rested between segments and repeated the process numerous times. The number and speed of repetitions increased each week until the endurance demands of the race were simulated. By breaking up the hard segments with rest periods, the overall stress of each workout was not as substantial as that required by a race. Whereas hard sustained effort tears the muscles down through gradual exhaustion, the rest intervals between speed accelerations keep the muscles from being overly fatigued.

The 8-week rule: After about 8 weeks of speedwork your performance will tend to peak. If you keep up intensive speedwork after this, you'll be risking injury, illness or fatigue.

Not for beginners: Speedwork isn't for everyone. If you don't have a time goal, you don't need it. It puts a lot of stress on your body and increases the chances of injury. Speed training is potentially more damaging than long runs. On the positive side, however, it can train tired legs to go farther and faster. You should stay in the base period for your first one or two years. During this time, an occasional speed session would consist of merely accelerating faster than normal pace for portions of the run.

Speedwork is described in more detail on pp. 81-91.

AFTER THE PYRAMID

When you have finished the speed phase of a pyramid and have run your "big" race, it's time to recycle and begin the base part of a new pyramid. Going back to another base period is a relief after a hard period of speed and races. The wear and tear of your peaking period will be repaired, muscle fibers restored, and you'll be ready with greater cardiovascular capacity the next time around.

Like a sand pyramid on the beach, the wider the base, the higher the peak. Start with a solid base, get plenty of rest, and you'll improve your condition and performances. One pyramid can be the base for the next one, if you plan it that way. For example, a 10K pyramid in the spring will give you the speedwork you need for use in your fall marathon pyramid—which gives you endurance for the next spring 10K and etc.... A series of increasingly difficult workouts will lead you from one stage to the next and make possible the fulfillment of your goals.

This has been an overall description of planning, goals, and the basic elements of this new approach to running. The chapters in the Racing *section of the book go into all the aspects of such a plan in greater detail.*

6 YOUR RUNNING LOG

	Date	Course	Distance	Time	Comments
M			11		up Hill By Rancho Baulines 1½ hrs
T			5		Stinson Beach
W		Row 20 Exercy 30	0		Sore calves
T			16		Thru woods to L. Ranch & Back. Last 4 mi = 32 [illegible] Felt tired but good
F			0		Cold still hanging on (sniffles) next time stick w treatment til it's gone
S			7½		
S		Row 20 Exer 30			
		* Week's Total	39½		
		Week's Average			
	Week #______	Year-to-Date			

MUST YOU KEEP A LOG? Not necessarily. Some people apparently make great progress with little or no planning and lots of luck. You don't need a plan to run, or even to make progress with your running. Indeed, some of your greatest experiences will be the unplanned ones: the spontaneity of the daily run, a beautiful day in the woods, coming upon an unexpected sunset, etc. But organization is what separates the runner from the jogger. Runners make more progress because they begin to schedule for their success, and schedule to avoid injuries, while joggers just get out there when they can.

Many runners will run for months, or years, without keeping a log. It seems like too much trouble, too fussy, or unnecessary. Yet eventually, perhaps through an injury, perhaps through the examples of friends, they'll start keeping a log, and then wonder how they ever ran without it.

	Date	Course	Distance	Time	Comments
M	12/5	up Hill, Down Road By R. Barn.	13		Rain Sore calves
T			7½		Easy, on roads
W			0		
T		Speed 6 mi @7	8		Cold just starting to fade
F			12		up canyon to ridge trail, back to Bolinas
S			0		
S			8		Feels like too much mileage
		Week's Total	48		
		Week's Average			
Week #____		Year-to-Date			

The log helps you analyze past mistakes as well as successes. Only with the details written down can you go back and see what led you up to the present. Ultimately you'll develop your own training program. You can do this efficiently by recording your daily work, analyzing the results, and re-designing your program. Not only can the log be used as a record of the past, it can also be used to schedule your training and races for the future.

Plan for Your Goal. You need a plan to make maximum progress toward a goal. Since a common goal is to run "injury-free" we must plot our activity to keep from over-doing it. Time goals especially require a plan. A plan is a tool, a guide for inspiration. Through a plan, a beginner can lay out an easier path, avoid injury and become addicted to running. A veteran can plan for variety, challenge and improvement.

An effective plan will stage a series of small successes starting from your present training program. Each step feeds on the confidence developed from the last. Every plan must have the right combination of stress and rest for *you.*

A plan must also be flexible. Things change daily. At every step you should re-evaluate progress and adjust the log to reflect your current condition, ability and other factors in your life. Successful plans are often changed en route to the goal.

A log helps speed up improvement and provides a sense of continuity over the long haul. Since a log is not only your plan for the future, but a record of your past improvement, it helps you pick things up when the doldrums set in. And a log can tell you exactly what you did to cause an injury so you can avoid the same mistakes next time.

Components of Your Log. Your log can be something like *Runner's Log, Jim Fixx's Calendar*, or just a wall calendar. In it you can schedule:

• *Long runs.* Relaxed challenges. You may not be able to run faster each year, but you can run farther. This gives you a continuing feeling of progress and accomplishment. You get to know yourself well on the long ones.

• *Hard runs* help you improve your speed. Competitors will schedule a hard run about once a week during their speed phase.

RUNNING LOG

DAY	WEATHER	TEMP	TIME (AM/PM)	TERRAIN	DATE	COMMENTS	1–7	TIME	GOAL	MILES
SUNDAY	Morn Pulse 49		AM PM			rainy cycled for 1 hour	1 2 3 4 5 6 7		0	0
MONDAY	Morn Pulse 48	56°	AM (circled) PM			felt fresh and bouncy	1 2 3 4 5 6 7		2-3	3
TUESDAY	Morn Pulse 50	76°	AM PM (circled)			hard speed workout 16 x 440 in 92 with 440 jog had trouble holding pace last 3 shin hurt form work	1 2 3 4 5 6 7		4-6	5
WEDNESDAY	Pulse (AM) 55	78°	AM PM (circled)			dragged – very tired might be dehydrated	1 2 3 4 5 6 7	25 min	3	2
THURSDAY	Pulse (AM) 55	65°	AM (circled) PM			felt better, but still took it easy form work	1 2 3 4 5 6 7		4-6	4
FRIDAY	Pulse (AM) 52		AM PM			rough week at work nice to take it off	1 2 3 4 5 6 7		0	0
SATURDAY	Pulse (AM) 53	59°	AM (circled) PM			Long run easy pace but ran a bit faster coming in right shin hurt	1 2 3 4 5 6 7	59 min	7	7

TOTAL MILES FOR YEAR [ ] WEIGHT [ ]

TOTAL MILEAGE OR TOTAL MINUTES: 21

Most runners should schedule some transition work, usually hills, before jumping into speedwork.

•*Social runs* give you a chance to chat as you run, or take a quiet run with a good friend. Long and hard days should be balanced with easy ones and the social run can provide the leisurely "Sunday Bar-B-Q" atmosphere.

•*Form work.* Accelerations performed twice a week, year round, teach you to improve your running.

•*Scenic runs* are trips to beautiful running areas near home. If you cover the same course every day, scenic runs can get you out of the rut to enjoy some different terrain and scenery.

•*Races* are not just competitive experiences, they are ways to evaluate your running progress. Anticipating a race gives far more meaning to your daily runs and keeps you motivated. It's inspiring to see hundreds of people working toward a common goal and helping one another along the way.

•*Trips* provide variety and excitement. You can run in different parts of the country on business trips or vacations, or schedule specific running excursions to scenic areas. Running in unfamiliar areas often introduces you to instant friends. You may have more in common with runners you meet in another town than you do with your non-running next-door neighbors.

•*Rewards.* Positive reinforcement helps keep you on track. Too often runners progress gradually and don't realize the extent of the improvement. Rewards are as varied as the individuals who appreciate them: dinner out, clothes, shoes, etc. Small things for small improvements in your training program; bigger rewards for more significant time or distance goals.

•*Easy runs.* The other runs (and all of the above except for speedwork, races and form work) are run at an easy, comfortable pace.

Filling Out the Log. Here are the components of your running program. Once you know what you're going to do, you can pursue your plan with more enthusiasm.

Plan Your "Pyramid." Designate the time you would like to "peak," and count back. A 10K runner on a six-month program would allow eight weeks for speedwork. A marathoner should allow at least 12

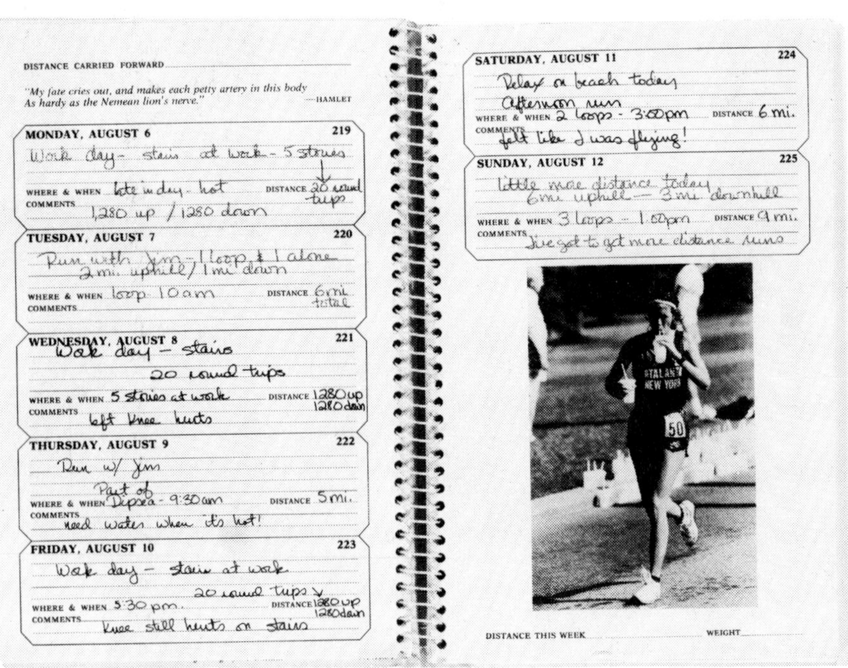

DISTANCE CARRIED FORWARD

"My fate cries out, and makes each petty artery in this body
As hardy as the Nemean lion's nerve." —HAMLET

MONDAY, AUGUST 6 219
Work day - stairs at work - 5 stories
WHERE & WHEN late in day - hot DISTANCE 20 round trips
COMMENTS 1,280 up / 1280 down

TUESDAY, AUGUST 7 220
Run with Jim - 1 loop, + 1 alone
2 mi. uphill / 1 mi down
WHERE & WHEN loop 10am DISTANCE 6 mi. total
COMMENTS

WEDNESDAY, AUGUST 8 221
Work day - stairs
20 round trips
WHERE & WHEN 5 stories at work DISTANCE 1280 up 1280 down
COMMENTS left knee hurts

THURSDAY, AUGUST 9 222
Run w/ Jim
WHERE & WHEN Part of Dipsea - 9:30 am DISTANCE 5 mi.
COMMENTS need water when it's hot!

FRIDAY, AUGUST 10 223
Work day - stairs at work
20 round trips
WHERE & WHEN 5:30 pm. DISTANCE 1280 up 1280 down
COMMENTS Knee still hurts on stairs

SATURDAY, AUGUST 11 224
Relax on beach today
Afternoon run
WHERE & WHEN 2 loops - 3:00pm DISTANCE 6 mi.
COMMENTS felt like I was flying!

SUNDAY, AUGUST 12 225
Little more distance today
6mi uphill — 3 mi downhill
WHERE & WHEN 3 loops - 1:00pm DISTANCE 9 mi.
COMMENTS I've got to get more distance runs

DISTANCE THIS WEEK WEIGHT

weeks. Preceding this, there would be four weeks of hill training and before this, the base period. This is a 32-week period for a marathon.

Pencil in the long runs, the hard runs and the races which will lead you to your goal. Look over the principles of daily and weekly mileage in the next chapter to help in your planning and see the charts on pp. 108-114 and 122-131. See how the whole picture looks and adjust where necessary.

Monitor Your Morning Pulse and Weight. A key entry for your daily log is your resting pulse rate, taken before you get out of bed each morning. Your body is less affected by external pressures like meals at this time. As soon as possible after waking, take your pulse and record it in the log. After two weeks, you should have a base line, an average. When morning pulse rises more than 10% above base, it's a sign you've been working too hard and you need one or more days of reduced activity. By keeping tabs on yourself this way, you'll monitor patterns in your training and be able to add rest days when needed.

Also, be aware of daily weight loss. It takes about 25 miles of running to lose a pound of fat. If you didn't run that far the day before, it's dehydration: water loss. Right after rising, weigh yourself and record it in your log. When you drop more than two percent of body weight in a day, take a *very* easy day. When it drops three percent or more, take the day off. Be sure to drink plenty of liquids to replenish, should this happen.

7 DAILY AND WEEKLY MILEAGE PROGRAMS

KENNY MOORE FINISHED 4TH in the 1972 Olympic Marathon. He says he wouldn't have come nearly this far if he hadn't discovered the importance of rest. In his high school track days, Kenny didn't win a single race. After a year and a half of training, on the University of Oregon track team, he began to improve. He started to "beat" some of the better Oregon runners—at least in practice.

Excited by the prospect of becoming a winner, Kenny decided to train harder for a coming indoor track meet against Stanford and sneaked in some extra workouts to get ready. Confident at the starting line, he knew that none of his competitors had worked as hard as he had coming into this two-mile race. At the crack of the starting gun, he went with the leaders, but at the halfway point ran out of gas. He finished in one of his slowest times in years, 9:48.

While sitting in misery in the locker room he saw his coach, Bill Bowerman, heading toward him. "Good," he thought, "Bill's going to cheer me up with an inspiring talk." The internationally respected mentor, however, put a hand on Kenny's shoulder and commenced to read him the riot act. Bowerman had noticed Moore's

THE IMPORTANCE OF REST

extra workouts. He made his point quickly: Moore would run no more than three easy miles per day for two weeks or be kicked off the team. Kenny was insulted. He had worked harder than anyone else and was now being criticized for it. He *knew* he'd lose fitness—and races—under such a program. Determined to show that his coach was wrong, he followed the instructions to the letter. When he lined up against Washington State two weeks later, he was confident he'd do poorly from lack of training and show up the "old man." This time he laid back at first, waiting for the out-of-shape "bear" to jump on his back. Instead, he found himself taking the lead at the mile and going on to win the race. His time: 8:48!

Although exalted by his fastest-ever time, he was humble as he thanked his coach. Bowerman knew Moore had pushed too hard without rest and that he'd come around if he took it easy. The sage of Eugene's Hayward Field track also knew that Kenny Moore was like most of us, and wouldn't rest unless confronted by the Wrath of God.

Getting Stronger. You cannot improve if you cannot run. *The single greatest cause of improvement is remaining injury-free.* If you're like most runners, you push it to the limit, and then mother nature steps in and forces you to rest. This slows your progress, for you must rebuild after each "down" period. But if you *build rest into your training program* you can avoid injuries and interruptions in your progress.

A common, overused running adage tells you to "listen to your body and you won't get injured." That would be great if it worked, but often either the signals are not strong enough or we're not listening attentively. A coveted goal will often cause us to push too far, to lose touch with the real condition of tired muscles. Or maybe we're preoccupied with other problems, and not paying careful enough attention to the warning signals.

When your muscles are overstressed, your body tries to mask the tiredness. For a while the body slavishly responds to the mind's commands. When exhausted, the body draws upon its reserves; but reserves are limited, and once they've run out, you're at the crash point. This can have three results: *injury, sickness* or *slump.*

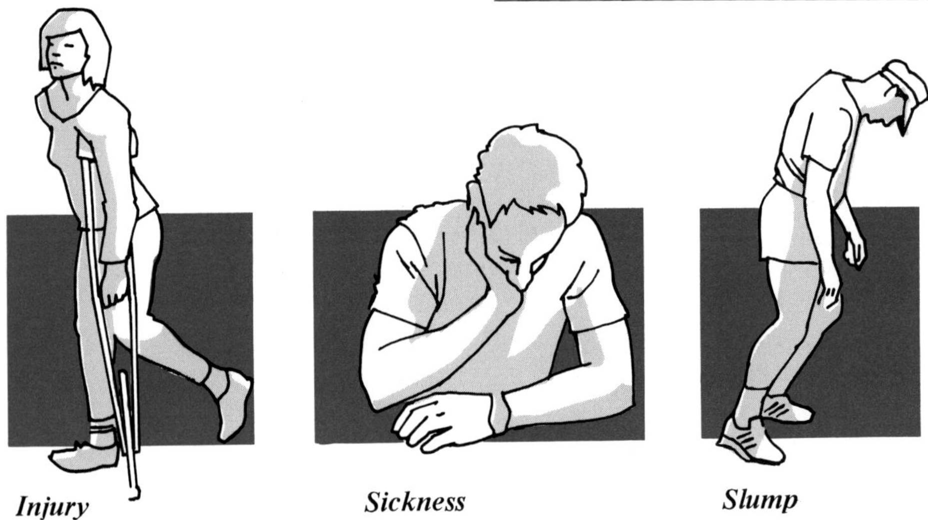

Injury *Sickness* *Slump*

Injury: With reserves gone, muscles are so exhausted they cannot function normally. Weaker muscles try to take over the job and are usually overwhelmed. For example, the calf muscle is designed to provide much of your running power. When it gets tired it may shift some of the burden to the weak muscles on the inside of the lower leg. Shin splints and other shin problems often result by continuing to push, especially if you're a pronator (where the forefoot rolls excessively to the inside). In this way, pushing too far will quickly show you the weak links.

Sickness: When the body is under prolonged stress, your resistance to disease is dramatically reduced. If a group of strong infectious germs wanders in, they're far more likely to find a comfortable home—at your expense and misery.

Slump: If you are lucky enough to avoid injury or sickness, there's a "slump" waiting for you at the end of your exhaustion trip. Once you've hit rock bottom, there's no backing off. Your muscles won't respond even if you muster the will to drive them. You're going to feel tired, lacking in energy, and probably depressed until you build up your reserves again. This can last for weeks or months.

How can you avoid the above three undesirable conditions? *Rest* is the answer. Since "listening to your body" doesn't always work, you must build rest into your program— before it becomes the only choice and you're forced to take a long vacation from running.

STRESS + REST

Rx For Maximum Improvement. A basic and simple principle of getting stronger has been recognized in recent years. Coaches, sport physiologists and top athletes agree that the most effective way to improve strength and endurance is to *stress*, and then *rest* the muscles. We've outlined the cellular aspects of stress/rest in the chapter on physiology (see pp. 40-42). Now we're going to cover the application of this equation to your daily and weekly mileage programs.

Rest is at least as important as stress in this formula. Muscles will rebuild stronger after being stressed, but *only* if they are given enough resting time. The trouble with most runners, and the cause of most injuries, is that the second half of the formula is neglected. You stress yourself–with speedwork, races, long runs, or weekly mileage increases. Then without adequate rest in between, you find yourself sidelined with an injury.

Individual muscle cells will do the work for which they have been prepared. When you push the muscles harder than you have before, they can become overwhelmed. They can no longer process oxygen and fuel efficiently and they build up large amounts of waste, primarily lactic acid. The mitochondria will try their best to process the energy needed, but are simply not able to do so. The circulation system becomes overloaded, the cell walls are physically "beaten up," swollen and even broken in places. You have an injury, but it may not be extensive enough to cause serious problems.

After 48 hours of reduced activity most of these problems should have been remedied. The walls of the cells, arteries and blood vessels have been rebuilt stronger. The mitochondria are recharged and can process more energy. The capillaries will be working to remove wastes and deliver nutrients. Most runners need two easy days after every hard day for the rebuilding to take place.

Here is a chart of the specific effects of stress and rest:

CHANGES INSIDE THE MUSCLE CELLS

	RESULTS OF HARD RUN	RESULTS AFTER REST
MITOCHONDRIA	SWOLLEN, ENERGY SUPPLIES DEPLETED	RECHARGED
CELL WALLS	TORN	TEARS HEALED
WASTE	LACTIC ACID BUILDUP	WASTES REMOVED, CELLS REPACKED WITH NUTRIENTS

THE DAILY MILEAGE PROGRAM

Many runners know they should run easy after each hard day. Oregon's Bill Bowerman is credited with this concept. This seems obvious today, but it wasn't in 1966 when I met Oregon steeplechaser Geoff Hollister. I was proud of my own progress under a system where I worked out hard each day. Back in the dark ages of my own running theories, it seemed that each day I slacked off, my competitors moved up a notch. I was amazed to learn from Geoff that the scores of national champions, recordholders and world-ranked runners from his alma mater thrived under a program that let them "loaf" every other day. We east coast runners still believed we had to run harder each day to improve—and we were also injured much of the time.

The Easy Day Rule. For most runners an easy day will mean fewer and slower miles rather than no running at all. This causes a gentle circulation of blood, oxygen and nutrients which speed the recovery (and strengthening) process. Dr. George Sheehan shifted to running every other day late in his running career. After several years of this he ran his fastest marathon (2:56) at age 62. Jack Foster, the New Zealander who ran a 2:11 marathon at age 41, also shifted to this program, running three, or at most four days a week because otherwise he "inevitably came up with an injury after about 10 days." After about two years of this, he ran a 2:20 marathon at age 50. Jack also does some cycling on one non-running day per week.

Each runner will find his or her own pattern of daily rest periods. Kenny Moore found that he needed two days of rest after hard days. He runs an easy 2-3 miles after a hard day, then an easy 8-10 miles the next day. We have to find the combination that works best.

Each of us responds differently to hard work or long runs. Some will feel very tired that night, others the next day. Some may feel fine the day after and then wake up exhausted the second day. Likewise, a tiring workout will produce lingering effects for some and only minor aches, pains and fatigue for others. Even if you don't feel tired, it's best to take one or two easy days after a hard one.

How Many Days Per Week? Research has shown that you need at least three days running per week for sustained improvement. One or two days do comparatively little for you. At three days the improvement curve rises dramatically. Each day thereafter, improvement continues, but at a decreasing rate.

When you consider the much greater injury risk from six or seven days running, five looks like the best compromise. Your rest days should be spaced fairly evenly throughout the week. If you want to exercise on non-running days, you can improve endurance and strength through cycling, swimming, rowing or other non-jarring activities. Only world-class runners can run seven days a week; but they, as well as other runners, can benefit physically as well as psychologically from a day or two of rest. (See chart at right.)

How Much Rest After Races? Jack Foster believes you need one easy day for each mile of a race. The sustained drain of a race takes its toll. You shouldn't run another race or do speedwork until you

HOW MANY DAYS A WEEK SHOULD YOU RUN?

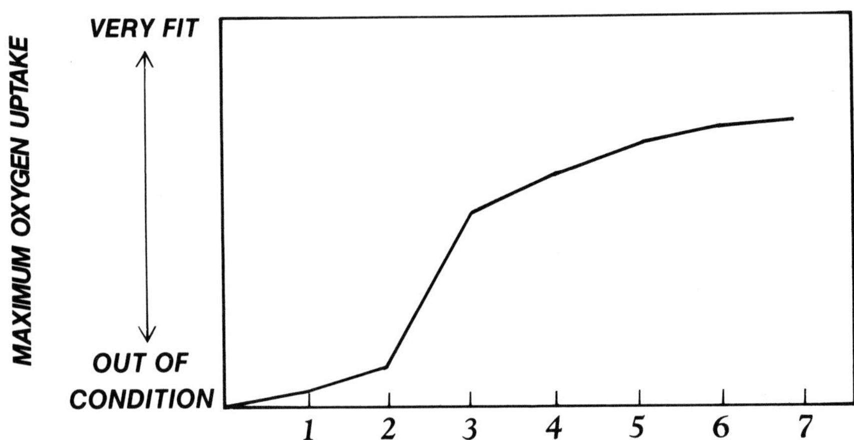

Note the dramatic increase in fitness from training three as opposed to two days a week. Over 95% of aerobic capacity is gained in training 4-5 days a week. Going beyond that point, the rate of orthopedic injuries rises drastically. (See p. 271 for reference.)

have served your time according to "Foster's Rule." You could run a light speed workout 3-4 days after a 10K race; but no hard work should be attempted for 2-3 weeks after a marathon. No race (except a 5K or shorter) should be run the weekend after a race longer than 4 miles. I've found that most runners should limit their race miles to 13 each month. This means you can run two 10K's or a half marathon each month.

After a Marathon. You face serious risk of injury if you return to hard running too soon. Many runners think they have recovered from this long race when they start feeling rested and the soreness has gone. But actually there is a *deep, lingering tiredness.* Don't be fooled by a feeling of recovery soon after the marathon. Many runners have felt so good they've run PR's (personal records) in races just a week after a marathon, only to be injured shortly thereafter because they pushed too hard too soon. I believe that after a marathon you should wait two months before racing again.

How Much Rest After Speed? In speedwork–either invervals or fartlek (see pp. 84-87)–you're resting after each hard effort. This isn't like the uninterrupted strain of a race, so you don't need as much rest time. Most runners should only do one speed session a week; this will not overstress the system. *(See Chapter 8, p. 81 for details on speedwork.)*

THE WEEKLY MILEAGE PROGRAM

It's not enough to merely have easy days each week. A steady mileage program, at whatever level, leaves a residual tiredness that builds up, and eventually produces injury. You not only need the rest days after stress, but regularly scheduled rest weeks with reduced mileage, allowing the body to rebuild.

As you increase stress or even maintain the same load, tired muscle cells break down and must be replaced with fresh ones. When one group of cells becomes exhausted, the burden of carrying on is shifted to other, usually weaker muscle groups. Small tears and broken tissues are not healed completely by a few rest days within a steady mileage program. If you don't reduce overall mileage you will dig into reserves which eventually run out and leave you exhausted. Over time, the isolated small tears in the muscle fibers accumulate enough to cause an injury. If you're increasing mileage, you are even more apt to face an injury.

The Easy Week Rule. If you cut your mileage by 30% the second week and 50% the fourth week you can avoid this mileage stress. This is a safety valve which allows your body to recover and shake off the accumulated stress and the physical abuse of running.

Some runners need more rest than others. Be conservative and find the pattern that works best for you. Don't be worried about losing conditioning. Studies have shown that athletes can cut their workouts by 50% for ten weeks and not lose significant fitness. In fact you gain rather than lose by cutting back, because you return rested and less prone to injury.

Low-Mileage Ultras? Steve Boyer, a friend of mine from college, is a doctor and has had to regulate his running and racing addiction. He has run several marathons (a best time of 2:42) for which his weekly training miles varied between 20 and 45.

In preparing for the 1983 Mt. Hood (Oregon) 40-miler, he decided to test my low-mileage/long run theory to its limits. A complicating factor was the altitude, and the rise and fall of the course (10,000 feet of gain and loss). Steve decided to spend his limited training time as specifically as possible for this difficult race.

He gradually built the long run to 30 miles with 2000 feet of vertical gain or did repeat hill repetitions with 7500 feet of vertical gain. Two weeks before the race he pre-ran the course very slowly. The day after each long run, he did not run, and gradually eased back into running (3-4 miles, 6-7 miles, etc.) The last week before the race he ran only 20 miles. Most weeks he ran less than 50 miles.

The results should be of interest to high-mileage advocates: In a strong field, including Bill Davis (third in one of the Western States 100's), Rae Clark (Tahoe 70-mile recordholder) and Frank Thomas (who holds the record for running across England), Steve finished second. He was six minutes behind the winner and later told me he thought he might have won had his ego not pushed him too fast (a 10-minute lead at 15 miles going up the first long hill).

Less Mileage For a Faster 10K. Lower mileage can also improve times for the middle distances. John Perkins found this out after three 2800-mile running years. He had reached plateaus with his marathon and 10K racing times despite his 50-70 miles per week, which included long runs and speedwork. After a disappointing finish in the New York City Marathon in 1981, he decided to give up racing and the hard training and run much fewer miles.

During an 18-month "vacation," John's competitive instincts didn't die. When he heard that a number of runners were improving performances with a program of reduced total mileage, a relaxed pace for the daily runs and weekly speedwork, John decided to test the new theories.

For about nine months John averaged 39 miles per week. He did a speed workout once a week with 8-10 440's at 82 seconds and gradually increased to 18 440's. Then he dropped to 10 440's, run at 74 seconds. This program helped him lower his 10K and 5K race times significantly.

John says he now feels strong from start to finish, whereas he used to feel lethargic, tired and unresponsive. He's not afraid to challenge other runners, or to increase the pace slightly after the first mile. Before, he was tired throughout each race and was looking for the finish line after the first mile.

On the next page is a comparison of John's previous program—weekly mileage, pace, and races—and his new one.

Previous Program	*New Program*
50-70 miles per week.	30-50 miles per week.
One hard 15+ mile run per week.	One easy 12-15 mile run every other week.
Pace for daily runs: 6:40-6:50.	Pace for daily runs: 7:45-8:00.
Raced most weeks.	Races every other week.
Best race times: 10K–37:27 5K–18:20	Best race times: 10K–36:34 5K–17:36

COLD WEATHER

Generally, cold weather makes running easier. Since there is less heat buildup, there is less body fluid lost, and the cool temperature makes running more invigorating. When the mercury drops below 50°, however, you'll have to start thinking of protective measures.

Head & hands: Cover them up: hat and gloves. Running causes a chill factor and if there is wind, things will be colder than the thermometer indicates. Wool or polypropylene are the best materials.

Lungs: There's no real evidence that you can freeze your lungs while running. There are protective barriers and buffer zones that protect these vital organs. Although cold air can be uncomfortable on your throat, I know of no case of "runner's frozen throat" either. You can reduce this discomfort by breathing through a ski mask or bandana.

Vital parts: Men, please wear more than nylon tricot shorts if you value your future family production. Penile frostbite is no joke. It comes on so gradually, you may not even notice it. When the injured member warms up, there is a great deal of pain. By wearing a tight-fitting underwear or a jock, and several layers (shorts, long underwear, warm-up pants), you will avoid this.

The layered look: A warm jacket with a heavy sweater may feel good to start with, but chances are you'll overheat and lose too much body fluid, so don't overdress. Several thin layers give you flexibility; you can add or remove a layer to stay comfortable.

Marine wool or polypropylene are the best materials to use next to your skin. They keep you warm but release excess heat as it builds up. Water is "wicked" to the outside and away from your skin. You want to get the sweat away from your skin, since cold weather can make it freeze.

Wind or rain suits: Nylon suits are usually treated to be water-repellent and will keep water out for a while, but it will eventually soak through. Goretex or the PTFE-film lightweight suits act like skin—they keep water out, but allow heat and air to escape. To be perfectly waterproof, seams must be treated. Goretex is the best material I've found for protecting the body from the wet and cold.

Into the wind: Don't start out running *with* the wind. If you heat up, you'll find that your sweat turns to ice when you turn around to run back. Run *against* the wind at first.

Vitamin C supplements will help heal the cracks that runners develop in their nasal passages in cold weather and, from my experience, it seems to be good insurance against colds.

HOT WEATHER

Everyone hates to run in the heat, but some cope with it better than others. You can make it easier on yourself if you train to run in the heat.

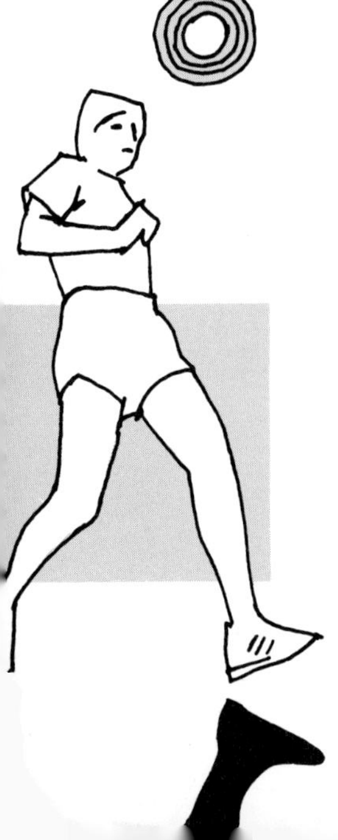

Physiology of Hot Weather Running. In hot weather, blood rushes to the surface of your skin and spreads out in thousands of tiny capillaries to release the heat. Small reservoirs of water in the sweat glands are squeezed out on the skin's surface by tiny "sweat muscles" to cool off the skin and body through evaporation. *This capillary action and sweating diverts needed blood away from the exercising muscles, reducing their work capacity.* There is also less blood to carry oxygen to the cells and remove waste. Although you may become adapted to the heat through training, even the best heat runner will feel discomfort and run slower as the mercury climbs above 55°.

Training For the Heat. The tiny sweat muscles can be exercised like any other muscles. As you continue to run in the heat they become stronger and more efficient, secreting enough water on the surface to cool you—but not a wasteful amount. Only by running in hot weather can you condition these muscles for maximum cooling efficiency. It often takes months before you see any improvement.

It's obviously best to train for heat *in* the heat. But if it's cold, wear extra clothing to simulate 80° temperatures. At first, run only a few minutes; gradually increase the length of the training runs until you're running the distance of the race you're training for. *Run slowly.* Two or three sessions a week are enough to develop this adaptation. Drink some water every waking hour.

Hot Weather Clothing. Obviously the object is to keep as cool as possible, so less blood will be needed in the surface capillaries and can go instead to the exercising muscles. Light, loose clothing will help, especially if it's wet or humid. It's better to wear *some* clothing than none, it keeps the sun partially off your skin. Cotton will hold any water you pour on, allowing it to evaporate slowly. Nylon and other synthetics do not absorb moisture. A light mesh with large holes is a good combination of coolness and absorption. I like 50-50 polyester/cotton blend best. To avoid chafing, don't wear tight garments or those with too much material in the armpits or between the legs.

Water in the Heat. You need a tremendous amount of fluid in the heat. Cold water is absorbed most quickly. Fluids and foods containing electrolytes (the salts of magnesium, potassium and calcium) should be consumed regularly during hot weather training. A recommended quota of water is ten 6-8 ounce glasses spread throughout the day, every day. Remember, coffee and alcohol are diuretics and will cause you to lose more water than you gain from them. The greatest heat problem is dehydration. Drink all day long and throughout your runs—especially the long ones. Stash water in the bushes along the route if necessary.

RACING
5

8 SPEED

TOP OF THE PYRAMID

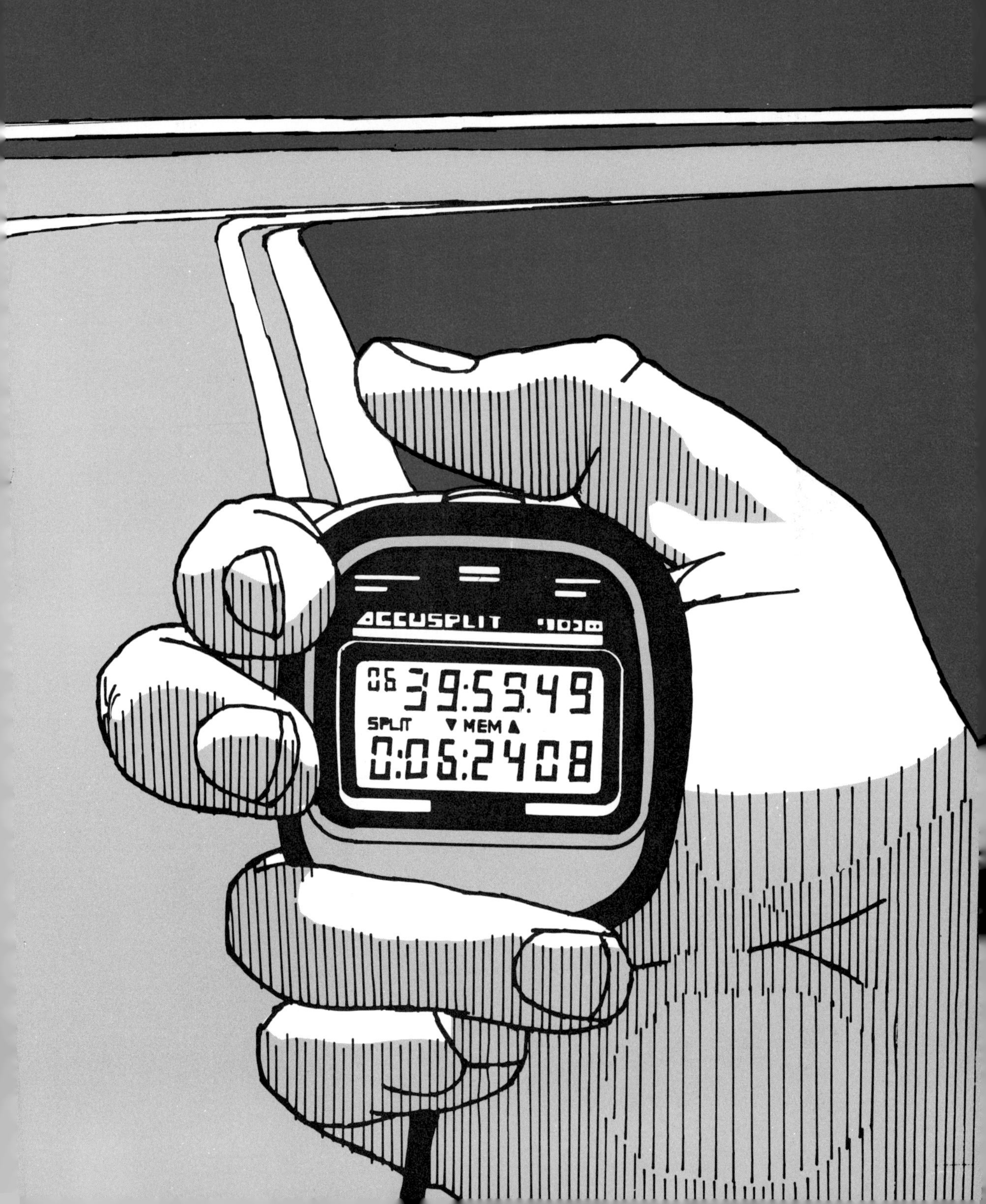
ACCUSPLIT
06 39:55.49
SPLIT
MEM
0:06:2408

YOU CAN RUN FASTER! I've seen thousands of runners improve by making simple changes such as:

- Rearranging their schedules.
- Adding rest.
- Doing speedwork.

The first rule is that your goals must be realistic. Setting a goal that is too ambitious will only lead to disappointment and frustration. But if you stage a series of goals that are within your reach, you'll build your running capacity *and* your confidence.

How Much Can You Expect to Improve?

Best performance last 6 months:	***Amount you might improve in 6-month pyramid:***
50 min. 10K; 4:30 marathon	3-5 min. 10K; 30 min. marathon
42-50 min. 10K; 3:30-4:30 marathon	2-3 min. 10K; 15-20 min. marathon
38-42 min. 10K; 3:05-3:30 marathon	1-2 min. 10K; 8-15 min. marathon
35-38 min. 10K; 2:40-3:05 marathon	40 sec.-1 min. 10K; 5-10 min. marathon
32-35 min. 10K; 2:30-2:40 marathon	20-40 sec. 10K; 2-5 min. marathon

Note: There's obviously a limit to how much you can improve. You'll reach plateaus at which your performance will level off, and sometimes even drop. A plateau may last a month or so, or even a year. As you get closer to your ultimate potential, the plateaus will tend to occur more often, and last longer.

Base Before Speed. *Before attempting any speedwork, you must have built a good base, consisting of:*

- One year of running.
- At least two months (and preferably three) of aerobic running.
- 4-6 weeks of hill training.
- *See pp. 55-59 for details.*

You're at the Top of the Pyramid

During the base period you get your cardiovascular system ready to handle future speed demands. Whether you've run speedwork before or not, your base period will improve cardiovascular efficiency. Veterans find that base training also cleans out waste from a recent speed program.

Your hill training strengthens the key running muscles in your lower legs, allowing you to shift your weight a bit farther forward on your feet and to use your ankles for efficient mechanical advantage—gaining a stronger push-off. Now you're ready for the fast stuff!

The primary benefit of speedwork is to teach the body how to run anaerobically—to run fast when the muscles can't get enough oxygen. To run faster than you have ever run before, you must go beyond your capacity. Speed workouts take you *beyond* in a regular series of small extensions. By the end of the speed session, you should have simulated the anaerobic demands of the race itself.

Each week you go beyond your efforts of the previous week. The lactic acid which pours into the muscles during the latter stages of a workout must be handled or the muscles will slow down. As the body restores the torn muscle cells and recharges the mitochondria (see p. 71), it is able to go farther and faster before producing lactic acid.

By dealing with this weekly dose of waste, the muscle cells learn how to cope with it. In some cases the muscles learn to process it out of the system more efficiently; in other cases they direct the waste into every available crevice. The mind learns that the body can go at least a bit farther even though it feels increasingly uncomfortable.

Speedwork brings you to a peak of performance and prepares you to race. When you have completed each of the small speed workouts in succession, you are at least physiologically ready to go. Of course you still have to take off at the crack of the gun and do it. Nevertheless you have the confidence of being prepared.

Endurance First. Before you can run a 10K fast, you must first be able to run a 10K without stopping. The first component of a speed program is a long run which increases each two weeks until it's longer than the race distance by at least 20%. Starting from the length of your longest run in the previous two weeks, add 1-2 miles once a week until you reach 11-12 miles. Then add 2-3 miles to each long one and run them every 14 days. You'll need this extra time between long runs.

Goal Race	*Minimum Miles*	*For Top Performance*
10K	8	15-17
half marathon	15	20-22
marathon	26	28-30

To avoid a long recovery period, run a slow pace during your long run, about 1½-2 minutes slower than your current 10K race pace. You can include walking breaks of 3-5 minutes, every 30-45 minutes, to make it easy for the body to adapt. These runs build endurance only and are not designed to improve speed. (Advanced runners should not take walking breaks.)

A Short History of Speedwork. Distance runners in the early 1900s believed that to run faster one must run repeated race simulations: full-speed races with rest in between. By the mid-1920s, athletes found they could improve more by breaking the race distance into many short segments and running each faster than race pace *with rest in between.* Two forms of speedwork thus emerged: *fartlek* and *interval training.*

FARTLEK

Fartlek is a Swedish word meaning *speed play.* It's a simple, natural form of speed training that can be worked into any daily run. During a run of a given distance, you accelerate—to the next telephone pole, to the end of the block, to any landmark. When you have pushed as long and as fast as you want (or can), you jog to recover. Then when you feel like it, you take off again.

Fartlek is speed training at your own pace. It is intuitive, free-form, without prescribed distances or speeds. You can run according to how you feel on that day, at that moment. Fartlek is speedwork, but it can be playful and creative.

Fartlek Variations. Two popular fartlek variations are *hill fartlek* and *timed segments.* Hill fartlek begins with a normal non-stressful pace (about one minute slower per mile than 10K race pace). When you come to a hill, accelerate up and over the top—then jog to recover. When you recover, resume your original pace until the next hill.

In timed segment fartlek, you run one minute, two minutes, three minutes, etc., slightly faster than race pace. After gentle warmup of 10-20 minutes of easy running, then 4-8 form accelerations (see pp. 154-55) precede the first segment. Rest enough in between segments for recovery. The total number of segments is up to you.

Not for Beginners. Fartlek does not give a beginner enough structure or feedback to learn a sense of pace. Many veterans who are already "pace-wise," however, can benefit from a fartlek session. While interval training gives the beginner exact feedback, it confines the veteran. Fartlek allows you to play with your limits of speed, tiredness and endurance without stopping at the end of the lap. In this way you learn to cope with race-like discomfort and the anxiety of not knowing how long you can cope before slowing down. Beginners run a high risk of injury in fartlek training while veterans, more sensitive to stress, should know when to back off.

One week before the 1973 National Track Championships I tried to complete my first track workout of the year. The only hard work I had done that season was fartlek, and I needed timed feedback for confidence. After only a few ovals around the track, however, things weren't going right and I decided to go in. But it was a beautiful day, so instead of heading for the showers I found myself running down some of my favorite country roads.

Without realizing it I increased the pace, accelerating for a while, letting off a little, then pouring it on again. I didn't feel particularly good that day, but my rhythm was smooth, so I just let it flow. Ironically, the workout was coming together although I felt bad and had to force myself to keep going.

I know now that this was one of the best workouts of my life and it led me to my best race. One week later, in the National AAU 6-mile at Bakersfield, California, I felt as I had when I started that earlier track workout: dumpy. For four miles I barely hung on in 12th place, and kept thinking about dropping out. Then my mind shifted into the same gear I had found on the roads. I moved up to fourth during the next mile and then took the lead. Although I was outkicked at the end I ran my fastest time, 27:21.

When you have a good sense of pace, fartlek will prepare you best for rigorous races; it helps your mind shift gears. It can teach you to use your often-hidden powers of mental concentration to get beyond the barriers of discomfort and anxiety.

INTERVAL TRAINING

What Is It? Interval training breaks up the race distance into segments, called repetitions, or "reps." You run each rep slightly faster than goal race pace, then either jog or walk during the rest interval to recover. The number of reps is gradually increased over a series of weekly workouts. When preparing for the 10K race or less, the eventual total will be close to race distance. But the total distance of speedwork for a marathon will add up to only about one half the race distance.

Repeating these segments may sometimes be boring, but the method gives you an invaluable lesson in judging pace. One of the most important skills of distance running is being able to judge whether you are running too fast or too slow.

Interval training is exact and has several advantages over fartlek:

- With a measured distance, you know exactly what you're doing.
- By controlling the pace of each rep you'll learn how to run an even pace.
- When you first do speedwork, you are often lost when you try fartlek because you can only guess at distance, speed and total amount of work.

Basic Interval Training Principles.

- *Choose the distance of your repetition: ¼ mile, ½ mile or one mile.* It's typical to use 440 yards for a 10K, one mile for a marathon.
- *Run each rep slightly faster (5-7 seconds per 440) than goal pace.* This makes race pace seem easier.
- *Hold back a little.* You need a tiring workout, but shouldn't "total" yourself. Finish the speed day feeling tired, yet capable of running more.

- *Jog very slowly in between to recover.* For 10K speedwork, jogging is better than walking, and a short rest interval is better than a long one. When you start each speed program, however, start with a long rest period—jogging the same distance as the repetition or more. If you recover easily, then decrease the rest interval. Walking is recommended for marathon speedwork.
- *Start with a few repetitions and increase the number in each weekly workout.* (See the charts on pp. 108-114 for a 10K, and pp. 123-131 for a marathon.) At the end of 10K speed training, you'll be doing 20 reps of a 440, with rest in between each one. At the end of marathon speed training you'll be doing 11-13 reps of one mile each, with rest in between.
- *Plenty of rest.* Take at least two days of easy running after each speed session. If speedwork leaves you feeling tired, rest even more to avoid injury.
- *Length of speed program.* Speed programs for the 10K or shorter events are intense and should last less than ten weeks. The marathon speedwork period is extended to 12-14 weeks.

Warmup for Speedwork. Warming up properly is essential. Jumping into a speed session with cold muscles puts tremendous stress on any of your weak links and causes injury.

- Walk 5-10 minutes if it's cold outside or you're stiff.
- Jog *slowly* for 10-20 minutes.
- Stretch *gently* if you usually stretch before running.
- Run accelerations (5-8 x 100-200 yards.) Gradually increase speed to race pace or slightly faster, then decelerate. Take plenty of rest between each acceleration.
- Jog slowly 3-5 minutes.
- Begin workout.

Warmdown After Speedwork. The warmdown is as important as the warmup. If you stop abruptly, the lactic acid in the blood pools and you'll feel stiff the next day. No matter how tired you feel, keep moving.

- Jog slowly for 10 minutes after your last repetition. (Sometimes I barely move one foot in front of the other.)
- Ease into a fast walk for 5-10 minutes.
- Then into a slow walk for 10 minutes.

You need to let the body down easy—don't drop it!

> ***Definitions of Pace***
>
> *Goal pace:* The speed which will lead you to your time goal. Example: 10K goal of 44 min. = 7 min./mile or 1:45/440.
>
> *Speed pace:* Your pace for speed workouts. Example: For a 10K, 440 reps are run 5-7 seconds faster than goal pace.

How Fast and How Long? The longer the reps, the slower the pace:

- 440 yards—5-7 seconds faster than goal pace.
- 880 yards—10 seconds faster than goal pace.
- 1 mile—15-20 seconds faster than goal pace for 10K speedwork.

There is obviously a trade-off here. The longer segments will more closely simulate race conditions, but make it harder to stay "on pace." The longer ones also take a longer recovery period.

Where? Accurate distance is very important. A 440-yard track is obviously a good choice for accuracy, but you can run roads, trails, athletic fields, anywhere, as long as the measurements are accurate. A car odometer and even highway markers are notoriously inaccurate.

Fighting Boredom. As the number of segments grows, speed workouts become more difficult, and often boring. Running in a small group or with another runner helps. Some running clubs devote a day each week to group speedwork, offering a choice of several distances. A workout partner will make these difficult sessions easier and more interesting. Choose someone who will run on pace and who doesn't need to "win" each lap. When you work out with several runners, each should take the lead, alternating laps; after the rest period, another runner takes over the lead.

How Often? You should run one speed workout per week for the 10K, one every other week for the marathon.

SPEEDWORK ALTERNATIVES

Back to the Track. Joe Henderson, one of the original runner-writers, came into running from a competitive track background. He led thousands of runners into fun running in the '70s through his *Runner's World* editorials on long slow runs. Track work practically dropped from his vocabulary.

During the past few years, Joe has returned to the track–but not for the exhausting 15 x 440-yard sessions of his youth. He believes that running four 440's at or slightly faster than your current mile race pace builds speed without undue risk of injury. This workout is done once a week. You take as much rest as needed between repetitions.

Example:

- Current mile race pace: 5:20.
- Average 440: 80 seconds.
- Workout: 4 x 440 with 440 or more jogging in between.
- Warmup and warmdown: 10-20 minutes slow jogging.
- This is a low-stress speed workout which should improve your speed if you are not doing regular speedwork. Improvement under this program is limited, however, because the shorter speed sessions do not develop endurance. Increasing the long run every other week (to 12-16 miles for a 10K, for example) will allow these light speed sessions to produce better results.

Speeding on Sunday. For years, Monica Leerman tried to break 50 minutes in the 10K. She increased mileage, ran more races and did regular speedwork, but nothing got her below the 50-minute threshold.

Then one winter, Monica changed tactics. Instead of running long on Sunday, she ran fast. Over a five-week period she ran a fast (7:15 pace average) three miles with some fartlek bursts. She shifted her weekly long run to mid-week, a 14-16 miler.

The new routine paid off. In a spring Avon 15K race, Monica ran the first 10K in 47:48, and held that pace to the end of the race.

She could probably run even faster if she did some fine tuning with 4-8 form accelerations twice a week and 4-6 440 repetitions at about 7-10 seconds faster than race pace.

MOST FREQUENT CAUSES OF SPEED INJURIES

Speedwork is the second most frequent cause of injury according to a 1980 survey of 4000 running injuries by the George Washington University Sports Medicine Clinic. (Increasing total weekly mileage is the first.) By understanding how they happen, you can avoid most injuries.

These are the main reasons for speed injuries:

• *Inadequate warmup or warmdown.* Be sure to follow a thorough warmup procedure (as described on p. 87). By gradually getting the muscles active, you can avoid the trauma incurred when cold muscles go to maximum exertion. Likewise, it's crucial to gradually ease off in a thorough warmdown.

• *Running too hard on easy days.* The speedwork and the long runs will take you to your goal. You must have easy running days in between these stress days to recover. If you run too fast on the easy days you'll gradually accumulate stress and tiredness which can lead to injury. A good easy day pacing rule is to add 1½-2 minutes per mile to your 10K race pace.

• *Sprinting.* Never run at top speed, not even in play, for there's great risk of injury. Even the form accelerations are designed to reach a maximum speed of only a hard one-mile pace.

• *Too many weeks of speed.* For races of 10K or less, speedwork should last no more than ten weeks. After this period, you run great injury risk by continuing. A marathon speed program should last no longer than 12-14 weeks.

• *Too many hard days.* If you pack too many speed sessions, long runs and races into a short period of time, you're asking for trouble. Running slowly on the long runs and alternating weekends with races or easy runs will reduce stress. It's more important to complete the quality speed workouts and the long runs while minimizing races.

• *Inadequate transition.* Some runners try a "shortcut" up the pyramid by minimizing or eliminating hill work and/or the first few sessions. This forces the body to move too quickly from long slow running to intense speedwork. Jolting the muscles this way tears them down and makes the rebuilding long and difficult. Each hill and speed workout is part of a gradual program, a series of stepping stones in which you gradually apply stress and then recover.

- *On a bad day.* If you're not up to an interval workout, quit. Try it the next day or the day after. If it still doesn't feel right, try a fartlek session or hill workout to simulate the intensity and duration of the interval work. If you suspect you're overly tired, take a low mileage week to recover and then try again.

Getting Off on the Wrong Foot. An early burst of speed doesn't mean much unless you're competing in a 100 yard dash. A would-be shoe thief found this out in our Atlanta store about four years ago. The young man came in, looked at several items, then grabbed a pair of shoes and sped out the door. He didn't realize he was in a true running store. The staff members–competitive runners to a man–drew straws to determine the lucky pursuer. While the thief gained ground in the first 200 yards, our salesman caught him at 600 yards and recovered the shoes from a quarry too tired to resist.

9 PACING

IT'S ALWAYS HARD to tell how fast you are running. Slight physiological changes, tiredness, the weather all affect your running speed. There are tests, however, which allow you to guess fairly accurately.

Speedwork as a test. When you follow a speed program as indicated on the 10K or marathon training charts you're preparing yourself for a goal. It's also a gauge of fitness. If you were able to complete the workout about 10 days before the race in the assigned time, you're ready to run at your goal pace. If you finished the workout easily, or faster than expected, you can expect to run slightly faster than goal pace. If you had trouble or couldn't complete the workout, you should expect a slower race performance.

Test races. If you schedule test races every other weekend leading up to the "big one," you'll get some valuable racing experience. After 2-3 such tests you should be able to estimate how fast your race goal should be. With a combination of speedwork and races as barometers, you can come up with an accurate estimate.

Race Pace. In my senior year in high school, my training for the mile was going well. As I lined up against the South's best milers at the Florida Relays, I knew it was *my* day. Around the first turn I didn't have to strain to move ahead of all but one of the 60 competitors and registered a 59-second second lap (instead of my goal pace of 67 seconds). Running the fastest first lap of my life didn't faze me; I felt strong and was running smoothly. Coming off the last turn into the stretch, I accelerated and could almost touch the leader. Suddenly a gigantic 400-pound "bear" jumped on my back—or so it seemed. A tremendous surge of lactic acid turned my muscles into concrete. I stumbled along to the finish line in a daze, almost oblivious to the stream of runners going by me. Had I run even 2-3 seconds slower on the first lap, I probably could have run with strength to the finish.

Start slow. Everyone knows you can get more out of a tank of gas by driving at an even speed. By stepping on the gas, then coasting, you ruin fuel economy. The same is true in racing. There's an old adage that for every second too fast per mile in the first half of the race, you'll run at least 2 seconds slower at the end. Moreover, the problem increases if you run the first 2-3 miles too fast; *for every second too fast per mile in the first 2-3 miles of the race, you can be as much as 10 seconds slower at the end.*

Your body becomes more efficient as it warms up. The muscles, tendons and joints work better after 10-20 minutes of activity. If you set up an inefficient situation at the beginning, it will be compounded throughout the rest of the race.

Recently I overheard one runner telling a friend he intended to run the first mile of the marathon in 8½ minutes. (His goal was a 7½ minute pace.) His more experienced friend just laughed. "You couldn't run the first mile that slow if you had three people hanging on your back!" Nevertheless, in spite of the adrenalin, excitement, and early-in-the-race speedsters, try to keep it down. You'll be glad later.

Run an even-paced effort. If the course is perfectly flat with no wind, you can run an even pace throughout. But since most courses have hills and most days have wind, you must be realistic. Miles with hills should be run with the same effort as flat miles. Uphill segments will therefore be slower than "pace," and downhill segments faster. The same "even-effort" principle applies to running into the wind, but you cannot quite make up for time lost to a headwind.

Account for heat. Most runners begin to slow down at 55° and start suffering at 65°. Of course, the body can adapt to heat stress and push the threshold up a bit, but you'll never be able to run as fast on a 75° day as on a 45° one. High humidity is also a major problem. It's like a wet blanket; it doesn't allow much evaporation or perspiration and your body heat builds up.

If you try to run too hard in hot or humid conditions you'll hit "the wall" sooner than expected. Trying to maintain a goal pace in heat is like going out too fast early in the race. Temperatures generally increase hour by hour; therefore you must adjust your pace for the temperature expected at the end of the race.

Note: This chart is based upon my own experience in the heat and talking to other runners. It has no scientific verification, but I think you get the general idea.

Adjusting Race Pace for Heat.

Estimated temperature at finish	*Slower than goal pace*	*8 min/mile pace becomes*
55-60°	1%	8:05
60-65°	3%	8:15
65-70°	5%	8:25
70-75°	7%	8:35
75-80°	12%	8:58
80-85°	20%	9:35
Above 85°	Forget it ... run for fun.	

Watch out for downhills. The Boston Marathon course goes sharply downhill for most of the first mile. On cool days, even experienced runners get caught up in the competition and fail to slow down when the course levels out. The results are often very fast times for the first ten miles and disappointing final results.

Be aware of your rhythm and pace after a hill. Time yourself carefully over the next mile or two and make sure you're not unconsciously going too fast.

Running "bursts" in the middle. Departing from an even pace can be disastrous at any point in the race. Competitive runners sometimes use "bursts" to gain a psychological edge. The idea is that these accelerations (usually 30-150 yards) put a runner ahead of an opponent or force him to spend energy to keep up. But the runner who does this is gambling that he's in better condition, or can demoralize the opposition and bluff into the lead. Bursts are an inefficient use of limited energy stores and I don't recommend them for the average runner.

What to do when you realize you've run too fast? Don't slow down significantly below pace to compensate for going out too fast. If you already feel too tired or hot, slow down a small amount below goal pace (5-10 seconds a mile) for 2-3 miles. Never slow down dramatically below your goal pace, for this probably won't help you rest any more than cutting 5-10 seconds a mile. Don't assume you've blown it. You probably still have it in you to reach your goal. Just try to maintain your goal pace for the rest of the run.

10 THE ART OF RACING

10K TO HALF MARATHON

JUST ABOUT ALL OF US have a competitive streak. Races can be an outlet for this tendency and give a special edge to running—whether you want to win, or just finish. On those days when motivation is low, the thought of an upcoming race can often get you out on the roads. You look forward to the excitement of a race—it's like a punctuation mark at the end of a sentence.

Races can actually be rewards for hard training. There's a positive atmosphere and contagious energy. Marking a race date on your calendar will give you a goal for structuring a running program.

Beware, however, for the excitement and stimulation of races can cause you to push your body too far and provoke injury. Races are intense. You may survive the race, but fail to rest afterward—and

---

Most of the information in this chapter refers to 10K races. Much of it can also be applied to half marathons or less-than-10K races, but the 10K is the standard.

become injured. The thrill of participation and achievement often lures runners into the "twilight zone" that is shared by both injury and success. If all goes well and luck is with you, you may run your best time ever. But unfortunately, things are often not in balance, and by pushing too hard in a race, some parts of the body will be overstressed.

Race euphoria can give you illusions of strength and invincibility. The mind recovers quickly from a hard race, but it takes the body longer. The race is really the ego icing on the cake. Your time "under the lights" may give more meaning to your daily run, but it's second in importance to your overall fitness. Remember, the true benefits of running come from the peace and physical and psychological strength found in the daily run, not from a 20-second improvement in your race time.

Setting Race Goals. Realism is the key to effective goal-setting. A 49-minute 10K runner cannot realistically project a 35-minute 10K by the end of the racing season. Even 40 minutes is too ambitious for that limited length of time.

Set goals you have a reasonable chance of achieving. We all have to deal with failure from time to time, but why push yourself into it? Set up a series of incremental goals, each leading to the other. Experiencing one success after another builds confidence. Then if you surprise yourself and do better than anticipated, it's an unexpected thrill. (See goal-setting chart, p. 82.)

PEAKING

"Peaking" refers to a careful scheduling of key workouts at the end of the speed phase that can raise your performance potential to its highest level. Speedwork and long runs are scheduled to build the racing muscles to top efficiency.

The marathon training schedules (see pp. 122-31) bring you to a peak for a marathon. Peaking schedules are normally designed, however, for more intense races: 10K and shorter. You must have enough quality work carefully planned to bring you up to—and keep you at—your peak.

Time your training peak to occur at a 10K race about two weeks before the goal race. This gives you a "dry run" to evaluate your fitness, readjust if necessary and work out any last-minute bugs in the system.

Peaking Principles for Half Marathon and Shorter

- Continue long runs every 14 days, alternating on weekends with speedwork or races. The long runs keep up your endurance and clean out waste products from speedwork or racing.
- Do your last hard speed workout (for example 20 x 440 for 10K) about 10 days before the first 10K dry run race.
- After this, cut your mileage in half for the rest of the peak period.
- Four days before the race, run a time trial—at race pace—of 8 x 440 for a 10K.

Peaking Formula for 10K and Longer

Week 1	***Tues***	***Sat***	***Sun***
	20 x 440	5K race	Long
Week 2	***Tues***	***Sun***	
	7-8 x 440	10K race	
Week 3	***Tues***	***Sat***	***Sun***
	7-8 x 440	5K race	Long
Week 4	***Tues***	***Sun***	
	7-8 x 440	Goal Race	

Riding the Peak. Like a surfer on a wave, you can ride the crest of a peak for an extended period of time—for about half the length of your base period. After you have reached the end of your speed program, use the peaking formula above. To continue after week number 4, repeat weeks 1, 2, 3 and 4 above, except substitute 7-8 x 440 for the first Tuesday's speedwork. To do this you need to fine-tune your training program—by cutting back 50% on total mileage and arranging your runs in proper sequence. You can maintain a peak even longer if your aerobic base period has been substantial. Some of my friends have spent May through September in Europe racing almost every week without a significant drop in performance level. But these same folks were running aerobically the previous September through February.

The Day Before. I've always felt better running a few miles rather than none at all the day before a race. This small amount doesn't tire me out, keeps the muscles moving and the blood circulating. I enter the race feeling rested and fresh.

Eating and Drinking Before the Race. A balanced diet is the best insurance against nutrition collapse. Don't change your diet right before a race, use the one that works best for you in daily life. As you get closer to the race, don't eat foods that are hard to digest, such as fried or fatty foods, milk, cheese or other large amounts of protein. Avoid too much roughage.

Anything you eat 12-18 hours before the race won't be processed in time to help you. Instead, you'll be carrying it along. Since you don't want to "carbo-unload" during the race, avoid this excess baggage in the first place. Make lunch the day before the race your last solid food meal. During the last 12-18 hours, cut solid foods and reduce total food intake. Fluids are crucial. Take 6-8 ounces of water or an electrolyte beverage every hour, especially the day before a race. This means 3-4 quarts a day—better safe than sorry.

Electrolytes are the minerals your body loses in exercising, particularly potassium and magnesium. Orange juice and the commercial drink ERG are good sources of these. Calcium is also important in maintaining heart rhythm, muscle contraction and healing. (For more details on food and water before a race, see *Fuel,* p. 236.)

Warming Up For the Race. Races bring you from a state of inactivity to top capacity in less than an hour. A warmup should start slowly and gradually get the body moving. Slow running warms up the muscles, tendons and other mechanical apparatus simultaneously with the internal organs—and gets everything working as a unit.

Warming up for a race is psychological as well as physical. Work out a routine that becomes automatic. You'll start slowly, increase intensity to simulate race conditions, then rest and store up energy so you're ready to go. This gives you confidence and eases pre-race anxiety.

Speed workouts are a chance to test out your pre-race warmups. (See p. 87 on speed warmups.) Try out several pre-race combinations and work them into a pattern that feels best for you. By the time you get to the race you'll have it down.

Relaxing is Part of the Warmup. As I started my warmup for the 1972 Olympic trials 10K, I felt the usual surge of nervous anxiety; this was compounded by the fact that I was running with two formidable veterans, Frank Shorter and Jack Bacheler. As we ran along, warming up, I nervously tried to joke with my running partners, but I got only negative feedback. Finally I gave up and we ran a mile in silence until Frank's terse statement about the weather: "Sorta windy." Jack quickly replied, "Yeah, just like the Texas Relays."

A tense silence followed. I remembered that earlier in the year, on a windy track in Austin, Frank had suffered one of his few bad days of the year and Jack had won the 10K. The rivalry between the two was surfacing. I realized that each of them was as nervous and tense as I was—maybe more—and I suddenly relaxed.

I began looking forward to the race. Looking around at the other runners on the starting line—most of whom had defeated me in every race we'd run together—I saw scared faces and tunnel vision. I was ready to run!

The gun fired and we took off. I didn't expect to do well and settled into the back of the pack to watch the leaders battle it out. Besides, it was 95° —too hot for a fast time. So I chuckled to myself as teammate Frank Shorter led the pack through a suicidal first mile of 4:21.

Later, when I passed that one-mile mark, I moved past someone and out of last place. By two miles I'd passed two others who had been burned by the heat and Shorter's pace. By the halfway mark I was in the middle of the pack and gloating about doing better than expected.

Then something happened. As I passed another two runners, I realized everyone was falling apart, while I felt fine. At four miles, when I moved into fourth place, I began to worry about a mistake I'd later pay for dearly.

But no problems occurred. With slightly more than a mile to go, I moved into third place, then into second behind Shorter and qualified for the Munich Olympics. I don't remember touching the track during the last mile. I had learned a powerful secret.

Race Pacing. As the gun fires, go with the flow of energy and adrenalin. You can accelerate for the first 100-200 yards without any bad effects, provided you slow down to race pace after that. An early burst will get you out of the crowd and give you some maneuvering room. Of course, big races like Bay to Breakers in San Francisco or Peachtree in Atlanta are so crowded you have no choice but to run them as fun runs.

Settle down. Don't let the energy of the crowd pull you faster than your race pace for more than a few hundred yards. You'll have a sense of pace from your interval speedwork repetitions. In fact, run the first mile of a marathon or a 10K about 10 seconds *slower* than race pace, to get thoroughly warmed up. Then get into your race pace and hold it; otherwise you'll miss your goal. Remember, for every second per mile you go too fast in the first half of the race, you'll run 5-10 seconds slower at the end.

I generally run my first mile of a marathon 15-20 seconds slower than goal pace. This warms me up and lets me relax. By the 2- or 3-mile points I've eased into my goal pace and I've never had trouble making up those few seconds during the last few miles.

Run steady. Even-paced running is the most effective strategy. Whatever your fitness level, you'll have a faster time if you keep a steady, even pace. Energy and oxygen are used more effectively at a steady pace, and you keep heat buildup to a minimum.

Beat the heat. Another reason to start slowly and to run your own steady-pace race during the first half is to keep cool. Getting too hot severely slows you down, so watch it when it's 60° or more. The faster your body temperature rises, the more blood flows to the skin to reduce heat, and the more you sweat. Both reduce the amount of blood available to the muscles, which in turn determines oxygen supply and waste removal. When capillaries near the skin dilate to cool you off, they use a substantial amount of blood. Sweat loss ultimately depletes the blood supply. If you maintain an even (and reasonable) pace in the first half you'll actually speed up slightly during the second half: your body mechanics become more efficient as you run.

Dehydration and Cooling. Drinking enough water is crucially important—especially in a race. Lately I've discovered that many of the undesirable aspects of racing—poor performance, muscle soreness, even injury—are partially or wholly attributable to dehydration. When you perspire, the water is drawn from the blood stream. If you haven't had enough water there'll be a shortage of this vital fluid for the cells and muscles. Glycogen won't be as efficiently converted to fuel, wastes won't be eliminated properly, and oxygen cannot be delivered quickly. With dehydration, all the stressful demands of racing are multiplied. To combat this:

- *Drink at least one full cup at each rest stop,* especially early in the race, even if you're not thirsty. (You become dehydrated before you realize you need water.)
- *Pour water on your head.* It cools your body, lowering your core temperature. I also believe, although I've seen no scientific verification, that in cooling your skin, you reduce the blood being diverted there. This makes more blood available for other vital body functions. Again, do this even if you don't feel hot in the early stages of the race.
- *Stay on pace.* Take pride in being close to your projected pace for the various check points. When you do you'll be amazed at the number of runners you'll pass later on. When you're tired at the end, it's reinforcing and inspiring to pass a stream of runners.

Hurting. If you're going to race competitively (rather than "just for fun") you'll have to learn how to cope with exhausting discomfort. You'll also have to distinguish between the feeling that goes along with pushing yourself to a peak performance and the pain that means injury. Experienced athletes have learned to walk this tightrope very well; think of the photos of Alberto Salazar finishing an all-out performance, or valiant Geoff Smith, who finished second to Rod Dixon in the 1983 New York Marathon, with his eyes rolling upward. Of course you won't push things to this extent, but it's helpful for anyone interested in racing to know why all-out performance hurts, and to experience these feelings in smaller doses before the big race.

When you're working the muscles harder than you have before, they cannot get enough oxygen to perform smoothly. The glucose fuel that feeds them is in a sense fermented, and in powering the muscles, produces more wastes than your body can handle. What speedwork does—and you can see why it's important to go at it gradually—is to increase the ability of the muscle to use a limited supply of oxygen, and to continue performing when waste is present. With each properly administered speed session you'll be pushing a little further and harder than before. The mitochondria will be slightly swollen, cell walls slightly torn and there'll be a buildup of lactic acid (see p. 71). It will hurt. But with proper rest everything will build up stronger, and the threshold will be higher the next time.

In training, you'll learn to live with this feeling. You'll take it in small doses in practice, so it's not overwhelming in a race, and gauge your tolerance. Although toward the end of the race you may feel that you'll *never* do this again, 30 minutes (or a few days) afterward, you'll be looking for the next one.

Note: *Certainly you should be careful. Heart patients must heed their physician's advice. Even seasoned athletes need to distinguish between discomfort on one hand, and true signs of spent muscles and actual endurance limits on the other.*

Creative Distractions. Distraction is a strong ally. When you get into the tired zone, try to bluff your way through with positive thoughts. When these wear out, try distractions: passing the next runner, making it to the next telephone pole, or merely maintaining the same rhythm for the next five steps. At this point you may drift into a "cruising" state and things will start to flow. Be creative in your distractions.

Tapping the Source. If you can occasionally overcome the tiredness, and speed up when you'd normally slow down, you'll find a great source of strength and power. Once you've tapped this source in running, you can do the same in other areas of your life when the going gets tough. You can discover this strength in a series of small excursions into the "twilight zone." At first you learn to tell when you've reached it. Next, you take small pushes into it. Next, bigger pushes. Some days you'll overestimate your capabilities and fall short. But if you're patient and keep at it, you can learn to utilize this strength on a regular basis.

In 1964 a U.S. Marine officer of American Indian heritage was training and racing toward his dream: to make the U.S. Olympic team. Although he wasn't expected to do well, he showed up for the 10K race and fought his way into the top three—in the shadow of America's great distance runner of the day, Jerry Lindgren.

Captain Billy Mills was excited about his trip to Tokyo and proudly wore his Olympic uniform. As the starting gun fired, Mills settled into the middle of the pack where he was expected to finish. As the race progressed, however, many of the lead athletes, including Lindgren, dropped back. Mills kept going. By the final mile he was as surprised as anyone to find himself in the lead group, which included world recordholder Ron Clarke of Australia.

As the three lead runners rounded the first curve of the last lap, Clarke was boxed in on the inside by Mills. Clarke tapped Mills on the arm to let him get out (so he'd have some room to pass the lead runner), but Mills didn't move. Clarke then burst through, shoving Mills out of the way. It looked like a two-man race, with Mills too far out of position to win.

Mills fought his way back into balance, regained his stride and moved back into the inside lane, significantly behind Clarke and Mohamed Gammoudi. Then something happened. Like a carbonated beverage bottle that had been shaken up, Mills built up pressure and exploded coming off the final turn. He passed Gammoudi and zoomed by Clarke to hit the tape. Under difficult circumstances, Billy Mills had found a hidden source of great strength.

THE COUNTDOWN

The Week Before. Your work is over. Don't push too hard now or you'll be too tired to race well. Run short, easy workouts, no more than 1-3 miles the last three days. Let your racing muscles rest and rebuild. Eat a normal diet and drink 4-6 ounces of water per hour.

Two Nights Before

Get a good night's sleep.

The Night Before

- Pack your bag.
- Eat a very light meal or nothing. (I don't believe in carbo-loading the night before races, even marathons.)
- Drink 4-6 ounces of water every waking hour.
- Try to relax so you can sleep. But if you can't sleep, the race isn't lost. (I've run some of my best races after sleepless nights.)

Check List

- Shoes, socks, shirt, shorts, sweats or running suit.
- Gloves, hat, turtleneck, etc., if cold.
- Water (about a quart).
- Bandages and Vaseline.
- $10-20 for registration, gas, food afterward, etc.
- Race number if sent to you in mail, 4 small safety pins.
- Copy of *Race Morning* instructions (see below).

Race Morning

It's hard to remember all these things at the last minute. Copy these pages and put them in your bag the night before.

- After you wake, drink 4-6 ounces of water every half hour.
- Drink your last water a half hour before the race.
- Don't eat, it won't get processed in time to do you any good.
- 30-40 minutes before, start your warmup.

Before You "Toe the Line"

- *Walk* 5-10 minutes to activate the running muscles gently and prepare the body for exertion.

- *Jog* slowly 10-20 minutes. Start *very* slowly, then speed up gradually to a relaxed warmup pace.
- *Stretch* gently if you usually stretch before running.
- *Walk* another 3-5 minutes to relax.
- About 10-15 minutes before the start, do some *accelerations* to get your body ready for race conditions. Do 5-10 x 150-300 yards. Start slowly, accelerate gradually to race pace, then ease back to a slow jog.
- *Walk* again, 3-5 minutes.
- About 5-10 minutes before the start, *relax,* sit down, walk around—whatever takes the edge off. Some runners put their legs above their heads, others meditate 5 minutes.
- *Shift gears* as you line up. Tense muscles don't work smoothly. Joke, and enjoy the festive air, energy and enthusiasm. This relaxes muscles throughout the body and gets them ready.

After the Gun

- Remember—go out slowly, settle into your pace and hold it.
- If it's hot, pour water over your head and dampen clothes about 10 minutes before the race. Drink at every water stop.
- Relax during the race—enjoy the experience.

Right After the Race

- Keep walking. Try to walk a mile right afterward.
- Drink 6 ounces of water or some other dilute fluid every 20 minutes for three hours.
- Walk or walk-jog about 30-40 minutes later in the day. It will help you recover.

The Morning After

- Walk-jog 30-40 minutes to get the stiffness out.
- Keep drinking 4-6 ounces of water every waking hour.
- Wait at least a week before you (a) schedule your next race or (b) vow never to race again.

10K TRAINING PROGRAM

On the following six pages are 10K training charts, geared to six different time goals. You should be familiar with the *Training* and *Racing* chapters in the book in order to understand the basic concepts behind the mileage and training elements listed.

Base Training

- Here you are building an aerobic base for the coming stages.
- Run slowly and comfortably.
- See *Base Training,* pp. 55-56, for details.

Hill Training

- Here you begin building leg strength for the speed phase.
- There are more weeks of hill work in these charts than in the marathon charts. This is because you need the driving leg muscles developed by hills more in a 10K than in a marathon.
- See *Hill Training,* pp. 57 & 155-56, for details.

Speed Training

- Speedwork trains you to run faster.
- 16 x 440 in 72 means sixteen 440-yard intervals, run at 72 seconds each with rest in between.
- See *Speed,* pp. 80-91, for details.

Form. Form work is done every Tuesday and Thursday, throughout the program. This consists of 4-8 accelerations during your daily runs. On the Tuesdays of the hill and speed phases, run your form accelerations as a warmup (after 10 minutes slow jogging). See pp. 154-55 for details.

10K GOAL: 50 MIN.

BASE TRAINING builds endurance.

Week Number	Mon	Tue (Form)	Wed	Thur (Form)	Fri	Sat	Sun (Longer runs)
1–10	0–2 mi.	3–4	0–2	3–4	0–2	0	Starting with longest run in last 2 weeks, increase 1 mile per week up to 12.
10–19	0–2	4–5	0–2	4–5	0–2	0	

HILL TRAINING develops leg strength (see pp. 57 & 155–56).

Week Number	Mon	Tue (Form)	Wed	Thur (Form)	Fri	Sat	Sun
20	0–2 mi.	4 (Hills)	0–2	4–5	0–2	0	12
21	0–2	5 (Hills)	0–2	2–3	0–2	0	6 easy
22	0–2	6 (Hills)	0–2	4–5	0–2	0	12
23	0–2	7–8 (Hills)	0–2	4–5	0–2	0	6

SPEEDWORK trains you to run faster (see pp. 80–91).

Week Number	Mon	Tue (Form)	Wed	Thur (Form)	Fri	Sat	Sun
24 easy	0–2 mi.	6×440 @1:52	0–2	2–3	0–2	0	6
25	0–2	8×440 @1:52	0–2	4–5	0–2	0	12
26	0–2	10×440 @1:50	0–2	4–5	0	10k dry run	2–5
27	0–2	6×440 @1:50	0–2	4–5	0	5k race	10
28	0–2	6×440 @1:50	0–2	2–3	1–2	0	10k race!

10K GOAL: 45 MIN.

BASE TRAINING builds endurance.

Week Number	Mon	Tue (Form)	Wed	Thur (Form)	Fri	Sat	Sun (Longer runs)
1–14	0–2 mi.	5–6	0–2	5–6	0–2	0	Starting with longest run in last 2 weeks, increase 1 mile per week up to 12.

HILL TRAINING develops leg strength (see pp. 57 & 155–56).

Week Number	Mon	Tue (Form)	Wed	Thur (Form)	Fri	Sat	Sun
15	0–2 mi.	5 (Hills)	0–4	5–6	0–2	0	12
16 easy	0–2	6 (Hills)	0–2	5–6	0–2	0	6
17	0–2	7–8 (Hills)	0–4	5–6	0–2	0	12
18	0–2	8–10 (Hills)	0–4	5–6	0–2	0	6
19	0–2	5–6 (Hills)	0–4	4–6	0–2	0	13
20 easy	0–2	4 (Hills)	0–2	4–6	0–2	0	6
21	0–2	5–6 (Hills)	0–4	4–6	0–2	0	14
22	0–2	5–6 (Hills)	0–4	6–7	0–2	0	6–7

SPEEDWORK trains you to run faster (see pp. 80–91).

Week Number	Mon	Tue (Form)	Wed	Thur (Form)	Fri	Sat	Sun
23	0–2 mi.	8×440 @1:42	0–4	4–6	0–2	0	15
24 easy	0–2	10×440 @1:42	0–2	4–6	0	5k	6–8
25	0–2	12×440 @1:42	0–4	5–7	0–2	0	15
26	0–2	14×440 @1:42	0–4	6–7	0	10k race	6–8
27	0–2	16×440 @1:42	0–4	5	0–2	0	15
28 easy	0–2	18×440 @1:42	0–2	4–6	0–2	0	6–8
29	0–2	20×440 @1:42	0–4	5–6	0	5k race	15
30	0–2	6–8×440 @1:40	0–4	4–6	0	10k dry run	6–8
31	0–2	7×440 @1:40	0–2	4–6	0	5k race	12–14
32	0–2	7×440 @1:40	0–2	4–6	0	10k goal race	

10K GOAL: 40 MIN.

BASE TRAINING builds endurance.

Week Number	Mon	Tue (Form)	Wed	Thur (Form)	Fri	Sat	Sun (Longer runs)
1–14	0–2 mi.	6–8	0–2	6–8	2–4	0	Starting with longest run in last 2 weeks, increase 1 mile per week up to 12.

HILL TRAINING develops leg strength (see pp. 57 & 155–56).

Week Number	Mon	Tue (Form)	Wed	Thur (Form)	Fri	Sat	Sun
15	0–2 mi.	5–6 (Hills)	0–2	6–7	2–4	0	12
16	0–2	6–8 (Hills)	0–2	4–6	2–4	0	6
17	0–2	8–10 (Hills)	0–2	6–7	2–4	0	14
18	0–2	10–12 (Hills)	0–2	6–7	2–4	0	7
19	0–2	6–8 (Hills)	0–4	7–8	2–4	0	16
20 easy	0–2	6–8 (Hills)	0–2	4–6	2–4	0	8
21	0–2	6–8 (Hills)	0–4	7–8	2–4	0	17
22	0–2	6–8 (Hills)	0–4	7–8	2–4	0	8

SPEEDWORK trains you to run faster (see pp. 80–91).

Week Number	Mon	Tue (Form)	Wed	Thur (Form)	Fri	Sat	Sun
23	0–2 mi.	8×440 @90	0–4	7–8	2–4	0	17
24 easy	0–2	10×440 @90	0–2	4–6	0	5k race	8
25	0–2	12×440 @90	0–4	7–8	2–4	0	17
26	0–2	14×440 @90	0–4	7–8	0	10k race	8
27	0–2	16×440 @90	0–4	5	2–4	0	17
28 easy	0–2	18×440 @90	0–2	4–6	0	0	8
29	0–2	20×440 @90	0–4	4–6	0	5k race	17
30	0–2	6–8×440 @90	0–4	6–7	0	10k dry run	8
31	0–2	7×440 @90	0–4	5–6	0	5k race	17
32	0–2	7×440 @90	0–2	5–6	0	10k goal race	8

10K GOAL: 38 MIN.

BASE TRAINING builds endurance.

Week Number	Mon	Tue (Form)	Wed	Thur (Form)	Fri	Sat	Sun (Longer runs)
1–16	0–2 mi.	8–10	2–4	8–10	2–4	0	Starting with longest run in last 2 weeks, increase 1 mile per week up to 12.

HILL TRAINING develops leg strength (see pp. 57 & 155–56).

Week Number	Mon	Tue (Form)	Wed	Thur (Form)	Fri	Sat	Sun
17	0–2	8–10 (Hills)	2–4	8–10	2–4	0	14
18	0–2	10 (Hills)	2–4	8–10	2–4	0	7
19	0–2	8–10 (Hills)	2–4	8–10	2–4	0	16
20 easy	0–2	8–10 (Hills)	2–4	4–6	2–4	0	8
21	0–2	8–10 (Hills)	2–4	8–10	2–4	0	18
22	0–2	8–10 (Hills)	2–4	8–10	2–4	0	8

SPEEDWORK trains you to run faster (see pp. 80–91).

Week Number	Mon	Tue (Form)	Wed	Thur (Form)	Fri	Sat	Sun
23	0–2 mi.	8×440 @85	2–4	8–10	2–4	0	18
24 easy	0–2	10×440 @85	2–4	4–6	0	5k race	6–8
25	0–2	12×440 @85	2–4	8–10	2–4	0	18
26	0–2	14×440 @85	2–4	8–10	0	10k race	8
27	0–2	16×440 @85	2–4	6	2–4	5k race	18
28 easy	0–2	18×440 @85	2–4	4–6	2–4	0	8
29	0–2	20×440 @85	2–4	4–6	0	5k race	18
30	0–2	6–8×440 @83	2–4	6–8	0	10k dry run	8
31	0–2	7×440 @83	2–4	4–6	0	5k race	18
32	0–2	7×440 @83	2–4	4–6	0	10k goal race	

10K GOAL: 35 MIN.

BASE TRAINING builds endurance.

Week Number	Mon	Tue (Form)	Wed	Thur (Form)	Fri	Sat	Sun (Longer runs)
1–15	2–5 mi.	10–12	4–5	10–12	4–5	0–3	Starting with longest run in last 2 weeks, increase 1 mile per week up to 12.

HILL TRAINING develops leg strength (see pp. 57 & 155–56).

Week Number	Mon	Tue (Form)	Wed	Thur (Form)	Fri	Sat	Sun
16	2–5	5 (Hills)	2–4	6–8	2–3	0	6
17	2–5	6 (Hills)	2–4	10–12	4–5	0–3	14
18	2–5	7 (Hills)	2–4	10–12	4–5	0–3	7
19	2–5	8 (Hills)	4–5	12	3–5	0–3	16
20 easy	2	9 (Hills)	2–3	6–8	3–5	0–3	8
21	2–5	10 (Hills)	4–5	12	3–5	0–3	18
22	2–5	12 (Hills)	4–5	12	3–5	0–3	8

SPEEDWORK trains you to run faster (see pp. 80–91).

Week Number	Mon	Tue (Form)	Wed	Thur (Form)	Fri	Sat	Sun
23	2–5 mi.	8×440 @78	4–5	12	3–5	0–3	18
24 easy	2	10×440 @78	2–3	6–8	0	5k race	8
25	2–5	12×440 @78	4–5	12	3–5	0	18
26	2–5	14×440 @78	4–5	10	0	10k race	8
27	2–5	16×440 @78	4–5	7	0	5k race	18
28 easy	2	18×440 @78	2–3	6–8	3–5	0	8
29	2–4	20×440 @78	4–5	7	0	5k race	18
30	2–3	7–8×440 @76	2–3	8	0	10k dry run	8
31	2–3	7×440 @76	2–3	8	0	5k race	18
32	2	7×440 @76	2–3	6–8	0	10k goal race	

10K GOAL: 32 MIN.

BASE TRAINING builds endurance.

Week Number	Mon	Tue (Form)	Wed	Thur (Form)	Fri	Sat	Sun (Longer runs)
1–15	2–5 mi.	12	4–5	12	4–5	0–3	Starting with longest run in last 2 weeks, increase 1 mile per week up to 12.

HILL TRAINING develops leg strength (see pp. 57 & 155–56).

Week Number	Mon	Tue (Form)	Wed	Thur (Form)	Fri	Sat	Sun
16	2–5	5 (Hills)	2–4	6–8	5	0–3	6
17	2–5	6 (Hills)	2–4	12	5	0–3	14
18	2–5	7 (Hills)	2–4	12	5	0–3	7
19	2–5	8 (Hills)	4–6	12	4–6	0–3	16
20 easy	2–5	9 (Hills)	3	6–8	4–6	0–3	8
21	2–5	10 (Hills)	4–6	12	4–6	0–3	18
22	2–5	12 (Hills)	4–6	12	4–6	0–3	8

SPEEDWORK trains you to run faster (see pp. 80–91).

Week Number	Mon	Tue (Form)	Wed	Thur (Form)	Fri	Sat	Sun
23	2–5 mi.	8×440 @72	4–6	12	4–6	0–3	18
24 easy	2–5	10×440 @72	3	6	4–6	0–3	8
25	2–5	12×440 @72	4–6	12	4–6	0–3	18
26	2–5	14×440 @72	4–6	12	0	5k race	8
27	2–5	16×440 @72	4–6	8	4–6	0	18
28 easy	2–5	18×440 @72	3	6	0	10k race	8
29	2–5	20×440 @72	4	8	0	5k race	18
30	2–5	7–8×440 @70	4	8	0	10k dry run	8
31	2–3	7×440 @69	4	8	0	5k race	18
32	2–5	7×440 @69	3	6	0	10k goal race	

CARS

Remember: be prepared to give in quickly. Avoid confrontations. It doesn't matter if you were "right" if you get hit. Survival is the goal.

- *Run on the sidewalk* when you can. Try to find secluded residential areas, parks. Obviously, paths and trails are even better.
- *Run facing traffic* if you must run on the roads. Always be aware of the shoulder, curb, etc.—a place to leap if necessary. Be aware of traffic behind you. Many runners have been killed by drunks or passing cars coming from behind them as they ran "facing traffic."
- *Wear reflective gear at night.* Use strips of reflective tape, reflective shoelaces or reflective vests.
- *Understand the driver's mentality.* He may be in a hurry. He may be drunk. He may be overweight, and hate you for being trim and in good health. Don't assume that drivers will behave rationally.

DOGS

It's usually a matter of territory. Your problem is to figure out the dog's boundary lines. If you're in his zone, let him bark to get some of the aggressiveness out, then slow down and make your way cautiously out of his territory. If he keeps coming toward you, bend down and pick up a rock or stick; this in itself will usually scare him off.

Throw the rock or stick if he's particularly aggressive and bend down to get another. Carry a stick in dangerous dog areas and if you have to, hit him on the nose. You can also carry dog spray. Some postmen use a strong pepper solution which will drive a dog away without causing lasting discomfort.

11 RUNNING THE MARATHON

ON AS LITTLE AS THREE MILES A DAY

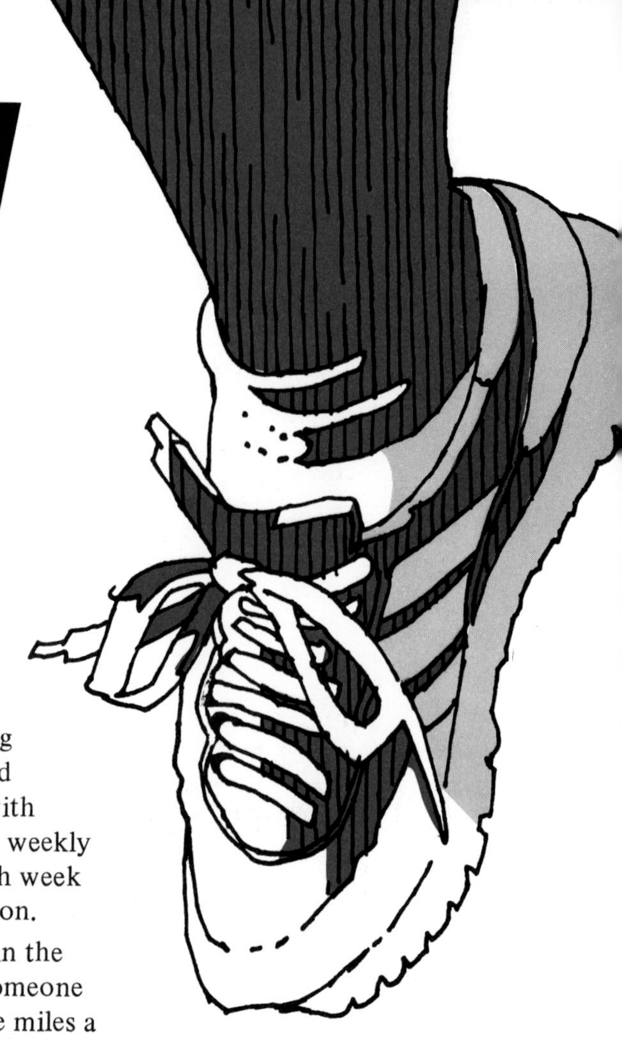

SEVERAL YEARS AGO I was giving a clinic on marathon training. During the question and answer session I responded to a request for marathon training advice with the usual recommended program: Increase weekly mileage to 65-70 miles, with a 20-miler each week for about four weeks leading to the marathon.

A non-"marathon-looking" person in the audience stood up and asked if I thought someone could train for a marathon by running three miles a day, and a long run increasing to 26 miles. I didn't feel this was enough and told him so.

He didn't mean to embarass me, but he replied that he'd been using this program to complete five marathons without injury and without hitting "the wall." I swallowed my 140 mile-a-week pride and started asking *him* questions.

His answers made sense. I wish I'd talked with this neighborhood runner before my first marathon. In 1963 at age 18, I entered the

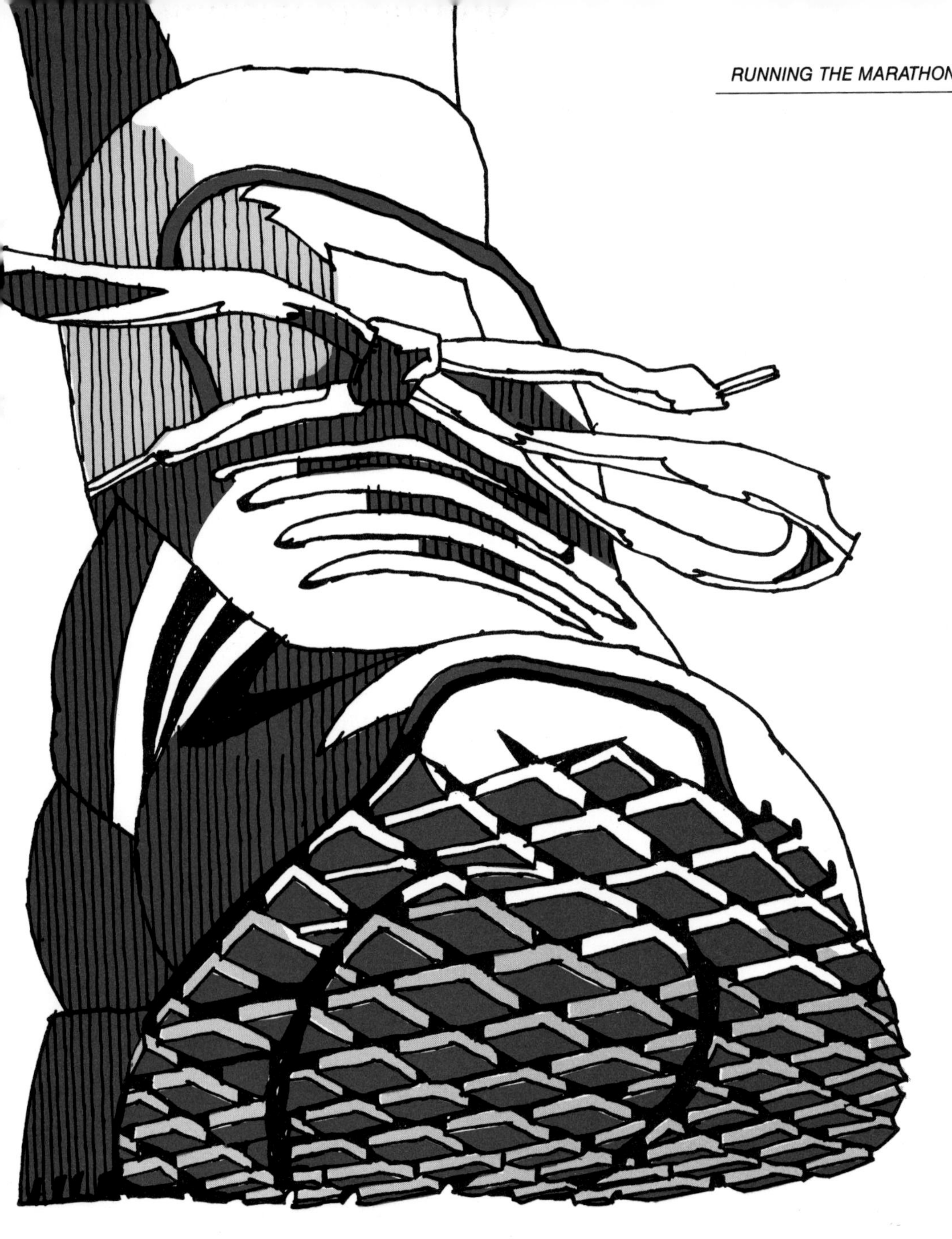

Atlanta marathon with a base of 30 miles a week and a long run of 15 miles. My weekly mileage seemed inadequate even then, but I falsely consoled myself with the thought that others were worse prepared.

I felt great for the first 10 miles. By 15, however, I began to tire. At 18 I went downhill rapidly and was so tired at 21 that I didn't realize it was time to quit. I walked most of the last five miles, propelled only by instinct and protected from injury by teenage resiliency.

Now, with the advantage of two more decades of running, some 50 marathons, and the knowledge gained from coaching hundreds of marathoners, I know where I went wrong. One simple addition to my schedule, as explained to me by that runner in the audience, would have made my marathon debut much more successful: *the long, easy run.*

A New Look at "The Wall." Even my 30 miles a week could have prepared me for Atlanta if I'd increased the length of my longest run. I've since learned that the body is only capable of what it's done in the recent past. My longest run had been 15 miles and that's exactly where I hit the wall in the race.

To run a marathon you need to run 26 continuous miles. The body is best prepared to do this by gradually increasing the long run to 26 miles, and preferably more. You often hear runners say: "The marathon is divided into two races–the first 20, and the last 6." They hit the wall at 20 because they've never gone beyond that in training. If your body has never traveled that distance before, it doesn't know how to handle the stress.

A race is the worst time to run your longest distance. By running the race distance (or longer) prior to a race, you're giving your body (and mind) notice that they will be called upon to go that far. So if you extend your long run to 26 miles or more, and run the race at the pace you've trained for, you can avoid encountering, much less hitting, the wall. (Breaking the race into two runs in morning and evening doesn't do the job, since you need the sustained effort without any *total* rest breaks.)

The Greatest Cause of Injury. Increasing *total weekly mileage* is not only an inefficient way to increase endurance, but is the greatest cause of injury among runners. Most marathoners are told to begin their program with 30 or 40 miles per week, then increase to 50, 60 and 70 miles per week in a 3- or 4-month marathon buildup. As a result, many of them break down from the increased strain. For example, approximately 2000 out of 16,000 runners had to drop out of the 1983 New York Marathon due to injuries.

THE LONG RUN

This program, which emphasizes the long run, and in many cases cuts down on the day-to-day mileage, with plenty of rest, is meant for runners of all levels. It can be used to *finish* a marathon–in four hours or more. Or it can be used by runners aiming for anything from a 3:30 time to a 2:45 performance or better. (Of course, 30 miles a week is too low for a sub-3-hour marathoner.) It's been a very successful program. Thousands of runners of all abilities have followed it and practically all of those who completed it and stayed within the boundaries have finished the race and achieved their goals. Here again, as with the training pyramid, the principles of sound injury-free running apply to runners of all levels.

The main components of this marathon program are:

- Keep the daily mileage you have been running. (Some runners may even decrease.)
- Increase the long run 1-2 miles every 14 days. This applies to runners of all abilities.
- Build to 26-28 miles before attempting the marathon. Do this last long run 2-3 weeks before the marathon.
- Run slowly, take walking breaks, enjoy each run.
- ***Key concept**: You increase your total mileage by lengthening the long run, not by an accumulation of daily increases.*

The Easy Week Rule. If you run long every week you develop a residual tiredness. Once your long run reaches 12 miles, do it only every other week. On the easy week, run about half the distance of the last long one.

Pacing the Long Run. Run at a comfortable pace and *if in doubt, go slower.* Most runners should run about 1½-2 minutes per mile slower than their current 10K race pace.

Take a Walk. From the ultra-distance runners I've learned you can walk for five minutes every 25-30 minutes and build endurance with less stress. Blood circulates better, which cleans out some of the wastes and allows you to run easier for a longer period. The goal is to stay on your feet for the prescribed distance. After you've finished a few marathons, and have set a time goal of 3:20 or faster for the next one, eliminate the walking breaks.

Prepare for the Long Run. Come into the long runs rested and ready to go. Don't run long after a race, speedwork or a hard workout. Arrange to race on weekends when you're not running long. The challenge of the long run adds spice to your training program, but too much stress will give the spice a bitter taste.

Tapering for the Marathon. Starting about 14 days before the marathon, cut mileage 30-50%. The last seven days before, you should run no more than 30% of normal mileage. The last 2-3 days, run only 1-3 miles. You cannot improve fitness during the last two weeks, and certainly not during the last week. You can, however, tire yourself out by running too much. Cut back and enjoy the rest.

Running Free. I have a friend, close to 50, who started using my marathon training schedule recently. Although he's now run in one marathon and says he might do one or two a year, the race itself isn't his primary motive for training. "I love those long runs. I'm out in the hills for 2-3 hours, alone, it's peaceful, just a pair of shoes and shorts, no hardware, no motors." He finds joy in the exertion, the solitude, the tiredness when it's over. He says he'd follow the program now, even without the marathon as an incentive.

That's the attitude I wish most runners would adopt toward the long run. Whether the race is a fixed goal or a hazy sometime-in-the-future dream, the long run should be fun, easy, relaxed and not too fast. It's obviously going to be much more enjoyable if you can run in the hills, the woods or the park as opposed to pounding monotonously down the same city blocks. But wherever you run, try to approach the long run as an enjoyable experience. Not coincidentally, relaxing and having fun will improve your conditioning and future performance more than any other single aspect of your training program.

IMPROVING MARATHON PERFORMANCE

When you've progressed to the point where you not only want to finish the marathon but have a time goal, some different elements are added to your training program. To improve *endurance,* you increase the long run to a final run a few weeks before the race of 28-30 miles. For *speed,* you run repeat miles, 20-30 seconds faster than race pace, to get used to the hard sustained effort of the marathon.

Starting with five one-milers (walking a few hundred yards between each) you increase by 1-2 miles each session until you run 13 one-milers in your last speed workout two weeks before the race. (See the chapter on speed, p. 80, for details.)

These workouts are strenuous and should be performed on alternate weeks. This gives you six days of easy running between each of the hard days.

It is the long run that develops endurance and the repeat miles that develop speed, so run slowly on the long ones. Your goal on the other days is to recover from the stress days. Social runs, easy runs, scenic routes can be planned for these in-between sessions.

Form. Runners of all levels can benefit from form drills—non-strenuous accelerations—twice a week. (This is covered in detail in the chapter on form, p. 146.)

During the Race

Pace. In your first marathon, don't worry about time. Just run to finish. Staying on your feet for 26 miles is a feat in itself. Then, after a marathon or two, you'll have an idea of what you can accomplish and you may want to run for time.

When you *do* have a time goal, run an even-paced race. During the first 15 miles, run no faster than the pace you want to average for the entire race. If, after 15 miles, things are going well, you can increase your pace by five seconds per mile.

Run your own race. The marathon is a contest between your will and your resources. Try not to get carried away by the competitive spirit, especially early in the race. Remember that most time goals are lost by going out too fast in the beginning.

Water. Drink at each water stop—at least one cup on cool days and two cups when it's hot. Be sure to drink at the early water stops, even if you're not thirsty; it's common for runners to become dehydrated even before feeling thirsty.

Cramping. If you feel your legs cramping in the latter stages of the marathon, *don't stop* at water stations—or at any other time. Instead sip your water while you jog very slowly. This keeps the muscles working in harmony. When you stop completely, the blood pools, circulation slows, and cramping and stiffness may increase.

Recovery After the Marathon

- *Immediately after race:* Walk 1 mile.
- *Later that afternoon:* Walk 3-5 miles.
- *Remember Foster's Rule:* A 26-mile race requires 26 days rest. (See pp. 72-73.)
- *Until "rest days" have been served:* Walk/jog for same number of minutes usually run on average days (before you started the speed section of your marathon program).
- *Long runs:* 12-14 miles about 10 days after marathon; 20+ miles about 21 days after race.

26 Miles, 385 Yards? The first marathon was run at the Olympic Games of 1896 from the village of Marathon to Athens, a distance of about 40 kilometers. In subsequent Olympics, the distance was roughly the same, varying slightly from year to year. In the London Olympics of 1908, the Princess of Wales was to start the race and it was decided to begin on the lawn at Windsor Castle so the royal grandchildren could see the start. The distance to the finish line at Shepherd's Bush Stadium? You guessed it: 26 miles, 385 yards and it's remained the same to this day.

MARATHON TRAINING PROGRAM

On the following eight pages are marathon training charts. These are *suggested* training programs geared proportionally to different time goals. You should be familiar with the basic concepts set forth in the *Training* and *Racing* chapters in the book in order to adapt these charts to your experience and ability.

Here are some notes on the three phases of each program:

Base Training

- Here you are slowly building an aerobic base for the coming stages.
- The daily runs, as well as the long run, should be relaxed and slow. Run at a comfortable pace and if in doubt, go slower.
- There may be more weeks in your base period than the 15 indicated; it's an individual matter.
- See *Base Training*, pp. 55-56, for details.

Hill Training

- Here you begin building leg strength for the speed phase.
- The only difference between hill training and base training is the hill workout one day per week.
- See *Hill Training,* pp. 57 & 155-56, for details.

Speed Training

- Speedwork trains you to run faster.
- 6x1 @ 7½ means run six 1-mile repeats, at 7 minutes, 30 seconds each with rest between.
- See *Speed,* pp. 80-91, for details.

Form work is done twice weekly, year round. Run 4-8 accelerations during your Tuesday and Thursday runs, concentrating on good form. See pp. 154-55, for details.

MARATHON GOAL: TO FINISH

Week Number	Mon	Tue (Form)	Wed	Thur (Form)	Fri	Sat	Sun
1	0–2 m.	2	0–2	2	0–2	0	2
2	0–2	2	0–2	2	0–2	0	3
3	0–2	2	0–2	3	0–2	0	4
4 easy	0	3	0	2	0	0	4
5	3	0–2	4	0–2	3	0	5
6	0–2	3	0–2	4	0–2	0	6
7	4	0–2	3	0–2	4	0	7
8 easy	0	4	0	3	0	0	8
9	4	0–2	3	0–2	4	0	9
10	0–2	4	0–2	4	0–2	0	10
11	4	0–2	4	0–2	4	0	11
12 easy	0	4	0	4	0	0	6
13	4	0–2	4	0–2	4	0	12
14	0–2	4	0–2	4	0–2	0	6
15	4	0–2	4	0–2	4	0	14
16 easy	0	4	0	4	0	0	7
17	4	0–2	4	0–2	4	0	16
18	0–2	4	0–2	4	0–2	0	8
19	4	0–2	4	0–2	4	0	18
20 easy	0	4	0	4	0	0	9
21	4	0–2	4	0–2	4	0	20
22	0–2	4	0–2	4	0–2	0	10
23	4	0–2	4	0–2	4	0	22
24 easy	0	4	0	4	0	0	11
25	4	0–2	4	0–2	4	0	24
26	0–2	4	0–2	4	2	0	12
27	4	0–2	4	0–2	2	0	26
28 easy	0	4	0	4	0	0	13
29	4	0–2	4	0–2	4	0	12 easy or 5k race
30	0	4	0	2	1	0	Marathon!

This program is not designed for speed, but for finishing a marathon comfortably and with reduced injury risk. Hence there will be no hills or speedwork in your training program. Thousands of runners have followed this program and successfully completed marathons. As you can see, it's quite a bit different from other marathon training schedules; the unique features are the low daily mileage and the long run every other week.

Shown here is a 30 week program. This assumes that your current long run is 2 miles. If your long run is longer than this, start with the week that has your current long run in it.

MARATHON GOAL: 4 HOURS

BASE TRAINING builds endurance.

Week Number	Mon	Tue (Form)	Wed	Thur (Form)	Fri	Sat	Sun (Longer runs)
1–15	0–2 mi.	4	0–2	4	1–2	0	Starting with longest run in last 2 weeks, increase 1 mile per week up to 12.

HILL TRAINING develops leg strength (see pp. 57 & 155–56).

Week Number	Mon	Tue	Wed	Thur (Form)	Fri	Sat	Sun
16	0–2 mi.	4–5	0–2	4–5	1–2	0	4 (Hills)
17	0–2	4–5	0–2	4–5	1–2	0	14
18	0	3	0	4	1	0	6 (Hills)

SPEEDWORK trains you to run faster (see pp. 80–91).

Week Number	Mon	Tue (Form)	Wed	Thur (Form)	Fri	Sat	Sun
19	1–2 mi.	2–3	1–3	4–5	1–2	0	16
20 easy	0	2–3	0–2	3–6	1–2	0	2×1 mile @8½ min.
21	1–3	4–5	0–2	4–5	1–2	0	18
22	0–2	2–3	1–3	4–6	1–2	0	4×1 @8½
23	1–3	4–5	0–2	4–5	1–2	0	20
24 easy	0	2–3	0–2	3–6	1–2	0	6×1 @8½
25	1–3	3–6	1–3	4–6	1–3	0	22
26	1–3	3–6	1–3	4–6	1–3	0	10k race in 50–54 min.
27	1–3	4–6	1–3	4–6	1–3	0	24
28 easy	0	2–3	0–2	3–6	1–2	0	10k race in 48–52 min.
29	1–3	4–6	1–3	4–6	1–3	0	26
30	1–3	4–6	1–3	4–6	1–3	0	10k race in 46–50 min.
31	0–2	2–3	0–2	3–6	1–2	0	12 easy
32	0	2–3	0	3–6	1–2	0	Marathon!

MARATHON GOAL: 3:30

BASE TRAINING builds endurance.

Week Number	Mon	Tue (Form)	Wed	Thur (Form)	Fri	Sat	Sun (Longer runs)
1–15	1–3 mi.	4–5	0–3	4–5	1–2	0	Starting with longest run in last 2 weeks, increase 1 mile per week up to 12.

HILL TRAINING develops leg strength (see pp. 57 & 155–56).

Week Number	Mon	Tue (Hills)	Wed	Thur (Form)	Fri	Sat	Sun
16	1–3 mi.	4–5	0–3	4–5	1–3	0	7
17	1–3	4–5	0–3	4–5	1–3	0	14
18	0	4–5	0	4	1–2	0	8

SPEEDWORK trains you to run faster (see pp. 80–91).

Week Number	Mon	Tue (Form)	Wed	Thur (Form)	Fri	Sat	Sun
19	3 mi.	5	0–4	5	1–3	0	16
20 easy	0	5	0–3	4	1–3	0	2×1 @7½ min.
21	3	5	0–4	5	1–3	0	18
22	3	5	0–4	5	1–3	0	4×1 @7½ min.
23	3	5	0–4	5	1–3	0	20
24 easy	0	5	0–3	4	1–3	0	6×1 @7½ min.
25	3	5	0–4	5	1–3	0	22–23
26	3	5	0–4	5	1–3	0	8×1 @7½ min.
27	3	5	0–4	5	1–3	0	24–25
28 easy	0	5	0–3	4	1–3	0	10×1 @7½ min.
29	3	5	0–4	5	1–3	0	26–28
30	3	5	0–4	5	1–3	0	11×1 @7½ min.
31	0–3	4	0–4	5	1–3	0	8–12 easy or 5k race
32	0	4	0	1–2	1–3	0	Marathon!

MARATHON GOAL: 3:20

BASE TRAINING builds endurance.

Week Number	Mon	Tue (Form)	Wed	Thur (Form)	Fri	Sat	Sun (Longer runs)
1–15	1–3 mi.	4–5	0–3	4–5	1–2	0	Starting with longest run in last 2 weeks, increase 1 mile per week up to 12.

HILL TRAINING develops leg strength (see pp. 57 & 155–56).

Week Number	Mon	Tue (Hills)	Wed	Thur (Form)	Fri	Sat	Sun
16	1–3 mi.	4–5	0–3	4–5	1–3	0	7
17	1–3	4–5	0–3	4–5	1–3	0	14
18	0	4–5	0–1	4–5	1–2	0	8

SPEEDWORK trains you to run faster (see pp. 80–91).

Week Number	Mon	Tue (Form)	Wed	Thur (Form)	Fri	Sat	Sun
19	3 miles	6	1–4	5	2–4	0	16
20 easy	0	5	0–4	5	1–3	0	2×1 @7:10 min.
21	3	6	1–4	5	2–4	0	18
22	3	6	1–4	5	2–4	0	4×1 @7:10 min.
23	3	6	1–4	5	2–4	0	20
24 easy	0	5	0–4	5	1–3	0	6×1 @7:10 min.
25	3	6	1–4	5	2–4	0	22–23
26	3	6	1–4	5	2–4	0	8×1 @7:10 min.
27	3	6	1–4	5	2–4	0	24–26
28 easy	0	5	0–4	5	1–3	0	10×1 @7:10 min.
29	3	5–7	1–4	5	2–4	0	26–28
30	3	5–7	1–4	5	2–4	0	12×1 @7:10 min.
31	0	4–5	0–4	5	2–4	0	8–12 easy or 5k race
32	0	4–5	0	1–2	1–5	0	Marathon!

MARATHON GOAL: 3:10

BASE TRAINING builds endurance.

Week Number	Mon	Tue (Form)	Wed	Thur (Form)	Fri	Sat	Sun (Longer runs)
1–15	2–4 mi.	7	0–4	7	2–4	0	Starting with longest run in last 2 weeks, increase 1 mile per week up to 12.

HILL TRAINING develops leg strength (see pp. 57 & 155–56).

Week Number	Mon	Tue (Hills)	Wed	Thur (Form)	Fri	Sat	Sun
16	2–4 mi.	7	0–4	8–9	2–4	0	8 or 5k race
17	2–4	7	0–4	8–9	2–4	0	14–16
18	0–2	5–6	0–3	5–6	1–3	0	8

SPEEDWORK trains you to run faster (see pp. 80–91).

Week Number	Mon	Tue (Form)	Wed	Thur (Form)	Fri	Sat	Sun
19	3 miles	7	2–4	7	2–5	0	16
20 easy	0	6	0–2	6	1–3	0	2×1 @6:45 min.
21	4	7	2–4	8	2–5	0	18–20
22	3	7	2–4	8	2–5	0	4×1 @6:45 min.
23	4	7	2–4	8	2–5	0	21–23
24 easy	0	6	0–2	6	1–3	0	6×1 @6:45 min.
25	4	8	2–4	7	2–5	0	22
26	3	7	2–4	8	2–5	0	8×1 @6:45 min.
27	3	8	2–4	7	2–5	0	24
28 easy	0	6	0–2	6	1–3	0	10×1 @6:45 min.
29	3	5–6	2–4	5–6	2–5	0	26–28
30	3	6–8	2–4	6–7	2–5	0	12×1 @6:45 min.
31	0	5–6	1–3	5–6	2–5	0	8–12 easy or 5k race
32	0	5–6	0	1–2	1–3	0	Marathon!

MARATHON GOAL: SUB-3:00

BASE TRAINING builds endurance.

Week Number	Mon	Tue (Form)	Wed	Thur (Form)	Fri	Sat	Sun (Longer runs)
1–15	2–4 mi.	8	2–4	8	2–4	0–3	Starting with longest run in last 2 weeks, increase 1 mile per week up to 12.

HILL TRAINING develops leg strength (see pp. 57 & 155–56).

Week Number	Mon	Tue (Hills)	Wed	Thur (Form)	Fri	Sat	Sun
16	2–5 mi.	8–9	0–4	9	2–4	0	8 or 5k race
17	2–5	8–9	0–4	9	2–4	0	14–16
18	0–2	6–8	0–4	6–8	1–3	0	8

SPEEDWORK trains you to run faster (see pp. 80–91).

Week Number	Mon	Tue (Form)	Wed	Thur (Form)	Fri	Sat	Sun
19	4 miles	9	2–4	9	4–6	0–4	16–18
20 easy	1–3	6	0–4	6	2–4	0–2	2×1 @6:25 min.
21	4	9	2–4	8	4–6	0–4	18–20
22	4	9	2–4	9	4–6	0–4	4×1 @6:25 min.
23	4	9	2–4	9	4–6	0–4	20–23
24 easy	1–3	6	0	6	2–4	0–2	6×1 @6:25 min.
25	4	9	2–4	9	4–6	0–4	23–25
26	3–4	9	2–4	10	4–6	0–4	8×1 @6:25 min.
27	4	9	2–4	9	4–6	0–4	25–27
28 easy	1–3	6	0	6	2–4	0–2	10×1 @6:25 min.
29	3–4	9	2–4	9	4–6	0–4	27–29
30	3–4	9	2–4	8	4–6	0–4	12×1 @6:25 min.
31	1–3	7	2–4	6	4–6	0–2	8–10 easy or 5k race
32	0	4	0–4	2	1–2	1–2	Marathon!

MARATHON GOAL: 2:50

BASE TRAINING builds endurance.

Week Number	Mon	Tue (Form)	Wed	Thur (Form)	Fri	Sat	Sun (Longer runs)
1–15	3–5 mi.	9	2–5	9	2–4	0–5	Starting with longest run in last 2 weeks, increase 1 mile per week up to 12.

HILL TRAINING develops leg strength (see pp. 57 & 155–56).

Week Number	Mon	Tue (Hills)	Wed	Thur (Form)	Fri	Sat	Sun
16	2–5 mi.	10–12	2–5	10–12	3–5	0–5	8–10 or 5k race
17	2–5	10–12	2–5	10–12	3–5	0–5	14–16
18	1–2	6–8	0–4	8–9	1–3	0–3	8–10

SPEEDWORK trains you to run faster (see pp. 80–91).

Week Number	Mon	Tue (Form)	Wed	Thur (Form)	Fri	Sat	Sun
19	5 miles	12	6	10	6–8	0–5	16
20 easy	2–4	6	0	6	3–4	0–3	3×1 @6:00 min.
21	5	12	6	11	6–8	0–5	18–19
22	5	12	6	12	6–8	0–5	5×1 @6:00 min.
23	5	12	6	12	6–8	0–5	19–21
24 easy	2–4	6	0	6	3–4	0–3	7×1 @6:00 min.
25	5	12	6	12	6–8	0–5	23
26	5	12	6	12	6–8	0–5	9×1 @6:00 min.
27	5	12	6	12	6–8	0–5	26–28
28 easy	2–4	6	0	6	3–4	0–3	11×1 @6:00 min.
29	5	12	6	12	6–8	0–5	28–30
30	5	12	6	12	6–8	0–5	13×1 @6:00 min.
31	2–5	8	0–4	6	5	0–3	12 easy or 5k race
32	2–4	4	0–4	2	1–2	1–2	Marathon!

MARATHON GOAL: 2:38

BASE TRAINING builds endurance.

Week Number	Mon	Tue (Form)	Wed	Thur (Form)	Fri	Sat	Sun (Longer runs)
1–15	4–6 mi.	9	4–6	9	2–4	0–5	Starting with longest run in last 2 weeks, increase 1 mile per week up to 12.

HILL TRAINING develops leg strength (see pp. 57 & 155–56).

Week Number	Mon	Tue (Hills)	Wed	Thur (Form)	Fri	Sat	Sun
16	2–5 mi.	10–12	2–5	10–12	3–5	0–5	8–10 or 5k race
17	2–5	10–12	2–5	10–12	3–5	0–5	14–16
18	1–2	6–8	0–4	6–8	1–3	0–3	8–10

SPEEDWORK trains you to run faster (see pp. 80–91).

Week Number	Mon	Tue (Form)	Wed	Thur (Form)	Fri	Sat	Sun
19	5–6 mi.	12	6–7	12	6–8	0–5	18
20 easy	2–4	6	0	6–7	3–4	0–3	3×1 @5:40 min.
21	5–6	12	6–7	12	6–8	0–5	21
22	5–6	12	2–4	12	6–8	0–5	5×1 @5:40 min.
23	5–6	12	2–4	12	6–8	0–5	24
24 easy	2–4	6	0	6–7	3–4	0–3	7×1 @5:40 min.
25	5–6	12	6–7	12	6–8	0–5	26
26	5–6	12	6–7	12	6–8	0–5	9×1 @5:40 min.
27	5–6	12	6–7	12	6–8	0–5	28
28 easy	2–4	6	0	6–7	3–4	0–3	11×1 @5:40 min.
29	5–6	12	6	12	6–8	0–5	30
30	5	12	6	12	6–8	0–5	13×1 @5:40 min.
31	4–5	8	0–4	6	5	0–3	12 easy
32	2–4	4	2–4	2	2–3	1–2	Marathon!

226
57

12 THE ADVANCED COMPETITIVE RUNNER

WORKOUTS FOR THE ADVANCED COMPETITIVE RUNNER

RUNNERS WITH at least four years of speedwork have often found the need for an extra "push" to top performance. These experienced runners usually have muscles and tendons that can handle more abuse, and their years of experience should (but don't always) keep them from overtraining. The principles here are the same; the workouts differ in degree, not kind.

If you try these workouts, follow all the guidelines in Chapter 7, pp. 66-78, especially the easy week concept. An easy week is especially important after these workouts, since you'll be pushing your body harder than other runners.

Don't be a slave to weekly mileage. The workouts that lead to your goal are the long runs, the speed days, and form work. Weekly mileage during the speed phase is unimportant. It's better to slack off before you need to, than to overtrain and suffer the consequences.

Note: Runners must often make sacrifices in order to excel. Performance work demands extra time, which may be taken away from work, family or friends. It can also make you high-strung or difficult to be with. I don't have a solution to this problem—it's really a matter of priorities. If you're an advanced competitor, being aware of the trade-off can make you think about balancing your running with other important elements in your life. Or if you have a friend who is training hard, perhaps this chapter will help you understand the demands of competitive running.

Greater Injury Risk. Advanced runners often feel invincible, immune to normal running problems. In fact, in spite of their greater experience and stronger running muscles, they are injured more often than the average runner for one simple reason: they run harder and longer.

Those who have been close to the fire know the meaning of warmth and have probably been burned. Usually, runners who have experienced injury-producing workouts become sensitive to early signs of overstress and hopefully will know when to stop. They have learned the necessity of strategic rest.

Greater Need for Rest. Greater stress means greater need for rest. Advanced runners *must* take their two easy weeks a month and two rest days after a hard or long day. Even when you feel recovered, you must take these breaks. When there is a hint of lingering tiredness you must have patience and realize that an extra rest day will do more for your ultimate performance than another hard day in a tired state. Rest cannot be compromised without disaster—sooner or later.

Pulse Rate and Weight Maintenance. It's very important for a veteran competitive runner to check pulse rate and body weight daily. As soon as you wake up—before getting out of bed—check your pulse. Then step on the scales. See p. 65 for details.

Common Mistakes

• *Pacing.* Advanced runners often run too fast in daily runs. Long runs build endurance, hills build strength and speedwork develops speed. Everyday runs should be slow, recovery experiences, about 1½-2 minutes per mile slower than 10K race pace.

• *High-powered weekends.* Don't run a race and a long run the same weekend. This stresses the system. Long-run weekends can be alternated with race weekends.

• *Too much speed.* Speedwork should not continue beyond the periods listed in the 10K and marathon charts or you will encounter fatigue, sickness or injury.

One Day Off Per Week. Yes, you too! Advanced runners tend to be compulsive. Force yourself to take at least one day off per week, usually before the long-run day. This must be scheduled and adhered to.

Goals. Like other runners, advanced competitors often have a general performance goal but are not specific about when they want to achieve that goal. They end up bouncing from one race to the next. They lose the edge gained by top European distance runners who plan for a specific performance peak and reach that goal by scheduling for it.

To make optimal progress, goals need to be scheduled at least six months in advance with a training pyramid (see pp. 53-59). Races, long runs and speed workouts can be carefully interwoven and strategically staged for maximum results.

Goals should not be too ambitious. By moving gently from one goal to the next, you build a foundation of success which leads to other successes.

THE ADVANCED TRAINING PROGRAM

Endurance. A long slow run should be taken every other week. Gradually increase to beyond the race distance. The maximum long run for a 10K is 15-17 miles, for the half marathon 20-22 miles, for the marathon 28-30. The extra distance builds extra endurance and almost assures better performance. When you have gone farther than the race distance, you can maintain a faster pace in the race. The extra long runs give you a better cardiovascular base, which will help you get more out of your speedwork.

Hills. Advanced runners can run a hill workout once a week during the base period. By running 4-8 hills (see p. 57), you can develop lower leg strength, which allows you to shift the body weight forward and push off strongly on your forefoot. This increases speed.

During the hill period of the pyramid, advanced runners can do two hill workouts per week. One could build to 8-12 hills of 100-200 yards, run at a 5K pace. The second workout should be shorter and faster: 3-5 hills, 60-100 yards, at the same effort as a one-mile pace. These must be coordinated with races; they're usually done on Tuesdays and Thursdays, with long runs or races on weekends. Be sure to warm up thoroughly before these workouts.

Speed. Advanced runners will find the speed workouts on pp. 86-87 excellent preparation for their goals. Because of your speedwork experience, you should be able to jog (rather than walk) between repetitions and take less rest between repetitions (half the repetition distance or less). The reduced rest gives the body a higher level of anaerobic conditioning. If more rest is needed to complete the number of reps in the time assigned, take it.

A second, faster speed session (usually Thursday) can be done each week. Here you lower the 440 pace of the main workout by about five seconds. This is a shorter workout and you take the complete rest in between reps.

Examples: 3-5 x 400, or 6-8 x 220, or 2 x 330; 1 x 440, 2 x 220.

The second, shorter hill workout could be alternated with this second speed workout, if you feel the need for strength or more hill training. The main hill workout is abandoned during the speed phase.

An alternative to the long speed sessions is training for a shorter race. Marathoners could do speedwork designed for the 10K; 10K specialists would train for the 5K, etc. Endurance is maintained through long runs and racing endurance is fine-tuned through hard, continuous runs.

Marathon runners would run the repeat 440's (of a 10K speed program, see pp. 109-114) on Thursday or Friday after a long run and again on Tuesday or Wednesday before the next long one. The repetitions would be run 5-7 seconds faster than the current 10K goal pace and would gradually build in number to 20.

10K runners would shift to a maximum of 12 x 440, but would run each about 3-5 seconds faster than a 5K goal pace.

Advanced Fartlek Principles. This trains your mind as it conditions your body. There is no end of the track to shoot for, so you quickly learn *your* limits. You want to push yourself to near the limit and stay there. As you make progress in your fartlek training, you learn your potential as never before. Because this workout more closely resembles a race, it takes more recovery time. For every easy day after an interval workout, take two easy days after these fartlek sessions. One of these every two weeks is plenty. In a race, you never know when the pace will pick up. Fartlek, with its intermittent accelerations–and no complete rest in between–gets you ready for this situation.

- Set distance at race distance (a maximum of 12 miles).
- Warm up by running an easy 1-2 miles.
- Run a fairly hard *base pace,* about 5-10% *slower* than race pace.
- Run *accelerations* 6-10% *faster* than race pace.
- Vary length of accelerations: 50-350 yards; 440-660 yards; 880-1000 yards. Occasionally throw in a fast 50. You can use the shorter ones to recover when you really need it.
- Return to base pace—not a jog—immediately after each acceleration. (This is the tough part.)
- Warm down the final 1-2 miles. Jog and relax after the hard running.
- Fartlek is free-form. You can be creative and tailor it to suit your exact speed needs. If you find yourself getting left in the dust at the end of a race, work hard on your accelerations at the end of a workout. If you find others pulling away from you in the middle, work on your mid-workout accelerations.

Advanced Interval Training. Interval workouts can also be creative. First, cover the basics by building the total number of reps to approximately race distance and keep the speed slightly below race pace. Then you can tailor your workouts to help you where you need it most.

Veterans should be able to take less rest between repetitions. You can jog between reps at a faster pace and still recover. Sometimes this also means you must take rest days, so listen to your body.

Longer repetition distances also help simulate race conditions. Instead of 20 x 440, you could run 10 x 880—or even 5 x 1 mile. There's no need to keep the same distance throughout. Run a 660, then a mile, then a 440. The guidelines are the same as for other runners: start with the equivalent of 6-8 x 440, gradually build up through the weeks to 20 x 440. Don't run more than eight weeks of this intense speedwork. After that, you must return to your aerobic base period.

Here's a fartlek/interval innovation that's worked well for me. Mile repeats are my base. My goal race pace is my "base pace" for the mile. Within the four laps I run several accelerations, one about

500 yards, and 2-3 others 50-100 yards. After each acceleration, I try to come back to the base pace.

Advanced runners may choose between fartlek or interval training or may mix them. In any case, these two stressful workouts need to be carefully mixed with races and long runs so there is adequate rest between each. *If you run more than one race or long run per week, you will run great risk of injury.*

The following workouts are listed only as guidelines that can be inserted into a 10K or marathon program. Remember, you are running these for form and speed. You don't have to complete them as listed. Your goal is to stay bouncy and strong throughout the workout. If you start feeling tired, or begin dragging, cut the distance of the reps in half. If this doesn't help, abandon the workout.

Sample 2-Week Schedule

Week	***Mon***	***Tue***	***Wed***	***Thur***	***Fri***	***Sat***	***Sun***
1	Easy	Inter-vals	Easy	Fast form	Easy	Off	Long (15-18)
2	Easy	Fart-lek	Easy	Fast form	Easy	Off	Easy (8-15) or race

Accelerations. Light acceleration work three times per week is crucial for the advanced competitor. Here the quick rhythm is maintained and improved and other refinements of style are made.

Never sprint. By running at your mile base pace, you can go fast enough to improve, yet avoid overstress. You want to feel light on your feet, and increase your rhythm. Don't try to increase your stride length, drive your arms or strain in any way.

These accelerations can be done as a warmup for hills, speedwork or races, or can be done in the middle of your daily run. As a warmup for accelerations, you should jog easily 10-20 minutes, and warm down adequately also.

Barefoot Running. Try to run one of your weekly acceleration sessions barefoot, since shoes block some of the crucial rhythmic feedback from your feet. Of course, you must have the right surface, such as a well-groomed golf course, or a smooth, clean, soft surface with no rocks or glass. Ease into barefoot running, at first doing only one or two 50-yard bursts. The next week, run 2-3, etc. By jumping into this too soon and too fast, you can injure vital muscles and tendons.

Only veteran barefoot runners should try loose sand. There are many potential hazards. Sand running is resistance work, not rhythmic running, and can be substituted for a hill workout with proper care. It gives you extra strength, but there is correspondingly extra stress.

Peaking. The veteran should be more "fine-tuned" than other runners and can therefore benefit most from a careful peaking strategy. Carefully follow the guidelines on pp. 98-99 for sustained improvement.

Beyond the Plateau. Often veteran runners will tell me they just can't seem to get beyond that 3:05 marathon, or 38-minute 10K, etc., try as they might. I've heard similar complaints over the years, have thought about it and come up with a few suggestions. If you've reached a plateau (it can be either slower or faster times than the above examples), here's what you might do to break through to a new performance level:

- Try a temporary reduction in job-related stress. Take your annual vacation 2-3 weeks before the marathon. Get away from the telephone.
- Train at a higher altitude than where you'll be racing.
- Switch to a lighter racing shoe. This will improve your efficiency and performance *provided* you're still getting enough cushion.
- Reduce your body fat (provided you have fat and weight to spare). Hold your food intake constant and increase your mileage slowly and gradually.

In the Long Run. Most runners don't realize how long it takes to fully develop their endurance running potential. Often after running two, three or four years, they reach a plateau and consider their best time unsurpassable. The truth is, and it will probably surprise you, it takes about ten years to build your strength, speed and endurance to its full potential in running—no matter what the starting age.

RACING STRATEGY FOR THE ADVANCED COMPETITIVE RUNNER

In the media, too much credit is given to the racing strategies of victorious athletes. From what I've seen, many runners win in spite of their strategies, or fail because they do not tailor their strategies to their abilities. An example of this was Steve Prefontaine, America's top 5K runner in the early 1970s. Pre was unbeatable in the U.S., but because of poor strategy couldn't win in Europe, where he raced each summer. In practically every race, less-talented runners would leave him behind with a finishing kick. After one of these summers, he told me that he merely needed more and faster speedwork—which he proceeded to do. The next summer, after finishing second, third and fourth in Europe, he discovered that determination and hard speedwork cannot install fast twitch muscle fibers that Mother Nature left out.

Leading up to the 1972 Olympics, Pre again changed his racing strategy. He decided to run hard for the last mile of the 5K race to put his competitors into oxygen debt and "burn the kick outta them." As planned, he took the lead with four laps to go and increased the pace. Unfortunately, he burned no one out but himself. Lasse Viren, the Finnish superstar, accelerated dramatically with two laps to go and held that hard pace until the end—hitting the tape far in front of everyone else. Had Pre waited until the last two laps, he probably would have given Viren a good race.

The Front Runner. Occasionally a front runner will win a race but usually he just sets up a fast race for the eventual winner. A front runner tries to build up a lead and demoralize the competition. Usually he becomes a victim of "the wall." He goes out at a much faster pace than he can maintain, slows down dramatically during the last third of the race, and is passed by the eventual winner who is running at a more even pace.

The front runner feeds on the confidence of being the leader. This mental energy and optimism propels the front runner to a hard, fast race. Although experienced front runners don't often win, they consistently finish high in their peer group.

By pushing the pace throughout the race, front runners get an excellent workout. If they don't overtrain in between races, they improve their condition race by race and are able to hold their fast pace for a longer distance in successive races.

Wait and Kick: The Lazy Method for Speedsters. If you're blessed with natural speed and find it's still there at the end of the race, you can afford to be lazy: wait and kick. The big kicker lets others do the pacing. As members of the lead pack jostle for position, he drops back and saves his energy.

The biggest problem for the kicker is staying with the leaders until the finish line is in sight. If he has dropped too far behind the pack, it takes great mental energy to catch up. Lead pack runners get increased energy from the exhilaration (and paranoia). They often try to "waste" the kickers by forcing a hard pace early on or by running a series of speed bursts.

As distance racing becomes more competitive at all levels, more races will be decided by the kick. Every runner, regardless of ability, can benefit from a regular program of accelerations that will develop speed. Runners with a kick who do regular quality speedwork and regular long runs are difficult to beat.

Stronger Arms for a More Powerful Kick. If everything else is equal between two runners, the runner with stronger arms and shoulders may run slightly faster in the sprint to the finish. For a short period, moving your arms faster makes you run faster. Jim Ryun lifted weights throughout his career. Frank Shorter recently said that weight training helps him run as much as three seconds faster for the last lap of a 10K, but added that he thinks only highly competitive endurance runners in the top of their age groups will benefit significantly from weight training.

How to Develop a Kick

- Continue two acceleration sessions per week year-round. Work on rhythm and driving quickly off each foot. Never run these at top speed; run at your current mile race pace, occasionally running at 880 race pace.
- During the speedwork phase, do an extra session of

accelerations after speedwork: 1 x 330, 1 x 220, 2 x 150 yards, etc. The 150's are run to the end of the track straightaway from the middle of the curve.

- Work on driving with strength and lightness. Don't let your hands get in the way: keep the palms down and let your wrists relax.
- Remember that you'll be tired at the end of these speed sessions. It's easy to injure yourself by pushing too hard. Monitor yourself carefully and back off if there's any feeling of strain.
- Warm down with at least one easy mile of *slow* jogging.

Bursting: A Strategy that Often Backfires. Some runners who have been frustrated by being out-sprinted at the end of races will try to "burn" the kick out of kickers by bursting (accelerating) in the middle or late stages of the race. The theory is the same as that of the front runner: by going with the burster, the kicker will use up his fast-twitch energy stores and reduce the power of the kick; but if he doesn't accelerate, the kicker lets the burster get so far ahead that the final kick can't carry him to victory.

The theory seldom works in a race. The burster usually gets worn out by the inefficiency of accelerating in a long race. Generally the kicker and others will let the burster go and then gradually and efficiently speed up and reel him in. Rarely does a kicker fall prey to the trick and match strides with the burster.

When it's common knowledge that a runner is the best in a given race, he can use bursting to separate himself from the rest of the pack. Otherwise, improving runners can hang on to a better runner and then run over their head in the final sprint. The "star" can sometimes discourage his competitors by a burst or two in the middle.

Pick it Up in the Final Mile. The smart runner maintains an even pace until the final stage of the race and then applies the strategy best suited to his or her capabilities. If you don't have much of a kick, your best strategy, in my opinion, is that of a sustained final mile or two.

Experiment to define *your* final stage of the race. For a 10K it might range from ½-2 miles. In a marathon, it might be the last mile or the last five. Most runners find they can concentrate best if the distance is around 1-1½ miles or less.

Until that point, an even pace is best. If you keep track of your peer group and maintain mental contact, you'll find yourself moving up on them as the miles pass. Then you'll have the added energy and enthusiasm of passing people in the last part of the race; it's also demoralizing to your competitors.

To run the kick (and determination) out of a speedster you must run hard for a sustained distance. Gradually accelerate and put the pressure on. Don't go so fast at first that you can't hold it to the end; but try to make it hurt a little. Then when you reach the half-way mark of your final push, go a bit harder. This long drive is hard on you, but it's harder on your opponents who haven't trained for it. They also don't know how long you can hold your acceleration. In many cases it wears the kicker's sprint muscles out so they cannot accelerate at the end.

TOO MUCH OF A GOOD THING

As I've mentioned, running is an addictive activity. Once you've run long enough to experience the stimulating effects of endurance exercise, it's hard to turn back. You feel so *good*, you never want to let it slide. Your body is used to its daily fix of oxygen, increased circulation and calming endorphins.

Yet running, like many other pursuits, can be carried too far—from habit to obsession. A highly motivated, hard-driving person may ride the pendulum swing from an overweight, sedentary lifestyle to an almost constant preoccupation with running, racing and weight. The solution soon becomes the problem.

Physical symptoms are obvious early warning signs of burnout. When activity is increased dramatically or too many races are run, injury is probably just down the road. There are also mental signs of going too far. You may not feel like running, you may be depressed, or you may experience radical behavior changes.

Early Warning Signs. Your body has hormones that keep you going under periods of stress. Sometimes you may feel even better than normal when overstressed. Try to be aware of the early signs of stress so you can back off when they occur and avoid injury or breakdown. These early signs are:

- *Restlessness at night.*
- *Higher pulse rate in the morning.* If it's 10% higher, cut back 50% on distance, run each mile one minute slower. If it's 20% higher, stop running for 3 days.
- *Soreness in the feet.* If your feet remain sore for a week, stop running for 2-3 days.
- *Pain in your "weak links."* If in doubt, take a day or two off to get the healing process started.
- *Change in appetite.* If you suddenly feel like eating more, or less, it may be overstress.
- *Lack of desire.* Usually your desire to run will be rekindled during the run, even if things were dragging at first. But if you have three or more days when the flame is not rekindled, take a 3-day rest.
- *Feeling dead at the beginning and end of a run.* Again, take a 3-day lay-off.

When running is no longer a joy and a release from the pressures of the world, but a manic pursuit, then family, friends and job are likely to suffer. Some runners—you probably know a few like this—jump into it so strongly they let everything *else* go. Ironically, they begin to lose the motivation even to run—although they keep pounding away, day after day. They're miserable, but don't know it.

I've seen many, many burnouts in my running career, with varying shades of disaster: divorce, separation, friendships ended, social contacts severed, careers interrupted, etc. The best advice I can give you to avoid this sad state of affairs is to first, be aware of the early warning signals—recurring injuries, depression, loss of motivation, irritability, fixation—and make necessary course corrections. Secondly, try to keep things balanced and in harmony, and let running enhance, not rule your life.

TUNING

13 FORM

HOW TO RUN STRONGER AND BETTER

FIRST, I HAVE A CONFESSION TO MAKE. Form was of no interest to me during my first 18 years of running. A friend and fellow runner at Wesleyan University, Karl Furstenberg, once asked if I was interested in improving my running form. He was a smooth runner—technically superior to me, so he was probably trying to be friendly and hint gracefully that I correct my ragged style. I didn't get the point. I remember telling him it didn't matter how you looked as long as you got there first. I believed that the body always found the most efficient path, and that each runner was limited by his or her own mechanical construction.

Sixteen running years later, however, my "lazy" form was getting me into trouble. In my earlier days, I had instinctively sprung off the forefoot—using the flick of each ankle for propulsion. Later I found I could rest the lower leg muscles by "cruising"—leaning slightly back and shuffling along. This more relaxed pattern allowed me to run slightly slower with less effort. As I slipped into this "cruise" mode for most of my workouts and races, I was losing power—and races. Since I wasn't using the springing and driving muscles, they were not strong and ready. The "cruise" muscles are not designed for power and acceleration—and they often were pulled or strained when I used them for that purpose. My running form was drifting.

Then I met Arthur Lydiard. The coach of New Zealand Olympic champions believed that form work helped good runners become great. I tried his suggestions and later developed some form principles of my own that have helped runners of all abilities run better and faster with the same effort.

One problem with learning form from a book (as opposed to a coach) is that you can read all the particulars, but then when you're out running it's impossible to remember everything. What I'll do here is list the general principles of good form. Some of them will ring a bell with you; you'll also recognize things in your own running style that need improvement.

But don't go out and practice all these tips at once. It'll only confuse you. The *Points on Form* section that follows is an overall review of good form and something which you can refer back to whenever you want to fine-tune things. The section after that, *Three Tips on Form*, lists three basic principles that are fairly easy to remember and that you can work on right away.

POINTS ON FORM

There is no single prescription for efficient running, for we are all put together differently. These points on form are general principles of body mechanics that can be applied to *all* runners. Be sensitive to your own structure and abilities and never force a particular running style on yourself that doesn't feel right.

One other thing: Good form is something all runners—regardless

The most efficient way to run is to have your head, neck and shoulders erect, as at right. When you run leaning forward, as at left, you're always fighting gravity.

of ability or experience—can work on. Racers are naturally interested in improving form, for it will help them run faster. But beginners and non-competitive runners will also benefit from understanding some of these principles, for good form will make anyone's running smoother and more enjoyable.

Erect Posture. Your running will be most efficient if your posture is erect, perpendicular to the ground (and the force of gravity). Check your form as you run by store fronts in a shopping center. If your body parts are lined up properly, you'll feel like you're moving forward as one unit—head, torso, hips, knees and ankles all together. The store front windows will tell you if your head or shoulders, etc., are leaning too far ahead or behind.

Relaxed Body. If your body is relaxed and balanced by being erect, you won't have to spend energy keeping your head, neck, shoulders, etc., aligned. The muscles of your jaw and face should be so relaxed that they bounce and shake as you run. Relax your upper body; it's just going along for the ride and you don't want to divert energy into this area.

Moving Forward. All motion should be directed straight ahead. Hips, shoulders, arms and legs should be pointing forward—not side-to-side and certainly not leaning back. This may sound obvious, but just look at the next runner you see for wobbles, sways and backward lean. I'll be charitable and not ask you to look at yourself—yet.

Arms. The main function of the arms is coordination with the legs. At the completion of each arm swing, a nerve signal tells the legs to work again. When held in a relaxed swing fairly low and close to the body very little effort is required to keep your arms in place and you'll tend to get a quicker response from your feet. But if you hold your arms out from your body, your arms and shoulders will tire quickly.

Let gravity do your arm work. Keep the top of your hands up, not to the side, and wrists relaxed and floppy. Let your legs lead and your arms follow your leg motion. Your hand can rise as high as the middle of your chest and back as far as the seam on your pants. *Most of your arm movement should be in the lower arms; the upper arms should not move very much.* Practice in front of a mirror. Don't try to run with your arms, just let them relax and follow the rhythm of your feet.

Armswing Tip: Keep your fingers slightly cupped and relaxed, palms down; let your hands slightly knick your shorts with each swing. If you find your hands and arms getting tight, shake them loosely and then put your thumb and forefinger together. This should keep the tension in a small arc between the two fingers.

Hips. Hips should be shifted forward in line with head and shoulders. Some of us slouch as we stand, walk or run and let the hips shift back and tilt one way or the other. This puts a major mechanical link out of position.

Legs. Sprinters lift their knees high. Endurance runners do not. Sprinters must achieve maximum stride length, leg speed and power. You can't run very *long* like that. You should also avoid a high back kick. Increasing speed in long runs comes from a quicker ankle action; high knee lift and back kick will slow this down and divert power up or behind you instead of pushing you down the road. A very slight knee lift is the result of an effective pushoff and will help keep your back kick from going too high.

Heel landing:
For cushion and to respond to your body alignment.

Ankle angle:
Quickly shift forward so ankle is in position to push strongly.

Foot push:
Take strong quick push.

Ankle Efficiency. The ankle is a highly efficient lever. As you strengthen your lower leg muscles and learn to shift your body weight forward, the ankles can do more of the work and save energy. Try to feel your calf muscles giving you a direct push on each step, taking over some of the load from the upper (hamstring) leg muscles. See drawing above on how to take advantage of ankle power.

Stride Length. Believe it or not, a longer stride will not lead to faster running. *Experienced competitive runners find that their stride length* *shortens as they run faster.* A key to faster running is stride frequency. If you increase the speed of your footfall and get a good strong pushoff you'll improve. Most runners I've worked with have too long a stride.

Quick and Light. You should bounce lightly off the ground. As your form improves, the sound of your feet decreases—as the direct force of each ankle-push increases. Top runners prance along, because they use the flick of the ankle and save energy that would otherwise be demanded by hamstrings and other major muscles.

Once you have overcome inertia by starting your run, you want to refine your form and use it to your advantage. You are trying to resist gravity rather than overcome it; you do this by bouncing lightly down the road with smooth, powerful strides.

Deep Breathing. When you are inactive you need only a small part of your lung capacity. When you run, you need to use much more. Deep breathing or "belly breathing" makes running easier. If your posture is erect you can utilize more of your lung capacity. With your chest forward you're better aligned for deep breathing.

To feel what it's like to get your chest forward, take a deep breath and maintain your forward (inhaled) position after exhaling. This helps you to use more of your lung capacity. When you breathe deeply you get better absorption of oxygen and in this way take fewer breaths.

THREE TIPS ON FORM: CHP

Here are three steps to efficient running form. These are the major aspects of improved mechanics, and when mastered can improve any running style.

Note: *It's hard to remember all the aspects of form when you're out running. If you forget everything else about form, try to remember these three points. A friend of mine from California tells me he remembers these three by thinking* ***CHP****—California Highway Patrol—for* ***C****hest/****H****ips/****P****ush:*

1. ***Chest Up.*** Lift your chest. Take a deep breath and hold that forward position as you exhale. Lydiard says to imagine you have a pulley attached to a harness around your chest. The other end of the pulley is attached to a three-story building a block away. As you run, lift your chest up and forward; it leads the way. Don't lean forward, just get your chest up and out. It will give you extended lung capacity. Don't change your shoulders or arms at all. Work only with your chest and you'll achieve better posture and lung efficiency.

2. ***Hips Forward.*** When you pull your chest up it helps pull your hips forward automatically. Before you start running, get your chest up; then put your hands on your butt and push forward. Your shoulders, head, hips and feet should all be lined up. In this position you can extend your legs for maximum power. Lydiard contrasts this with the typical runner's position, which he calls "sitting in the bucket." When your hips are under and forward you'll feel the muscles of the calf being used and hardly any exertion in the hamstrings. You should feel light on your feet and run quieter when hips are forward.

3. ***Push Off*** strongly with your foot. With your ankle brought into position by a forward chest and hips, a small amount of work from the calf muscle can produce a major effect in push-off power from your feet.

Most runners lean slightly back as they run and must overcome gravity with each step. A wear spot on the shoe heel indicates this. It's fine to land on your heel, but don't stay there. It's harmful to the knees. The knee cap is pulled tightly into the knee, grinding the cartilage against the bones. When your ankle does the work, this knee tension is reduced considerably.

If you naturally land on the heel, don't try to shift suddenly to your forefoot. After landing, shift your weight to the midfoot and let the ankle exert its leverage. Gradually make your running an *ankle reflex action*, which will give you a feeling of floating, more than pounding.

Practice These Three Tips. These three tips work together; they're not isolated factors. Try this standing up: Lift your chest and shift your hips; you should feel yourself roll off on your toes. Lining yourself up properly generates forward momentum. By running in proper alignment, you reduce wasted motion. You're directing energy and generating power in the right direction.

WEEKLY FORM WORK

Form work will improve your running if you practice it twice weekly, year-round. A man in his '70s taught me the value of this one summer. Dr. Miguel Dobrinski celebrated his 74th birthday with us at our Tahoe Trails running camp. He was impressively active and joined us in all our activities. But during the form sessions when accelerating or bounding, he could barely get off the ground. I didn't want to offer false hope and frankly explained to him that it was probably too late to build spring into his legs.

The following year, in our first form session, what did we see but a bouncing Dobrinski in the mountains! As he celebrated his 75th birthday, he explained that he had practiced his accelerations regularly. He had restored 30 years of bounce in one year.

FORM ACCELERATIONS

The Procedure

- Warm up with at least 10 minutes slow jogging.
- Stop, shake shoulders, arms, head until they feel relaxed.
- Take a deep breath, exhale, and keep the forward chest orientation.
- Push hips forward with hands on butt.
- Roll off on your toes and spring off.
- Run 4-8 times this way, according to how you feel.

Why? Running accelerations with good form teaches you to run faster. Through repeated outings, you get in touch with your body mechanics, and stay in touch. You instinctively become aware of inefficiencies and learn to correct them.

When? Twice a week, year-round. The idea is to set aside these periods to concentrate on form and not worry about it constantly. You needn't always be preoccupied with form. You may use the form accelerations as warmups for a hill workout, speed session or race; or simply put them in the middle of a normal run. A common practice is to run one on Tuesday, another on Thursday.

Where? A level surface is normally best, but use any even surface that feels good. I've found that running barefoot on a golf course or the beach gives the best biofeedback. (If you do this, break into it very slowly. Too much barefoot running too soon can cause injuries.)

How Far? 100-300 yards.

How Fast? About your race pace for one mile. This is fast but not all out. Never sprint. Gradually build into this pace, hold it for 60-100 yards, then ease off gradually.

RUNNING FORM FOR HILLS

Making Molehills Out of Mountains. Training on hills makes running easier on any surface. Specifically, hill training will:

- Greatly strengthen lower leg muscles and quadriceps, getting you prepared for speedwork.
- Teach you rhythm—probably the most overlooked and crucial ingredient in distance racing. Good rhythm can pull you through periods of tiredness.
- Give you a good hard workout with relatively little pounding.

Erect Posture. Keep your chest out and up. Good posture will help your body mechanics, whether running up or downhill. Try not to compromise the maximum lift from each step by leaning either forward or backward as you ascend or decline. You'll get the greatest push from each step if your main elements—head, chest, hips and feet—are perpendicular to an imaginary horizontal. They are therefore lined up to best defy gravity.

Running Uphill. Hills can be a great advantage to you in a race if you understand a few principles. As your competitors struggle against the force of gravity, you can conserve energy and actually let it work for you. It may be hard to imagine when you're in the midst of a steep incline, but a hill can be a great opportunity.

- *Maintain the successful rhythm* you have established on the flat.

- *Maintain the same effort level.* Don't try to keep up the same pace on the hills as on the flat or you'll soon be worn out. A good check of this "same effort level" is your breathing.
- *Shorten your stride* and let yourself slow down gradually as you ascend. Conserve energy for the rest of the run.
- *Pick up the rhythm* slightly as you near the top. Some runners find a slight increase in arm rhythm helps them do this. Don't increase length or power of the arm swing, just pick up the rhythm. This helps pull you over the top and gets you ready to take advantage of gravity on the other side.
- *Think of running over the top:* You don't want to let down there.

Running Downhill. At the crest, the effort required for each step decreases. Be sensitive to this and gradually let the pace increase as gravity allows.

- *Let gravity do the work.* Gravity and increased rhythm should pull you downhill, with little energy required.
- *Increase stride length slightly.* If it becomes too long you lose control and must expend energy to slow down. Too long a stride can pound your knees unmercifully.
- *Experiment with your stride length* going down. Practice will show you the length that lets you take maximum advantage of gravity, yet keeps you under control.
- *Lean slightly forward.*

What If You Live in Kansas? Not everyone lives where there are hills. Much of the mid-west, Texas, the East Coast along the beach, the Carolinas, Florida and Alabama are flat. One alternative–if a beach is available–is to run on the sand. (Wear your running shoes.) Warm up as you would for hills, then run 100-200 yards in sand that is neither hard-packed nor too loose. Other possibilities are parking garage inclines (hopefully when there's little traffic and fumes), stadium steps, a treadmill, or running up 5-10 flights of stairs in an office building. The other rules of hill training described previously apply in all these cases.

TROUBLESHOOTING

Now that you know the principles of good running form, you'll be more sensitive to some form-related problems. We'll cover some of the most common ones here.

Shoulder tension. If you feel this after a run, you're probably leaning too far forward or back with your head or shoulders: you're not balanced. Watch in store front windows as you run by; your hips may be too far back. Shift your hips forward, take a deep breath and maintain this forward position. Shoulder tension may also be due to your shoulders being too high instead of relaxed, or by holding your arms too far out from your body. Whenever you feel tension building up, stop, shake your arms and shoulders and let them relax.

Tight hamstrings. You're probably not using your ankles, feet and calves enough. Work on shifting the major effort to the calves and give the hamstrings a break. Push off with your feet.

Rapid, quick breaths and/or side cramps. You're probably running too fast, especially at first. If you still can't get deep breaths when you slow down, you may be slumping your chest. Try the deep breath described above (shoulder tension) to get the chest forward. Keep it forward, breathe deeply and slowly, and the problem should go away. The ultimate solution is to use deep breathing throughout your run. Caution: If the problem persists, see a doctor.

Shoulder roll. When you run by a store front do you see your shoulders rolling either up and down or forward and back? If so, you're probably throwing your arms across your body. Cut down on your arm swing, keeping arms low and moving forward and back. Try not to move your upper arms much.

Tight neck. Your head may not be directly over your shoulders. If your body leans too far forward, you may be leaning your head back to compensate. Bring your chest back. Or if you run leaning too far back, your head is probably too far forward. Bring your hips forward. Check this out in store front windows also. Massage your neck after running.

A Final Note on Form. One of the great beauties of running is its free-form nature. Don't destroy this by working on form every time you run. *Most of your runs should be fun and flowing.* During those two or three times a week when you concentrate on form, focus on just that. You want each step to take you directly ahead and eliminate any excess motion and run quietly. Relax and enjoy the ride.

14 STRETCHING AND STRENGTHENING

RELAXING AND BALANCING

STRETCHING CAN HELP–but it can also hurt. Stretching regularly and properly will help you avoid tight muscles and injuries. But it's a two-edged sword. The wrong type of stretching is actually the third leading cause of runner's injuries, after too much mileage and speedwork.

I learned about the dangers of stretching the hard way. Some years back, after reading an impressive article on the benefits of stretching, I tried to reverse the tightness of 16 non-stretching years in six months and developed a sciatic problem. Instead of gently holding a relaxed extension, I was pushing each stretch until I "felt it." The tension I was putting on my hamstring muscles was actually triggering a stretch reflex (the body's automatic protective mechanism) that shortened the muscle and caused me to become tighter each day. When the sciatica came along, I gave up stretching for a while.

Four non-stretching years later I was married. Barbara had a background in physical education and I guess she didn't look forward to spending her later years with someone who had to hobble around tightly strung like an archery bow (bent over backward). She watched me stretch and didn't hesitate to criticize. She knew that stretching had to be relaxed and told me so. With her help, I've gradually evolved the simple program of exercises that follows. In the process I've learned how regular and gentle stretching can combat 25 years of distance running tightness. The *right method* of stretching means more relaxed running muscles and less chance of injury.

Although important in its long-term benefits, stretching will not instantly improve running. In the mid '70s many running articles claimed stretching could chase away injuries and improve speed. Since nothing could deliver all the benefits promised, unrealized hopes produced great despair as runners became injured, or failed to zoom away into the sunset.

We runners are often wishful thinkers. If a little stretching is good, then a lot must be wonderful. We think that if stretching "this far" is good, then pushing a few inches farther will turn us into fast pretzels. So stretching injuries occurred, and then multiplied. Then when the word got around that it was the third leading cause of injury, a lot of runners went to the opposite extreme and stopped stretching.

The fact is that regular *and proper* stretching will reduce chances of injury. By understanding and fine-tuning a few simple principles, you can safely become more flexible—and you needn't spend much time doing it.

Why Stretch? Running strengthens the massive muscle groups on the back of the body: the calf, hamstring and lower back. As these become stronger they also become tighter, pulling at the connecting points. Unless you develop a regular, gentle stretching program, you can look forward to a gradual tightening of these crucial muscles—and increased risk of injury. Touching your toes will become almost impossible.

Our *lower back* muscles are incredibly strong. A further strength increase through running pulls on the curve of the spine, often putting pressure on the nerves and weakened or damaged discs. Proper stretching will fight the tendency of the spine to become more "bowed" (swaybacked) or inflexible with aging.

Knee problems are often the result of structural inefficiencies being pushed too far, when strong hamstring (rear upper leg) muscles overcome weaker quadriceps (upper front leg) muscles. *Shin splints* (see pp. 222-25) may result when strong calf (rear lower leg) muscles overpower weak ones in the anterior tibial (lower front leg) area. As the months pass you may not notice the gradual tightening of these backside muscles. But over a period of 2-4 years or more, your running power will be reduced considerably if you don't stretch.

How Runners Should Stretch. Only a relaxed muscle can be extended safely and comfortably.

• *Start with a gentle massage.* By gently kneading the calf, hamstring, butt and lower back, you increase blood flow and loosen up the muscles. For about 5 minutes use your 10 magic fingers to work out any knots, but don't apply any deep penetrating pressure.

• *Gradually and slowly move into the stretch.* Back off from any tension and hold that relaxed extension for at least 10-20 seconds. If you feel the slightest pressure, pain, or the muscle starts shaking, you've gone too far. Ease back until you're relaxed again.

• *Finish* the stretch by slowly easing out of it.

The Principles of Stretching

• *Be regular.* Benefits come through steady, regular sessions of gentle muscle extension. Just as tightness builds up through years of standing, walking and running, so will it subside only gradually—through months of gentle extension.

• *Don't bounce.* Decades ago, runners did bouncing stretches. It was thought that a jolt to the muscle gave it the extension it needed. More recent research has shown, however, that bouncing shortens and tightens the muscles. It engages the *stretch reflex,* the body's automatic defense device against injury, which causes the muscle to tighten rather than extend.

• *Don't compete.* Don't try to stretch as far as someone else. Everyone is different in terms of flexibility. And don't try to equal your best stretch of yesterday. Some days you'll be relatively limber, others fairly tight. Just relax and move into the comfortable position that feels good that day.

When to Stretch—A New Approach

Before running? Most runners think they should stretch just before running. You see them everywhere, legs up on benches, leaning against buildings—getting ready to run. I don't recommend this. Just before running, the muscles are tight and may pull or strain easily. You are particularly at risk early in the morning when you're cold and blood flow is minimal. Pushing a cold muscle, tendon or joint often leads to injury. Research by Dr. Ned Frederick at the Honolulu Marathon showed that runners who stretched before running had a greater tendency to be injured. Bob Anderson, author of *Stretching*, contends that it's not the stretching itself, it's that they're stretching the wrong way. Bob insists that if you are relaxed, don't push too far and take it gently, stretching gets the muscles ready for movement.

After running? Stretching right after running is also a risky proposition. The muscles don't simply stop all activity when you stop running. They are still "revved up" and ready to respond for about 30 minutes; stretching may cause them to spasm. When they are working hard like this, a stretch often activates the stretch reflex—leaving you tighter than before.

When, then? The best time to stretch is after the body is warmed up, relaxed, and when the blood is moving. Since many runners *do* stretch incorrectly, it's best to wait and stretch after warming up. Don't stretch to warm the muscles up; it won't work. Stretch in the evening, for example, or throughout the day as you have time. Many of my friends use stretching as a nice way to prepare for sleep.

Think of stretching as preventive maintenance. It gives long-term rather than short-term results. Try to stretch regularly, a minimum of three times a week. If you do that, month after month, year after year, you'll cut down on the tightening effect of running and other endurance exercises.

Tight During a Run? Some runners find that when they become tight during a run, to stop and gently stretch helps. It sometimes helps if you contract the tight muscle very hard, then relax, massage gently and stretch gently. Don't stretch too far. Other runners find that a light massage works, while others walk a few minutes to relieve tightness.

THREE RUNNERS' STRETCHES

Three muscle groups are strengthened and tightened in running:

- Calf and Achilles (back of lower leg below knee).
- Hamstring (back of upper leg between knee and butt).
- Lower back (butt, lower back area).

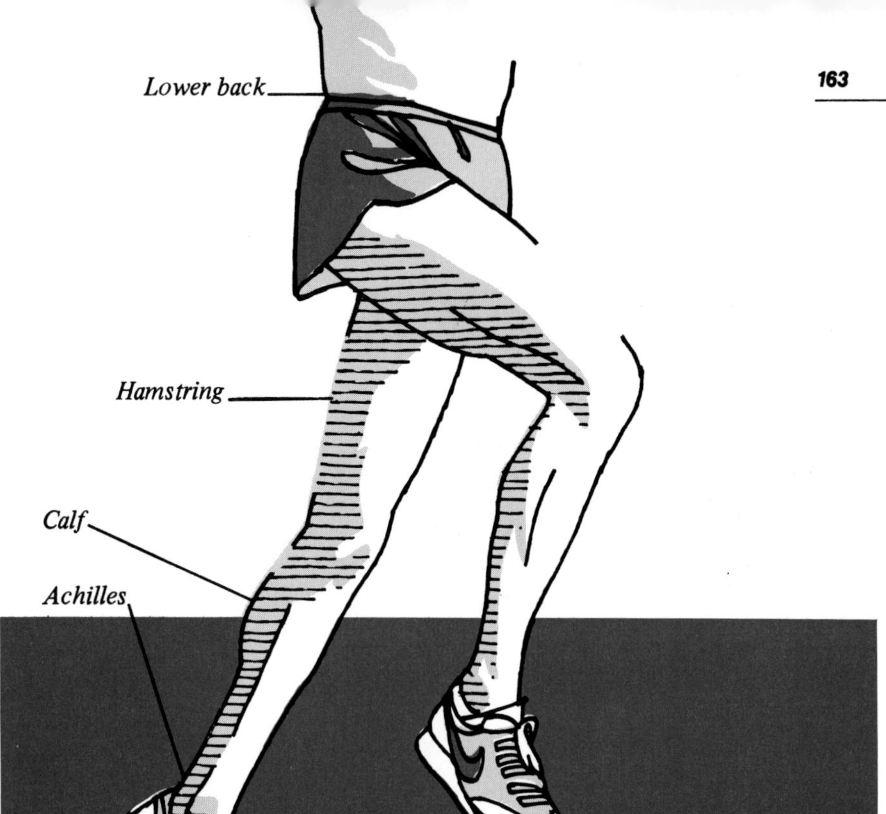

To get good results you need to stretch each group in isolation. Of the dozens of exercises for these muscle groups, we've chosen the three that have worked well for runners and that pose little injury risk. We have avoided stretches that are likely to cause injuries by their design, as well as those likely to be performed incorrectly.

How To Do These Stretches. Make sure the muscles are "warm." If not, gently massage 3-5 minutes each.

- Ease into the stretching position.
- Hold each stretch at least 10-20 seconds.
- Do three times a week at first.
- Increase the length of time you hold each stretch.
- Stretch longer for any of the muscles that need it.

You can add other stretches to these basic three, depending upon your individual needs. Each session of stretching will take only 5-15 minutes, a small investment of time for such beneficial results.

Calf stretch *Achilles stretch*

Calf and Achilles Stretch. Brace your hands against a wall or pole. Extend your back leg and bend the front one. Gradually support the body weight on the back leg, keeping it *slightly* bent. This stretches the upper calf muscle. Now stop, bend the knee of the back leg more and create a slight stretch. This stretches the Achilles tendon and lower calf. Do both legs. Be careful. Stretch the muscles and tendons, don't pull them.

Hamstring Stretch. Lying on your back, loop a towel over your foot. If you don't have a towel, use pants, or a T-shirt. Don't lock the knee, but keep it slightly bent. Tighten the towel gently until you're stretching the hamstring. This is a better hamstring stretch than the familiar one you see of putting the leg up on a chair or other object, because you're less likely to overstretch. The chair puts you in a position where you can put too much stress on the hamstring. With a towel, you have the

Hamstring stretch

flexibility to move into the exact position your muscles need. After stretching hamstrings of both legs, you can stretch your butt muscles by continuing to use the towel, bending the knee more and pulling your leg across your body.

Lower Back Stretch. Move into a squatting position. Make sure lower back is curved, neck and back relaxed. Let your head drop forward toward a resting position on your chest. Normally, heels will rest on the ground and your Achilles tendon will get another stretch. If you are tight like I am, they'll rise; every other session, hold on to a pole or door knob and stretch with heels resting on the ground.

Lower back stretch

STRENGTHENING EXERCISES

In running, the rear leg muscles become strong, while the front leg muscles just go along for the ride. Running, except for hard sprinting, doesn't develop these front muscles much, and a strength imbalance develops between front and back.

The front muscles help balance the back ones. When they're weak, they're overpowered by forces of the rear, leading to problems in the knee, shins and lower back. Stretching will reduce tension in the back muscles, but a regular strengthening program for the front groups is needed, however, to keep them in tone and to maintain a balanced ratio.

I believe that regular stretching and strengthening work together to produce a running body that is in tune and in touch with itself. As with stretching, the time required is not great; you need only be regular. Following are four of the best *strengthening exercises* for runners. After that we show three *potentially harmful exercises* that are often prescribed for runners.

Four Runners' Strength Exercises. To do these strengthening exercises you needn't join a gym or set one up in your basement. They can be done entirely without weights and will take only five minutes to perform. As with stretching, these exercises should be done 2-3 days a week for best results.

Stronger Quadriceps: The Stiff Leg Lift

Knee Problems may develop when the quadriceps (front of thigh) muscles are not strong enough. A strong quadriceps supports the body's weight and acts to absorb the shock of landing. It also keeps the knee cap in its track by tightening the connections.

Sit on a table, bench or chair. Lift one leg at a time with knee locked and leg straight. Start with 5-10 lifts each leg and increase by 2-3 each week until you can do 40-50 with each leg. You may add some weight at this point, if you wish. Remember, *don't bend your knee.* (See p. 169.)

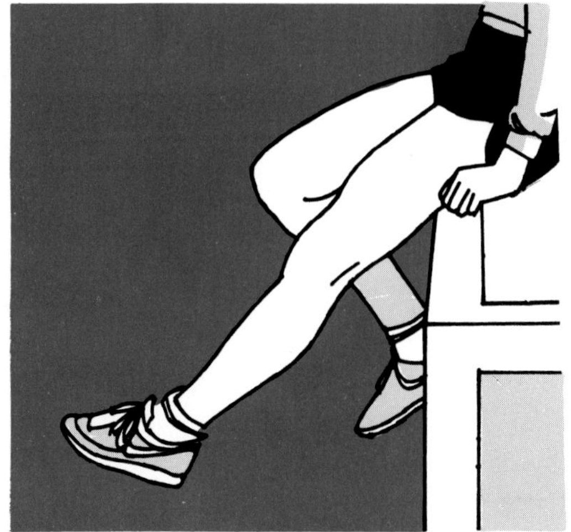

Stiff leg lift, down.

Stiff leg lift, up.

Lift straight up and down

Lift up and toward inside

Stronger Shin Muscles: The Foot Lift

Shin problems or "shin splints" result from increasing mileage too suddenly, running on a hard surface or downhill, or from new shoes. (See pp. 222-25 for a detailed description of shin problems.) If you haven't had shin problems, you're lucky. If you have, here is an exercise that will strengthen the attachment of the tibialis anterior muscle to the leg.

Sit on a table or stool and hook a bucket, old purse or weights with a cloth loop over your foot. Start with one pound. Lift *foot* 5-10 times in two separate motions; this is an ankle motion:

- Straight up and down.
- Up and toward the inside.
- Remember to *lift only your foot.* Don't try to lift the whole leg as in a "stiff leg lift."

Gradually increase number of lifts to 30-50 or increase weight from one pound to 3-4. If you are one of the few runners who lands on the outside of your foot (supinates) you can strengthen the small muscles on the outside by rolling the foot up and to the outside. This will help prevent ankle turns or sprains.

Lie on your back, knees bent.

Raise head 10-12".

Stronger Stomach: Bent Knee Situps

Lower back problems can often be avoided by having strong stomach muscles, which will control the pull of a strong back and release pressure on the spine and the many nerves in that area.

Lie on your back with knees bent. Leaving feet on floor, raise shoulders slowly to a 30° angle (10-12") and return. Going higher than 30° does not develop the muscle any better, and may cause back problems. Don't jerk yourself up as this doesn't use the stomach muscles; go slowly. Cross your arms on your chest so you won't use them for propulsion.

For years I couldn't do this exercise without hooking my feet under something. At Barbara's urging I tried several times each night to do it without such aid and at first I couldn't get up off the ground. But the isometric effect of the effort paid off, for in about a month I could do my first one—with no help. Now I can do 30 or more.

Foot Strength: The Toe Squincher

Foot pain in the morning (which goes away as you warm up) may be caused by weak foot muscles. Running does not strengthen these muscles. A more serious problem is *plantar fasciitis,* where the pounding and weight of your body causes a strain in the strong ligament that runs from the heel to the ball of the foot. The "toe squincher" strengthens the muscles which support this ligament, helping the foot to push off with more force and support the body's weight better. It also seems to stretch the plantar tendon and balance the pulling effect of muscles that pull the tendons on the top of the foot.

Point your toes, then contract the muscles very hard for 7-10 seconds. Relax. Do this 5-10 times daily, throughout the day. Don't be surprised if the muscles cramp when you first try it; this merely shows that the muscles are weak and need work.

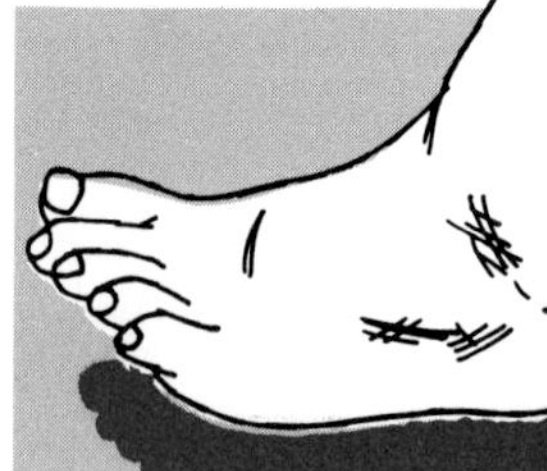

Point toes.

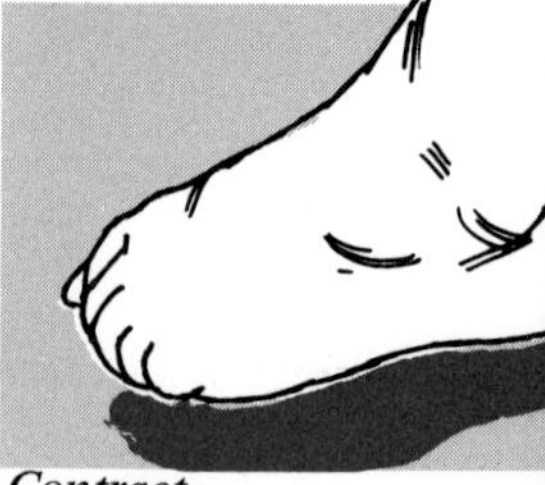

Contract.

CAUTION! THESE EXERCISES MAY BE HARMFUL

The Chair Hurdle. This popular stretch puts too much pressure on the hamstring and has caused many muscle pulls. The hamstring stretch with a towel (p. 165) does the job with less risk.

The Plow. As you bring feet and legs over your body, gravity can take you too far and put too much pressure on the neck and spine. You may do this for years and have no problems, but it's risky. The lower back stretch stretches the back gently, without risk.

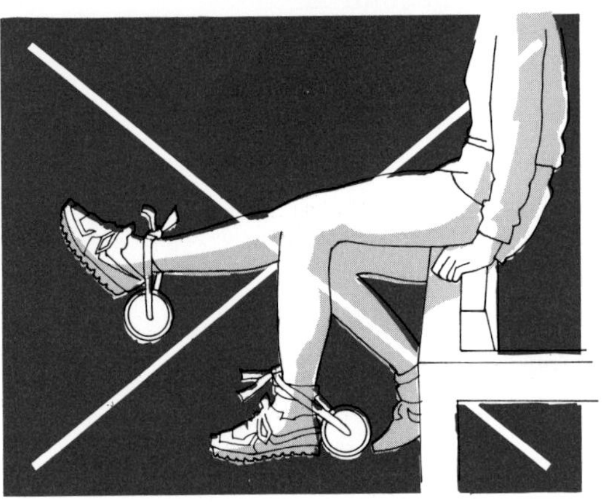

Bent Knee Extension. Usually performed on a weight bench, you lift your leg from a 90° position to a stiff leg position with weights. This will strengthen the quads as well as the stiff leg lift, but can aggravate a knee problem. It's not worth the risk. The stiff leg lift strengthens the same muscles without the risk.

15 RUNNING EXERCISES AND DRILLS

HOW TO STRENGTHEN AND IMPROVE FORM

RUNNING DRILLS HAVE BEEN USED by generations of great coaches around the world. In 1977 Arthur Lydiard showed me a special set of exercises that has improved my running ever since. Arthur observed these exercises in Europe, and then experimented first on himself, then on his young Olympic athletes. He believes they strengthen key running muscles and improve rhythm. I agree.

The great New Zealand coach showed me these exercises at our mountain retreat running camp at Lake Tahoe, California. After watching Arthur's athletes perform, I can see why he believes these exercises make the difference that can push an athlete like three-time gold medalist Peter Snell from "good" to "great." From his clinics at Tahoe I have learned the principles behind these exercises. They've not only been a major influence on my own running form and theory, but tools that have aided me in helping runners of all abilities.

Hill training (see p. 57) prepares the major propulsion muscles for speedwork and the four exercises shown here. These exercises specifically develop the lower leg muscles, the quadriceps and hip flexors, and improve running reflexes. As your lower legs get stronger, they support more body weight and allow the ankle to maximize the power of the lower leg muscles. These exercises work on the entire sequence of the running motion, from the push-off of the foot to the carry-through of the leg.

As in all training, these exercises over-develop some muscles so they'll be strong enough to carry you throughout the run and the race. It's good to have someone help you with these, to correct your form as necessary. "Hands-on" instructional clinics offer the best type of guidance.

Don't be discouraged if you don't pick them up right away. It took me a year of hard work to start realizing the benefits of these drills. It takes time for the coordination of all the nerves, muscles, etc. involved to come together. For best results, these exercises should be done gently and regularly. They train the various body parts to work together and to produce the desired results.

Rules of Running Exercises and Drills

1. Warm up by jogging at least a mile before, and warm down with at least an easy mile afterward.

2. Don't try any radical changes. Let the exercises give you the strength to change gradually.

3. Don't just jump into these! Ease into them. At first, do only 2-3 of each.

4. Slowly work up to about 50-100 meters of each exercise, 2-3 times a week.

5. These are non-strenuous exercises. If they're not easy to do, or if you wear yourself out, you're either doing them wrong, you're not ready to do them, or you're doing too much.

6. Do these exercises twice a week for best results. After a good warm up, you may combine them with your form accelerations to get warmed up for hills, speedwork or races. They may also be done by themselves, in the middle of an easy run.

Quick knee lifters

Quick Knee Lifters: Walking on Ice

Purpose: Strengthens lower leg muscles, quadriceps, hip flexors, driving muscles of butt, helps improve running rhythm.

- Taking short quick strides, lift knees to waist level.
- Stay forward on your feet.
- Be quick and light, as if you were walking on ice.
- Avoid long strides and don't go down the course fast. This is for knee lift and quick reflexes.

Kick outs

Kick Outs**: **The Majorette

Purpose: Develops ankle action and good leg motion.

- First walk through it.
- Lift knee to waist level, bringing foot under butt—almost touching it.
- Kick lead foot out in front.
- As lead leg kicks out, push off with other foot with burst of power at ankle.
- As kicked-out foot reaches about 45^0, bring it down directly under your body.
- Work on a quick follow-through of the foot from the time it pushes off, until the time it kicks out.

The "Kicking Skip": This is Lydiard's innovation of this exercise where you spring off the ankle then skip by landing on the same foot. Do same with other foot and "kick-skip" along.

Hill springs

Hill Springs

Purpose: Strengthens muscles of hips, legs and feet and moves body into position for ankle to do its work.

- Pick a moderate hill (10% grade).
- Bounce off one foot and leap into air lifting lead knee.
- Hang in the air until the last second.
- Very quickly bring the leading leg down for a landing, and spring off with leg *almost* straight. Here's where the ankle has to do its work.
- Never let the push-off leg be perfectly straight. Keep the knee slightly bent to avoid spraining the weak and slow-healing muscles behind the knee.
- Keep a short stride length, just work on floating and maintaining form.
- Start with a few "springs"; gradually work up to 50-100 yards.
- Don't worry about lifting knees high.

Bounding drill

Running tall

Bounding

Purpose: Develops more quadricep strength and driving power.

Bounding is the same as hill springing, with these exceptions:

- Lift knees higher.
- Take longer strides.
- Do it on a flat or slightly inclined surface.
- Follow directions for hill springing (except for the short stride).
- On each step you are driving with greater power, extending your stride and developing your calf muscles.

Running Tall. This is a summary exercise. Put all the elements of these drills together into a running stride—high knee lift, erect posture, strong push-off, quick follow-through of each leg with the foot tucked under the butt, and a chest that extends forward and upward. Run no faster than your 10K pace. Keep things under control and let all the elements come together.

16 WILL POWER

HOW TO RUN FASTER WITHOUT TRAINING

CHANCES ARE YOU CAN RUN FASTER, farther and *better* than you do right now. At your fingertips is an untapped source of strength and power that—when called upon—can not only help you run faster, but have more fun.

Unleashing "The Monster." Dick Gregory, the entertainer and also a non-competitive ultra-marathoner, talks about the deep reservoir of strength we all have inside us. He calls it "the monster." In the days of his high school and college track competition, Dick says he would call upon the monster to help him battle insecurity and uncertainty. He'd wait until he absolutely needed it, and then call it up to help him run better and faster.

I've seen a number of monsters at work. In the 1972 U.S. Olympic trials, Dave Wottle, a middle distance runner, had beaten the best of the American 800-meter crop, including a Kansan named Jim Ryun. As we traveled to Norway to prepare for the games, however, Dave complained of a knee problem that wouldn't go away. After several frustrating speed sessions which had to be quickly terminated, Dave took 2-3 weeks off to let it heal.

One day as my roommate, Doug Brown, and I were starting an easy run in the forest, we saw Wottle, full of optimism and ready to resume hard training, starting on his first run after the layoff. When we returned from our short run, we came upon Dave limping along, in tears. The rest had done nothing for his knee. He was certain his career was over, just as he was reaching his peak.

After a few more days of rest and depression, however, we began to see a new Wottle at meals and on the track. Able to joke about his problem, he ran when he could and improvised workouts to get in at least *some* training without aggravating the knee. By the time we arrived in Munich for the first trial heats, Wottle—though weakened by the prolonged layoff—was able to run enough to enter his race.

In the first qualification round he struggled to stay at the end of the pack. As he came off the final turn in last place we were ready to rush out and congratulate him for his courage in staying up with athletes who were now in much better condition. But somehow he threaded his way through the mass of bodies and finished third, qualifying for the next round. He ran two more qualifying rounds the same way, struggling to stay up, then fighting his way into the last qualifying position. We were amazed: Wottle had qualified for the 800-meter finals.

It was a bright sunny afternoon in the Munich Sports Stadium when the world's best 800-meter runners toed the line. At the gun they sprinted for position and strategic advantage, and Wottle strained to stay up with the slowest runners. As the runners rounded the final turn, we could see that Dave was boxed in at the rear of the pack. Though our own sportscasters were describing his effort as an unfortunate strategy that would keep him from a medal, we knew he was lucky to be close to the next-to-last runner.

Then something happened. At the toughest time of the race, when all the runners were trying to pull every ounce of power from muscles overfilled with waste products, Dave found a hidden source of energy. His body had reached its limits, but his mind pulled ahead. He squeezed between two runners, stepped quickly to the outside, then the inside, and drove forward in hopes of getting out of last place. Just at this moment, the other runners were slowing, having run too fast at the start. Dave found himself streaming by the other runners, finally lunging at the tape—a gold medal winner!

Dave Wottle's story is dramatic but the fact is, each of us can run better right now—the power is there for the asking. The monster lurks within. Dave went inside himself and pulled together all his inner resources. In the same way, each of us can draw strength from a hidden reservoir.

Body and Mind. The mind can have a great influence in pulling our bodies beyond their limits. Unfortunately most of us usually experience this in a negative way. As the mind pulls us away from a designated course of action, we get distracted into non-productive or destructive activities. In running, such negativity may cause us to believe we're not capable of achieving our goals.

When you get the body and mind working together, you'll find yourself a better competitor than someone who is a stronger runner but lacks this body/mind integration. Just as a team with good teamwork can defeat a team of outstanding but not synchronized individuals, you'll be able to outperform others who may be more "capable" in the particulars, but can't get them working together. The mind is the captain of the ship, and it must be in constant communication with all the body systems so they work in harmony and keep you moving strongly ahead.

Problem-Solving. The problems that have caused me the most trouble have been the ones I didn't attack systematically. The worst enemy wasn't the problem itself, but the confusion that went along with it. Before the 1973 Boston Marathon I was in the best condition of my life. I felt so good and was responding so well to training that I felt invincible. I didn't feel the need to plan my training, but ran as I felt each day.

A series of two speed sessions and a hard hill run hadn't seemed to tire me, when I suddenly realized it was only eight days before Boston. My Sunday 15-miler was therefore going to be an easy one, but I felt wonderful. Without thinking about it, I ran that training run like a race and noticed, as I walked up my driveway, that I had run my best time ever for that distance. I was pleased and excited when I should have been concerned by my lack of caution so soon before a race. During the next week I felt like I had legs of lead. I ran well at Boston (fifth), but not nearly as well as I could have with planning.

If we don't concentrate on our problems, they will confuse and worry us, and often get worse. Once I understood this, I developed a way of looking at problems, and solving them. Whether it is how to hold myself back when I feel great, or push harder when I don't feel like it, I generally try three steps:

- Define the problem.
- Analyze my strengths and décide if I need outside help.
- Attack the problem.

Define the Problem. Figure out what's bothering you. Discomfort, boredom, low energy, tiredness, doubt. Sometimes you'll just feel uneasy and when you trace that to its source, you'll feel a lot better. It's easier to work on something specific than on a general feeling of uneasiness. As you become sensitive to the onset of negative feelings, you can attack them. If I had really analyzed my training before Boston '73, I'd have realized there was a reason behind my lingering tiredness and the pre-race anxiety it generated. Such an understanding would have caused me to enter the race with a gentle, no-pressure approach. Instead, I worried for weeks afterward about my body betraying me on race day when I had felt so great in training.

Analyze Your Strengths and Get Help When You Need It. Once you've seen the problem clearly, you can usually find the means for dealing with it. You'll learn to draw on strengths you never knew existed. Still, we all need help sometimes and you shouldn't hesitate to go to someone you respect and trust for advice and support.

Attack the Problem. Just having a plan gives you confidence. Taking into account your own strengths and the help you can count on from others, you'll figure out a direct approach and work on overcoming the problem as soon as possible. As you do this repeatedly you'll gain self-confidence. By developing a system of problem-solving you're showing yourself you can cope and have what it takes to overcome setbacks.

The Power of Positive Running. Just as the mind can lead you astray or hold you back, it can also lead you forward. If your thoughts are negative, you'll feel worse, slow down and have bad feelings about the run. But if you can "accentuate the positive," you'll hold your pace or speed up and feel better. Here are some techniques I've developed through many years of running, that help turn negative thoughts around—during a race, or any time I don't feel like continuing:

Ignoring. When you feel bad, try to let the thoughts just pass through. When the negative thoughts have gone their way, you'll be on a positive track.

Distraction. In the last part of a hard run, you feel bad. You're tired, hot, you want to stop, your legs ache. You may even feel you no longer care about the run. Everyone gets these messages, even those in the lead. These needn't become real problems unless you dwell on them. When I'm tired, for example, I've found that by concentrating on things around me I forget how I feel. Almost anything will do: a passing car, a house, a line on the road. I'll look at the object and describe it to myself. "A blue Chevy, I think 1978, needs a wax job, got a small dent right front fender." Concentrate on the specific. Or focus on one object that leads to another: a series of telephone poles, the next runner, mileage markers—a progression of distractions.

Projection. First concentrate on a realistic goal, then project yourself through it. Projection is pretending, very strongly; so strongly, in fact, that you make things happen. You assume you've already achieved the goal, and are going to do it again. This can give you confidence.

During a 4-6 month training period, you can "brainwash" yourself. Over this period, you capture your goal mentally and it becomes part of you. When you've finished training, just let your body do what it's been trained to do, and you'll run your desired time or distance.

You can also combat negative thoughts by projecting yourself through the race itself. Imagine nearing the finishing line, with everything under control; you can see the time on the clock. This will help you maintain the rhythm and pace you need to get there.

Relax. When you're relaxed you're conserving energy and have a better chance of achieving your goal. Since tension usually comes from the fear of being out of control, the best defense is to tell yourself you *are* in control. When I'm tense or tired, I like to repeat three words to myself: *glide, ease, power.* This helps get my thoughts on the right track. The more I say these words, the more I convince myself I'm demonstrating what they mean.

You're the Captain of the Ship. If you're realistic, positive and relaxed, you'll get the most out of your body. When problems come up during a run—heat, hills, injury—you can assess them accurately if your mind is free of negative thoughts.

Set up a system that works for you. You'll gain unexpected strength and security from tapping this reservoir of mental energy. As the system starts working, you'll gain even more strength and have more control when you next need it.

17 WOMEN'S RUNNING

BY BARBARA GALLOWAY

My wife Barbara has been a serious runner for years. In fact, we met at a track meet in Florida when she was on the Florida State women's track team. She has a master's degree in physical education and conducts running clinics (for women and men) in various parts of the country. She's frequently asked questions about special training considerations for women and especially about running during pregnancy. As a result she's done some research and a good deal of thinking on the subject. Everything else in this book applies to runners of both sexes, but in this chapter Barbara relates what she's learned about the relation of a woman's reproductive system to running, as well as her own experiences "running with a passenger."

–J.G.

AWKWARD! That's how I felt when first giving a talk on women's running. All my college and graduate courses in training and physiology had told me that women respond to training the same way as men. It was difficult to find enough "women only" information to fill a 30-minute clinic.

One pregnancy (and a boy) later, I've learned that there are some very real differences. Although deep inside the muscle cells and throughout the cardiovascular system there is no sex discrimination, our reproductive systems cause us to face some problems men don't have to worry about.

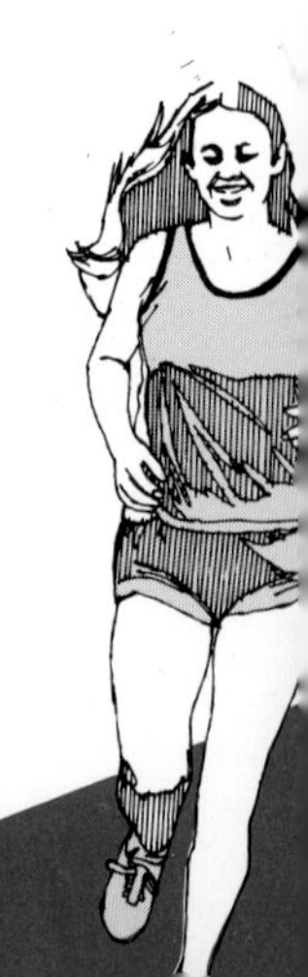

Structural Differences in Women. Physiologists have found that a man and a woman with the same ability, exercise background and training program will have the same oxygen-carrying capacity, the same blood system development and the same muscle cell development from training. Why then, does the man run faster?

For one thing, men do not have the extra flexibility and width in their hips to support a developing child. Their pelvis and hips are more efficiently designed for speed and strength. Men can run faster than women with the same amount of effort. Although women can increase the size and strength of their muscles, the inherent capacity for this type of development is greater in men.

When it comes to long races, however, the scales begin to tip toward the women. At 50 miles, for example, speed and muscle are no longer an advantage and they are possibly a burden. Marathon and ultra-distance performance is based largely on the body's ability to burn fat. Women not only have an extra amount of this usually unwanted commodity, but may metabolize it more easily than men. Of course, I don't recommend these ultra-long events (over 26 miles), because they may break down muscles for a long, long time. The women pioneers who try them may have great success in the event, but risk long-term injuries.

Starting. Most women begin a running program without a substantial exercise background. Past generations of mothers and fathers have implied that little girls might melt if they sweat. Tomboys were warned that they'd never get a man unless they quit running around and playing so hard. Boys of the same age were climbing trees, running full speed, swinging on ropes, throwing balls and chasing them—with full parental approval.

Not only may women's muscles be weak, but connecting tendons, ligaments and bones may not be prepared for hard exercise. These are the weak links in the fitness chain. Most women must begin more slowly than men and be more careful as they increase their fitness base. The suggestions in Chapter 3, *Getting Started* (see pp. 32-35), apply to women as well as men, and to people of all abilities. Start by walking and add running to your program gradually.

Losing Weight. Running is one of the best ways to lose fat and keep it off. It's a better approach than dieting and it has the added advantage of providing a health base which will last for the rest of your life.

Through childhood many girls will have little fat on their bodies. In the teenage years, the female hormone, estrogen, begins to cause many changes, including the deposit of fat.

Men usually build fat on the outside of their muscles—and it quickly shows. Women, however, will "marble" their fat, adding deposits in the muscle itself. This kind of fat buildup doesn't show at first, because it's interspersed among the muscle cells throughout the body. But once a muscle fills up its inner storage areas, fat is stored on the hips, breasts and in thin layers over the body.

Endurance exercise stimulates fat-burning muscles to work day and night. Because these muscle cells weigh more than fat cells, you may not lose weight and may even gain some. Weight is also added because you are increasing your blood volume through exercise. At the same time, though, you are losing inches, dress sizes and unhealthy fat. (See Chapter 22, *Running Off Fat.)*

If, however, you have increased your exercise for several months, have gained weight, and not reduced your dress size, you need to watch your consumption of calories. The worst offender is dietary fat, the second sugar.

Don't be a slave to your scale. Weight lost in diets and fasting is mostly water. This will cause dehydration and may lead to illness. Exercise, over time, is the best way to control your weight and also produces lasting health benefits.

FOUR AREAS OF FEMALE CONCERN ABOUT EXERCISE

Whether we want to have children or not, it's natural to be concerned about how running might affect our reproductive systems. Those of us who choose to have a child are also protective of the baby and want the best conditions for its natural and healthy development.

Dr. Edwin Dale, a specialist in female reproductive physiology in Atlanta, has become an expert on the influence of exercise on women's menstrual periods and pregnancy. During the running boom in the latter part of the '70s, scores of women asked their doctors questions they couldn't answer. When the professionals consulted Dr. Dale, he discovered that the research hadn't yet been done.

Finally, Dale conducted studies of his own, working with hundreds of women and comparing notes with other specialists. According to him, there are four major areas of female concern about exercise.

Menstrual Irregularities. Though there are still a lot of questions as to why it happens, long distance running does seem to be linked to interruption or cessation of menstrual periods in some women. Recent research indicates that a special area of the brain, the hypothalamus, closely monitors total body fat and stress, and when it perceives that the person is "too stressed," may shut off estrogen production. When body fat in a woman falls below the level at which the hypothalamus judges she could handle a pregnancy, estrogen production stops. This could be a protective mechanism used by our ancestors during periods of famine.

The good news is that there's little evidence that this loss of fertility is permanent (although it may take some time to reverse). However, don't depend upon lack of periods for birth control! Irregular or absent menses do not guarantee infertility and many runners have been surprised to find themselves pregnant.

To women runners who are seeking to normalize menstrual activity, Dr. Dale recommends the following:

- Make sure you are getting the right balance of daily protein, grains, fat, fresh vegetables, fruits, vitamins and minerals. A diet high in complex carbohydrates and low in fat and protein is important to all runners. (A certain amount of cholesterol is necessary for estrogen production.)
- Cut back on mileage by 50% or more to reduce stress and stimulate hormone production. Cutting back one week won't be enough; it will probably be necessary to continue at a reduced rate for several months. For extra exercise, try swimming. For some reason, even world-class swimmers tend to have few menstrual problems. This may be due to lack of weight-bearing stress.
- If neither of these methods works, see your physician. He or she will investigate the case, rule out serious disease and may prescribe hormone shots. However, most women would rather cut back on their running programs than take hormone shots, for some of the side effects are often dangerous.

Note: In early 1984, medical researchers at the University of California Medical School in San Francisco reported that women who exercise enough to stop menstruating may be suffering loss of bone tissue similar to that seen in elderly women. Ten women in a test conducted were under 50, had ceased menstruating due to vigorous exercise and had very little body fat and relatively low levels of estrogen. The scientists were concerned that the bone loss (in this case 22-29% less than normal) observed in this small test group might predispose women to osteoporosis (a condition where bones are easily broken) at an earlier age than normal. It will be worth watching for future tests and research on the subject. Adequate calcium should be included in the diet to help prevent this condition.

Feminine Image. Another area of concern to women, according to Dr. Dale, is how exercise may change the image of the new runner. Although it was not always the case, exercise is now regarded as a natural part of a woman's life—desirable and necessary for women and men alike. TV ads, the movies, newspapers and magazines depict healthy, vigorous athletic women in a variety of pursuits. Fashion designers have made "sweat clothes" into attractive, feminine apparel. The image has changed.

Breast Support. Many women wonder if the jarring effects of running can damage the breasts. Dr. Dale reports that there is no known evidence that running causes the breasts to drop, or injures them in any way. However, most women find that some support is a lot more comfortable in a regular running program, particularly on longer runs. Many bras have lightweight elastic straps, which stretch and are not suitable for running, though they are adequate for everyday wear. Non-elastic straps, while they "support," can cut into the shoulders. Underwiring should also be avoided.

Sports bra manufacturers have come up with a bra that suits many women. 100% cotton, without hooks, it has wide elastic straps, crossing at the back. This gives firm control and eliminates uncomfortable movement. Some women have found a "minimizer" bra to be more comfortable, because of their special design for "distribution" and support.

Female Organs. In spite of a few unresearched articles warning of uterine collapse due to running, there is, according to Dr. Dale, no known medical evidence for such a condition. (Of course, if there is a structural weakness in the bladder or uterus, running can make things worse.) Some women will lose urine while running, especially during hard runs or races, and this is a sign that pelvic floor strength should be improved before resuming running. (See "Kegel" exercises, p. 193.)

An excellent book for women runners is Joan Ullyot's *Running Free.* (See *Selected Reading List,* p. 278.)

RUNNING THROUGH PREGNANCY

For all that's been written about running, there isn't much first-hand information for pregnant women. For that reason, I'll relate some of my experiences, as well as what I've learned in talking to various experts on the subject. To begin with, there are three important points:

- Little is known about the effects of a mother's exercise on the fetus. Hopefully more research will be done in the near future.
- I was a runner for many years before becoming pregnant. Pregnancy is not a good time to *start* a running program; the combination of beginning running and pregnancy puts too much stress on the back, hips, knees and other joints and muscles. If you want to begin exercising, try either a pregnancy aerobics program or swimming. If you are already running, you can probably continue doing so, modifying it as pregnancy advances—according to how you feel and what your doctor recommends. Much of what follows applies to experienced runners who become pregnant.
- A woman, especially during pregnancy, has to make sure she has good pelvic floor and abdominal muscle support before even jogging. Check this out with your doctor as soon as possible. As pregnancy puts such a strain on these two muscle groups, most pregnant women runners give up jogging after the fifth month. Again, discuss this with your physician.

Conception—Thanks to a Bad Knee. Strange as it may seem, we owe our boy to a knee injury. After four years of marriage, Jeff and I decided to have a baby, but decision and reality turned out to be two years apart. Being in good health, we assumed conception would be quick and simple. We were somewhat shocked to find my ten years of running, 17 marathons and hundreds of races might be the reasons we weren't becoming parents.

About a year before we started "trying," menstrual irregularities gave me warning signs that my reproductive system wasn't working normally. When I increased my mileage from 25 to 40 miles per week, my menses became irregular. When the weekly count went to 50 miles and beyond, they ceased entirely. For a year I waited in vain for my next period—partially happy about being relieved of the burden. As the months passed, however, I began to wonder if this might be a permanent upsetting of nature's balance and lead to future problems.

Armed with research, I was assured there was no need for concern. This was, in effect, a natural method of birth control (although certainly not foolproof). Feeling a need for fertility reassurance, I reduced my weekly mileage. My periods came back, although they were unpredictable. The cycle varied from 40-50 days and occasionally skipped entirely.

My doctors told me I may have been ovulating, even when I was missing periods. I'd participated in Dr. Dale's study of women runners, and knew that running more than 30 miles per week can reduce the secretion of reproductive hormones. For over a year we tried to conceive in vain; then a blessing came, disguised as a knee injury.

Running five marathons in six months was a mistake, compounded by my running the last three of them within three minutes of my best time. At first the knee pain was only sporadic and I could run with a dull pain some of the time. After several months, I found myself suffering with each step and was forced to cut back to 10 miles a week. My physicians now tell me that this six-week reduction allowed crucial hormones to rebuild. Finally, we had a baby on the way!

Running With a Passenger. When I first became pregnant, I was afraid I'd have to give up running. It was to be my method of coping with the mood changes and other emotional adjustments of pregnancy. But my knees still bothered me, even at only 10 miles a week, and I began to dread the coming months.

I finally stopped running altogether and enrolled in an aerobic dance class to get some exercise and burn off a few calories. Suddenly the knee pain was gone, and it didn't come back. The healing had started, undoubtedly, because of the reduced mileage. My orthopedist theorized that the sudden reduction of pain was produced by a pregnancy hormone. (It is common for pregnant women to have a reduced sensation of pain in labor due to this natural drug.) I was elated, and decided to resume my normal running.

Second thoughts were more prudent. Although I wanted to get back to my usual mileage, I was lugging around a body that was increasingly strange. Each week the weight gain was noticeable, and my center of gravity played tricks during each run. Frequent internal changes also kept me guessing.

Convinced that this was *not* the time to go for long runs or run fast, I kept all runs below those of pre-pregnancy days. What used to be a 60-70 mile week would now top out at 45 miles. As my "time" drew near, my mileage decreased.

From the fifth until the eighth month I held it to 35 miles a week. From that point until birth I cut back to 18-20 miles per week, walking some of it during the last few runs.

Precautionary Measures. If you're already running, you probably don't have to stop. If your doctor understands aerobic exercise (hopefully from current first-hand experience), ask his or her advice. If you are told not to run or exercise, and the reasons given do not seem good enough, talk to other pregnant women runners and find a specialist more familiar with exercise. It never hurts to get a second or third opinion. Many women give up their running or other exercise when there seems to be no reason to do so; they lose a wonderful source of needed relaxation, oxygen infusion and stamina development. *Of course you must ultimately listen to your doctor, as there are good reasons why some women should not run.*

Stay cool. If you run while pregnant, don't let your body temperature rise too high, because it can damage the fetus. If you feel too hot, walk and cool off before you continue. Drink water at every chance, as sweating is your best cooling mechanism. Avoid both extreme heat and extreme cold. Be sensible, make adjustments and you'll usually be able to get in a run. Hot tubs and saunas should be avoided during pregnancy, especially during the early phases because of their effects on body temperature.

Walk, you don't have to run! The psychological and physical benefits of endurance exercise are based upon keeping your pulse rate up for three half-hour sessions per week. Most pregnant women don't actually have to run to keep the pulse up. Walk briskly and if you want to run, do so for short distances.

While several studies have shown no adverse effects on the baby from *aerobic* exercise, little is known about effects on blood flow and oxygen to the baby during *anaerobic exercise.* (See pp. 42-43 for definitions.) So, when running during pregnancy, you should always be in an aerobic state—able to conduct a conversation. If you are out of breath and cannot talk, *slow down.*

Don't worry about mileage. If you can walk for 30 minutes, three times a week, during pregnancy, you'll stay in shape and you'll feel better. Never push yourself to the point of stress. If you do run, make it fun. Walk at the first sign of any undue stress. Remember, every person is different. Don't try to match the exercise program of anyone else; make up your own.

Take early precautions. If you think you may have conceived, be especially careful. These early weeks are critical for the baby. All the "warnings" in this chapter, especially those concerning overheating and anaerobic exercise should be heeded if there is a chance you could be pregnant.

Pay attention to your changing body. As you gain weight, your center of gravity changes. Because you're carrying such a large "package," your back may hurt and you may pull some muscles. Listen to your body and make daily adjustments in your exercise program.

How Did It Feel? I had three types of discomfort on runs. I felt sluggish when I ran. Most runners feel sluggish the first mile or two; my pregnant sluggishness lasted at least three. Miles 4-6 were often enjoyable and more than made up for the earlier discomfort. Feeling this way naturally made for a slow pace. The overall effect of the run was so good, however, that the early sluggish feelings never dampened my enthusiasm. I was invigorated after and felt better the rest of the day.

As the baby grew, running put more pressure and mechanical stress on the pelvic area. Ligaments do not have much flexibility and they became tighter as I grew. Particularly pressing was the band that stretches from the iliac crest (hip bones) to the abdominal wall, which supports the uterus and the abdominal cavity. During a run this structure would get very tight and seem to "pull."

This was such a pressing and seemingly serious problem I was worried that my pregnancy-running days were just about over. I knew that many women stop running about this time (fourth month). Imagining myself at birth with sagging abdominal muscles and loose ligaments, I read all I could on the subject, consulted with doctors and my fears were gradually calmed. I kept on running, but most women take this problem as a signal—at about the fourth or fifth month—to stop running, and substitute walking or swimming.

Running During the Last Trimester. "Practice" contractions, called Braxton-Hicks contractions, may occur in the later stages of normal pregnancy. I experienced these mildly and sporadically while running in the sixth and seventh months. In the eighth and ninth months, they became increasingly harder to handle and, despite my doctor's assurances, I was sure I was going to have my baby out on the trails. The breathing exercises I learned in our natural childbirth classes helped, and of course I walked or stopped and rested while the contractions were going on.

Important note: Many doctors believe you should not run when experiencing contractions. If *sporadic* contractions occur and are not worsened by exercise, fine, but if they get worse, slow down, stop or switch exercises.

Again, you should consult your doctor should any of these questions arise. As I said, most women stop running before this stage of pregnancy.

Don't get out of breath. By the seventh or eighth month the demand for oxygen increases about 10%. This makes it very easy to become anaerobic during a run, so you have to slow down and walk.

Elizabeth Noble, director of the Maternal and Child Health Center in Cambridge, Massachusetts, emphasizes the need to keep the breathing normal and avoid breathlessness. Interruption in the oxygen supply may have physiological effects on the fetus, she explains, and psychological effects as well.

Again, my romance with running isn't for everyone. Listen to your own physician—and to your own body. This is especially important if, like many women, you experience balance problems and tend to fall. It is also, of course, extremely important if you have any special health problems.

GETTING BACK INTO SHAPE AFTER THE BABY

Returning to fitness after Brennan was harder than I'd expected. The reproductive part of my body required rest. But I wanted my running "mind release" more than ever to cope with the instant responsibility of caring for one who depended upon me for everything. There were some frustrating times—for about four months my body and emotions were out of balance.

You must rest. A body weakened by the tremendous physical drain of labor and sleep loss will not heal as fast as usual. The birth process puts a great strain on the inside and outside of one's body and it takes many weeks to recover. Rest is a prime ingredient, along with good nutrition and exercise.

Walk before you run. Most women runners can *begin* running about two weeks after birth. Go slowly at first, even on flat surfaces, and stop whenever you're tired. Even if you feel great, hold back; you could overstress your body and prolong your postpartum recovery. A walking program of three 30-minute sessions a week will keep you fit and reduce stress so you can recover. There are very few women who can't walk after a few days' recovery.

Exercises. The abdominal muscles are stretched out of shape during pregnancy. Postpartum bent-knee curl-ups starting soon after childbirth are very important in rebuilding abdominal tone and helping to prevent back problems. Raise your head, then shoulders, about 10-12 inches, then lower back down. (See p. 168.)

I'd also recommend "Kegel" pelvic floor exercises. Many women, especially those over 30 who have had a child, experience involuntary leakage of urine when running. The term used to describe this condition is "stress incontinence." One interim solution is to wear a sanitary pad while running. Another, better approach is to strengthen the perineal muscles that control this function. Joan Ullyot, in *Running Free*, offers a thorough description of strengthening the proper muscles. You alternate by squeezing, then releasing the "... muscles of the perineum, which surround the bladder neck and vagina." You can also strengthen the bladder sphincter itself by tightening, then relaxing the sphincter. When urinating, stop and start the flow; this is the sphincter muscle you're using. You can do these exercises at any time: contract hard for a second, then release completely. Do this about 10 times in a row for one exercise, then work your way up to doing 20 sets of 10.

See also *Essential Exercises for the Child Bearing Year* by Elizabeth Noble (Houghton Mifflin Co., Boston, Mass., 1982), a book on health care for child-bearing women that includes information on body mechanics, posture and movement, as well as exercises.

Drink liquids. Be very careful about dehydration. Drink plenty of water, juices or milk—small amounts (4-8 oz.) every hour rather than large amounts less frequently. Make sure your urine is always pale yellow—not darker.

Get Help. If the father can take time off to be with you and the baby the first week or two, it will help build a strong family relationship and a natural interdependence. Don't be shy about asking him for help. Too many mothers push the father out of the nest early. If he becomes a part of the experience and shares in the duties, he'll be more likely to identify with your problems—particularly your need to run.

Two big problems of a new mother who wants to run are finding the time, and a babysitter. Try to work this out before the birth. If the father can't help, try to find a relative, a friend or a child care program. Establish, early on, that you need your 30-60 minutes of exercise. Life flows better for all if an exercise-addicted mother gets her daily dose.

A Postpartum Exercise Program

First 2-4 weeks: Exercise the pelvic floor and abdominal muscles. Walk or run a little every day if you feel like it. Check with your doctor if there are problems.

Next 4-8 weeks: Run every other day at most. Start by jogging in short stretches as in a beginners program. Gradually increase the amount.

Next 4 weeks: Gradually ease into your normal running program. If you're a beginner, follow the beginner's plan (pp. 32-35).

Anytime during your recovery: If you feel bad for any reason, *stop.* Don't be afraid to back off, take more rest or run less than the previous day or week. You may feel you're taking one step ahead, then one back, but small steps are better than none. Again, listen to your body!

Note: Caesarean mothers must obviously take more recovery time.

If You Nurse. Be extra careful when you are the baby's only source of food.

- If milk quality or quantity drops, stop running for at least three days or until milk returns to normal; also increase fluid intake. Drink 4-6 ounces of fluid each hour you are awake.
- Try to nurse just before running.
- You need extra calories: 400-500 more than when pregnant, *plus* extra for running or exercising.
- Use a bra with the greatest support. Use absorbing pads to absorb "leaks."
- Fall asleep with your baby at naptime. Get as much sleep as you can.

Regain Fitness and Lose Fat. You know the old wives' tale about how you gain fat during pregnancy that you can never remove? If you're determined, you'll be gently persistent and eventually lose that weight. Don't rush.

A Final Note. In the chapter on *The Advanced Competitive Runner,* there's a section called "Too Much of a Good Thing" (pp. 143-44), where hard-driving ambition and competitive instincts may push a runner beyond enjoyment and fitness to a fixation with training and/or racing. The same thing—on a different scale—can happen to a competitive woman runner who becomes pregnant. She will be addicted to the beneficial effects of running and may be so determined to continue with her exercise that she overrides some of the natural governing mechanisms that the body calls forth when a child is developing within.

Elizabeth Noble, author of several books on childbirth, points out that although runners may be addicted to their activity, a new dimension might be added to their lives if they could learn to ". . . flow with the contemplation, introspection and slowing down that naturally occurs during pregnancy. It is a time for getting in touch with the body's natural wisdom . . . . Women must be encouraged to take note of bodily signs and symptoms, and to trust their natural instincts."

INJURIES

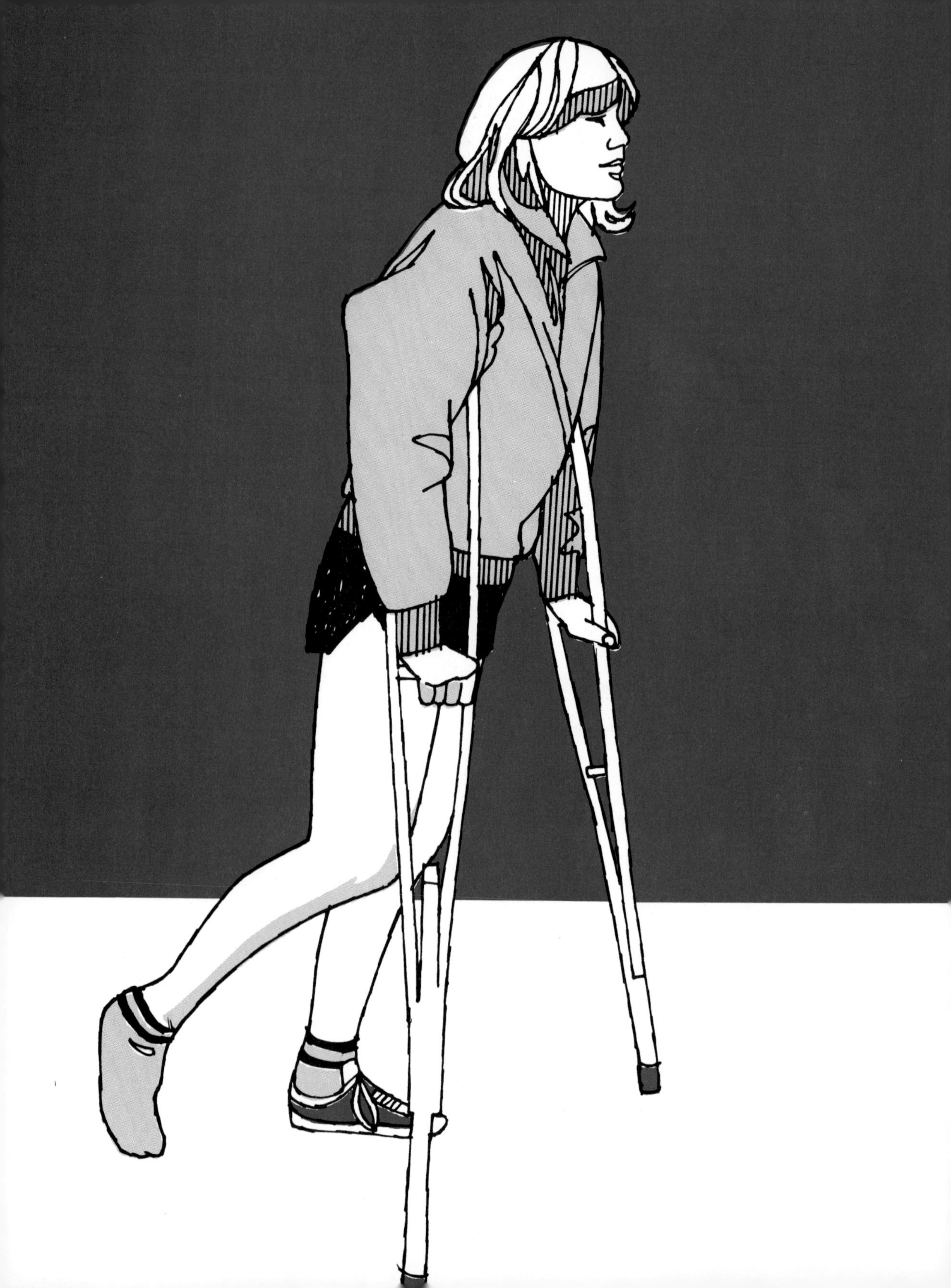

18 THE WALKING WOUNDED

LET'S FACE IT. Running is an addiction. Once you get that daily fix of aerobic exercise, improved circulation and capillary stimulation, you feel too good to ever stop. *But* when an injury crops up and you become one of the "walking wounded," you are faced with a problem: How do you rest long enough to let it heal?

Sooner or later every runner is injured. Very few injuries last longer than 3-4 weeks; with proper care and when treated early, most injuries will be gone in a few days, with no loss of conditioning.

Note: *I'm not a physician and not qualified to dispense medical advice. But having run continuously for over a quarter century, I've had just about every injury possible: strained Achilles tendons, pulled muscles, shin splints, etc. In the process of trying to recover and get on with my addiction, I've learned some helpful things I'd like to pass along. What follows in this chapter and the next is offered as advice from one runner to another and not meant to be expert medical advice. If you are ever in doubt about any injury, see your physician.*

When Is It an Injury? Some runners have little aches and pains every day. Most of these are temporary. These everyday aches and pains indicate the breakdown of weaker tissues and gradual buildup of stronger ones. Through experience, you'll learn to tell the difference between a passing ache and an injury. Here are some helpful guidelines to help you distinguish between the two. It's an injury if it's:

- *Functional*–If it keeps you from running in a natural way.
- *Continual*–If it goes on for more than a week.
- *Increasing*–It gets worse.
- *Swollen*–Compare the two knees, ankles, etc., to see if one is swollen.
- *Painful*–Pain is the body's way of telling you to pay attention. Dr. Richard Schuster, a New York podiatrist, tells you to "run with annoyance, not pain." Don't use an artificial expedient such as medicine to override your body's signals and keep running.

When in doubt, consult a running doctor: either a podiatrist (who treats only foot problems and problems that radiate from the foot) or an orthopedist (who treats foot, leg and other limb problems). (See pp. 209-210.)

Take a Day Off . . . Or More. By running on an injury you aggravate the problem and geometrically increase the time needed for repair. It's always better to be conservative and take a day or two off as a safety measure when you suspect an injury. Even if there's nothing wrong, taking a few days off won't hurt your overall fitness level, and may spare you weeks or months of forced rest later.

Treating an Injury. Good medical help is the first step in treating an injury. There is a running underground which can recommend local doctors who treat runners. Talk with some long-term runners. Every injury requires special treatment and you want to find the specialist who has successfully treated the greatest number of similar problems.

Before You See the Doctor. Here are some guidelines for treating yourself until you can see a doctor. Be particularly sensitive to pain in the knee, Achilles tendon, heel and shin. These sites can produce some long-lasting problems.

• *Stop running* for a few days. Almost all runners will benefit from the restorative effect of a few days off.

• *Learn* as much as you can. Talk to runners who may have had similar problems. Read some good books like *The Foot Book* by Harry Hlavac, D.P.M., or *Listen To Your Pain* by Ben E. Benjamin.

• *Ice* the injured area. Ice helps reduce inflammation and stimulates circulation: when blood returns to an "iced" area, it returns in abundance. Use an ice bag, a bag of frozen peas (which can conform to uneven surfaces) or a commercial preparation. The frozen ice popsicle works best. Keep a few styrofoam cups of ice in your freezer; peel off the top of the foam and apply to the injury. This way your fingers don't freeze. Get the area very cold for 10 minutes, let it warm up for 20 minutes, then ice it again.

• *Compression.* If there's swelling, wrap the area firmly–but not so tightly that it becomes a tourniquet and cuts off blood flow. If it throbs or the color next to the compressed area changes, then it's wrapped too tight. During the day, as the swelling increases, it may be necessary to release the compression. Elevate the foot for a few minutes before, then apply the compression from the distal (away from) to the proximal (close to). The compression is used to pump the distal swelling back toward the heart. This and ice help prevent the pooling of blood which leaves scar tissue.

• *Elevation.* Keep the injured area higher than your head or at least off the floor as long as you can. This helps remove blood from the injury so that fresh blood can flow in greater abundance.

> ***ICE:*** *Remember the above three injury measures by ICE: Ice, Compression, Elevation. Or RICE, adding the obvious element of **R**est.*

• *Supplement your diet* with vitamin C, which promotes healing. Take moderate amounts, 250-500 mg three times a day. (Timed-release tablets of larger dosages are generally wasted in the intestine where absorption is low.) Calcium is also important in healing; be sure it's included in your diet.

• *Don't stretch* the injured area unless a doctor advises you to. Many injuries are actually tears in the tendons, muscles or other tissue and stretching will only aggravate the problem.

• *Aspirin* reduces inflammation and kills pain and if it does not irritate the stomach, you can take several per day, preferably with meals. Aspirin is more effective in reducing swelling than substitutes like Tylenol. However, too much can be dangerous. A friend of mine, a runner in good shape, developed a bleeding ulcer from taking eight aspirin a day (sometimes on an empty stomach) to help an injury. This is rare, but it can happen.

ALTERNATIVE EXERCISES: HOW TO STAY FIT AND SANE

There's a real problem when you're injured. You're used to that daily fix of oxygen and exertion. Without it you're sluggish and cranky. Running, with all the pounding, is mechanically stressful and often the worst thing you can do. Luckily, most injuries will allow you to perform an alternate activity. If you can reduce the force of gravity and minimize the trauma of hitting the ground, you can let the injury heal, yet stay in shape.

We runners are spoiled. No other activity is as simple or convenient as running. Now that you're hurt, you'll have to get some equipment, or travel to a gym or pool to maintain your hard-earned fitness. It's going to be more complicated than running. Oh, the price of addiction!

When You Can't Run

Exercise effectiveness of alternatives (in simulating the cardiovascular and strengthening effects of running):

Activity	Effectiveness
Running in swimming pool	90-100%
Cycling on stationary bike	60-80%
Race walking	50-80%
Cross-country skiing, or rowing	50-80%
Swimming	30-60%

Note: Percentages are based upon performing at approximate intensity and duration of running. Figures were arrived at by my personal experience and talking with other runners.

Running in a Swimming Pool. This exercise simulates running better than any other activity and can keep you in fine condition. Many athletes who couldn't run for 3-4 weeks have come out of the pool and run their best times ever.

Horses are taught to run this way. When you run against the resistance of water, it forces you to lift your knees and drive them straight forward. If there is an imbalance, the water will exaggerate the leg movement. Thus this is a good exercise even for athletes who are not injured.

There are two ways to do this:

• Run in thigh-deep water, about halfway between knee and hip. If this puts pressure on the injury, try deeper water where the feet can still touch bottom.

Note: You need to run in a vertical position rather than kick in a horizontal position.

• Use an inner tube or float and run in deep water. Some runners can do without the float and stay afloat by their quick running movement and treading motions with the arms.

Your goal is to simulate running conditions as closely as possible. If you can put your legs through the same motions as running you'll stay in good running shape. Stay in the water the same amount of time you'd be running. On scheduled speed days, do speedwork by moving your legs very fast and hard for the same time as for your interval distance. Simulate the workout as closely as possible.

You may be surprised by how quickly the body will find just the right amount of exertion in the new activity. You're used to a certain level of exercise in running and you'll find yourself soon approximating this same amount of stress.

Cycling on an Exercycle. This is the next best exercise in simulating the effects of running. In fact, this "cross-training" will strengthen your quadriceps, which reduces pressure on the knees. The back of the lower legs are not worked in cycling as they are in running. If you use toe clips, however, you simulate running more closely. Cycling doesn't produce the gravity stress (pounding) of running and therefore will not aggravate *most* injuries.

An exercycle is actually better than a real bike for several reasons: It's safer and you can maintain a steady and controlled pace without interruptions for traffic stop lights or coasting downhill. You can also do it at home, and even read a book or watch TV while working out.

You'll generate a lot of heat so it's best to have a fan or good cross breeze. As with running in the pool, simulate the long runs and speedwork on the cycle; to gain the same benefits you need to add about 20%-40% more time to each session.

Race Walking. This is an activity which seldom aggravates an injury, but don't do it if there is even a *hint* of aggravation. The object is to rotate your hips and shift your legs quickly, keeping one leg on the ground at all times. This reduces the pounding of running, but uses the same muscles (plus many others). Again, you simulate your running sessions. To get the same benefits, you must cover the same amount of miles you would running. This obviously will take more time.

Cross-Country Skiing or Rowing Machines. If you live where there's snow, you can ski cross-country. If not, you can use the ski or rowing machines available in many health clubs. These two activities are excellent substitutes for running. They also strengthen your upper body. To simulate running, spend about the same amount of time you would on the roads.

Swimming. Although it's an excellent cardiovascular exercise, swimming does not keep your legs in running shape. You'll need to train about 30-60% longer, depending on how hard you swim, to roughly simulate the cardiovascular work of running.

IF YOU CAN'T EXERCISE AT ALL

You'll be surprised to learn how little conditioning you'll lose in five days of complete rest. For each week thereafter you'll lose about 25% of your fitness level. After a month you'll need to start like a beginner.

Rule of Thumb: If you were unable to do alternative exercises, you'll need at least *twice the number of weeks you took off* to gradually build back to pre-injury level.

Note: This is based on my experiences with over a hundred layoffs after injuries.

How Much Conditioning Do You Lose?

Rest Time Without Any Exercise	*Estimated % of Conditioning Lost*
1-5 days	0-1%
7 days	10%
14 days	35%
21 days	60%
28 days	85%
35 or more	100%

GETTING BACK ON THE ROAD

If the healing process has begun and you're responding to treatment, your doctor may let you start running before the pain is completely gone. As long as you have a solid healing effect started, you may return gently to running, but be very sensitive to the old problem. At the first sign of aggravation, back off and rest some more. *Be conservative.* It's better to take a few extra rest days than to go through the whole process again.

Even if the injured area suddenly feels 100%, it's not totally healed. You'll feel strong once enough of the cells have been healed, replaced or supported by scar tissue. But there are still many damaged cells, and scar tissue is fragile.

Coming back requires patience and adequate rest. It may seem like you're taking one step forward and two back. Actually, you're taking one forward and two in place. This is certainly better than taking no steps forward at all.

Even if you take a long layoff, you haven't lost the conditioning you previously gained. The strength, tone and performance of the muscles is lost when you don't run, but the deeper cardiovascular improvements are not hard to regain. You'll need some time to recondition the exercise muscles and open up the deeper "plumbing" passages. At first it will seem like a depressing second beginning, but once you regain your conditioning base, improvement will be rapid and you'll soon be back to normal. While you're coming back, continue your alternative activities. This will give you some variety during the frustrating days of rebuilding.

STARTING BACK WORKOUTS

If you were able to do alternative exercises as often and at the same relative intensity as your running during the layoff, you should take one easy "beginners" week and then two or three more transition weeks before resuming pre-injury workouts. If you couldn't exercise at all or did less than three days a week alternative exercise, you'll need at least twice the number of weeks you took off to gradually build back to pre-injury levels. Here are some guidelines for both situations:

If you've had four or more days a week alternative exercise:

- The first week, jog easy one day (with liberal walking breaks). Walk the next day.
- For 2-3 transition weeks, you can start running every other day, slower than you did before the injury, and take walking breaks whenever you feel like it. Walk every other day. Increase the length of your long run each week (only on one day) by ½-1 mile.
- For the next month ease back into your schedule by gradually increasing the running days.
- Be sensitive to the injured area and back off at the first feeling of re-injury.

If you've had three or less days of alternative exercise:

- Set aside 30-40 minutes, three days per week. Walk, inserting short jogs of 100-300 yards, never pushing too hard. Walk until you're completely ready to run again.
- Over several weeks replace the walking with slow jogging—continue 3-4 days per week.
- For the next month, ease back into your schedule by gradually increasing the running days.
- Be sensitive to the injured area and back off at the first feeling of re-injury.

WHAT WENT WRONG?

You can actually benefit from an injury: If you analyze what went wrong, you can use this knowledge to prevent not only recurrence of the same injury, but other injuries as well. Most injuries have the same general causes: you increased total mileage too quickly; you didn't rest enough between hard days; you didn't warm up enough for a speed workout; you let the adrenalin rush of a race push you too far. I've also come to believe that dehydration is one of the major underlying causes of injury. The lack of vital fluids in the exercising cells causes them to break down sooner and it will take them longer to recover. Drinking 4-6 ounces of water during every waking hour will minimize this effect.

Once you've had to stay off the roads for a few weeks (or months) you'll be highly motivated to build some preventive measures into your training program. In some ways, the mistakes that led to the injury can be the best learning experiences of your running career.

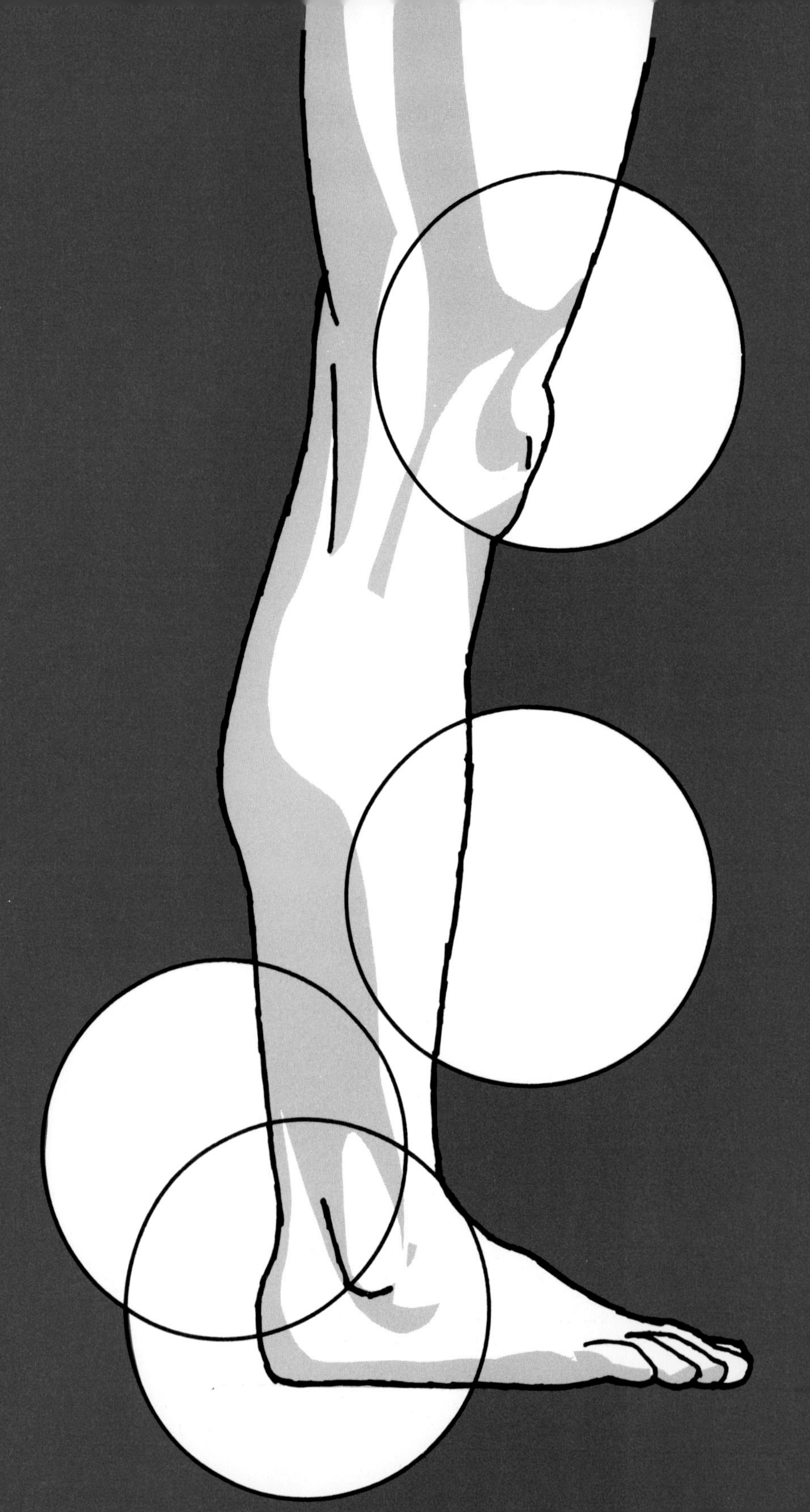

19 INJURY ANALYSIS AND TREATMENT

WHEN AN INJURY OCCURS, there's no substitute for expert advice. If you get a good diagnosis in the beginning, you can avoid complications and get on the healing path. Generally a doctor who works with runners is your best bet. The running underground will help you find such a person. (It's even better if the doctor is a runner, but this is certainly not a requirement.)

With a leg or foot injury, there are two types of doctors to consider: a podiatrist or an orthopedist.

Podiatrists are trained as physicians and surgeons of the foot. Leg or knee injuries are also treated by podiatrists when they relate to the foot. For example, knee problems are often caused by improper alignment of the feet and can be remedied by corrective foot devices, which a podiatrist will prescribe. Most podiatrists are fully aware of the mechanics of the entire lower extremity.

Orthopedists are M.D.'s who have taken surgical training and specialize in the bones and muscles of the body. Most are primarily surgeons and not much interested in biomechanics. However, if you can find an orthopedist who is known for treating runners and is interested in the mechanics of injuries, you'll be in good hands.

If the problem is only in the foot or has its cause there, you can see either specialist. If the problem is in the leg or foot and the *cause* is probably not in the foot, see an orthopedist.

Beware of surgery. Orthopedists are trained in surgery and are often oriented toward this form of treatment. When the knife goes in, there is a good chance that the area will not work as well as before. As a last resort you may have to let a good surgeon operate, but get several opinions and try everything else. It's also best to choose a surgeon who has successfully performed the same operation many times.

If surgery is inevitable, *arthroscopy* may be considered. Arthroscopy is the use of a small sterile metal tube and fiber optic light source to look inside the body without cutting things open. It is commonly used diagnostically, and surgery can be done through the arthroscope. Arthroscopy, if used appropriately, can be helpful to the athlete by producing minimal trauma, thus a rapid return to activity is possible.

What Caused It? Think about the most obvious causes of the injury and make adjustments. Worn shoes are often the culprits. Check your shoes, inside and out, before you see a specialist. Another factor often overlooked is the crown of the road. Your injury may be caused by running on a surface that slants one way or another. For example, if you run against traffic, your left foot will generally be lower than your right, due to the road sloping toward the shoulder; this puts more pressure on your left knee. Avoiding these obvious problems can often start you on the road to recovery without medical treatment.

DIAGNOSIS AND TREATMENT

Note: *The previous chapter shows a standard treatment and recovery program for injuries in general. Be sure to read it before you look at the following specific treatments for the four most common trouble areas: knee, Achilles, heel and shin.*

KNEE PROBLEMS

The knee is the most common site of running injuries in all sports. Unlike the multi-directional ball-and-socket construction of the hip joint, the knee is a one-directional hinge joint. Four bones converge at the knee and are held together primarily by ligaments on either side and secondarily by connective tissue over the front of the knee.

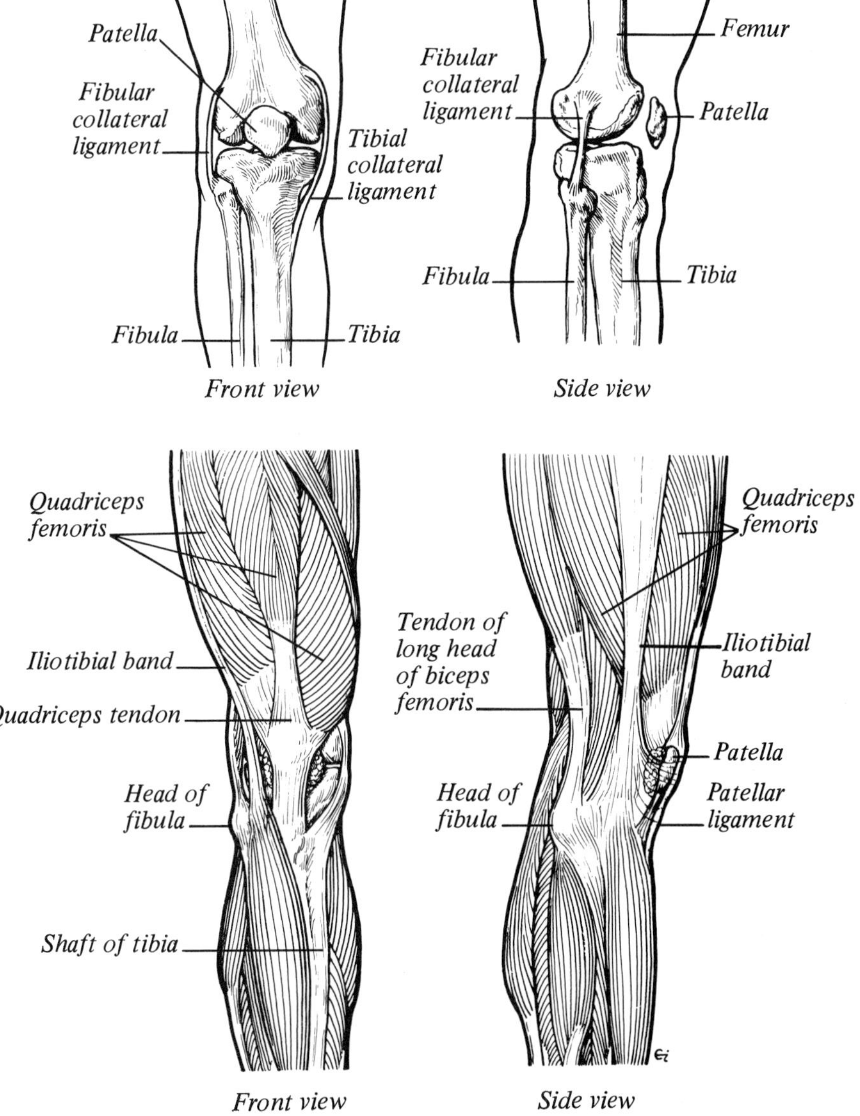

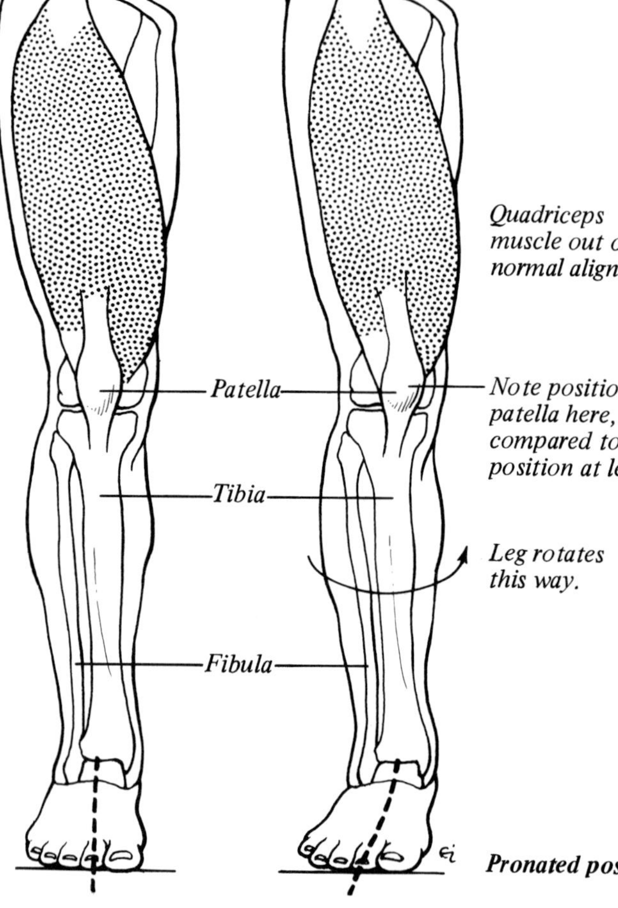

Pronated foot (at right) forces knee out of alignment. As weight of body comes down, there is abnormal pressure on cartilage under kneecap. This can lead to chondromalacia, *or runner's knee.*

Neutral position **Pronated position**

The femur, or thigh bone, ends in two rounded projections with a groove between them. The patella, or knee cap, slides up and down in this groove. From the lower leg, the tibia–the full weight-bearing bone–rises and joins the femur at the knee.

On the lateral (outside) is the iliotibial band, a thick, strong tendon which combines with the collateral ligament and a muscle called the biceps femoris to support the knee on the outside. The weaker tendon and ligament on the inside are more prone to injury, due either to rotational stress or an outside blow to the knee.

In the front of the knee is the patella or knee cap. It is attached at the top to the quadriceps or thigh muscle. When strong, this muscle keeps the patella in its groove. At the lower end of the patella, the patella tendon attaches and connects to the tibia.

As long as the foot is in a neutral position, the knee is aligned harmoniously between the hip and foot. The weight of the body actually helps to keep a "normal" knee in place, especially when a strong quadriceps keeps the knee cap tight and in position.

Pronation, where the foot rolls from the outside to inside, is the normal shock-absorbing mechanism in running. But when it is excessive, to the point where the arch is flat or the heel is tilted over, it causes overuse problems of the foot and leg. The knee is often forced into a weaker position on the medial side, and out of alignment. As the weight of the body comes down on the improperly aligned knee, problems arise.

Causes of Knee Injuries

Rigid-footed runners tend to move their feet forward and back, with a strong pushoff, and often have problems on the outside of the knee. The *iliotibial band* is very strong and will rarely, if ever, give way. But it can become inflamed and irritated when the foot rolls too far to the outside. *Causes* of iliotibial (outside of knee) pain are usually associated with:

- Worn-out shoes (especially mid-sole breakdown on the outside).
- Too much mileage.
- Sudden increase in mileage.
- Inadequate shoe cushion.

Rigid-footed runners push and land so hard that shock may not be adequately absorbed. At first there is pressure on the bottom where the foot pushes hard. Blisters may form here, then thick callouses. Repeated abuse will send the shock up the knee.

Floppy-footed runners tend to roll from side to side. There may be wear on the outside of the heel, but also on the inside of the forefoot. Floppy-footed runners who pronate tend to have problems on the inside of the knee, or in the knee itself.

(See pp. 251-52 for how to determine whether you are a rigid-footed or floppy-footed runner.)

Types of Knee Injuries

Runner's Knee. The first symptom is usually stiffness, especially after sitting for a long time. There's pain inside and around the knee—a general ache. This condition can occur when the (floppy) foot rolls in and puts great pressure on the inside and middle of the knee. The leg rotates and the patella often moves outside its normal path, wearing out the cartilage. As time passes, this may become *chondromalacia*—a true medical problem where the cartilage softens and begins to disintegrate. Early *chondromalacia* is felt as a "creaky" joint, with a rough feeling under the knee cap.

Tendonitis. This is pain on the inside or outside of the knee. Tendons connect muscles to bones and they can become inflamed from a direct injury or overuse. Floppy feet tend to get tendonitis on the inside, rigid feet on the outside.

Patella Tendonitis. This is pain and inflammation in the soft tissue just below the knee cap, or where it connects to the tibia, just below.

Plica syndrome is another, but rarer problem of pronators. It involves a pinching and folding of the membrane at the knee joint. Symptoms are similar to *chondromalacia* with pain around the joint line, either medially or laterally, but not always under the knee cap. There may be a clicking sensation, which indicates damage to the meniscus, a shock-absorbing structure inside the joint.

Treatment of Knee Injuries

- Ice massage. Keep a styrofoam cup in the freezer for this. Ice twice a day, 10 minutes on, 20 off, 10 on.
- Don't run for at least 2-3 days to get the healing started, longer for a more advanced injury.
- When you start back, run very little at first, every other day.
- No speedwork or hills for at least two weeks, or until the soreness is gone.
- Knee injuries usually take more time because we run on them and aggravate them.
- Even when it seems healed, continue icing, reduce mileage and avoid speed and hills for two more weeks.

Correcting the Cause of Knee Injuries. The following steps have helped runners in the past and can be used along with advice from a good doctor:

Shoes:

Rigid foot. Replace worn shoes and look for better cushioning and flexibility.

Floppy foot. Get a more stable shoe. A "board last" shoe gives more support than a "slip last" one (see p. 251). Shoes with anti-pronation devices may help. If these measures don't do enough, ask your podiatrist about a custom orthotic which is custom-molded to your foot with the correction built in.

Foot Support. I've found that pronation problems are best treated with a firm arch support. If that isn't enough, take a foot support system (an insole with arch support built in, and sometimes the heel "cupped") or insole, and layer it on the bottom with cork or felt. Keep adding layers under the arch until it supports your arch firmly and equalizes pressure. Many runners extend some of the buildup into the heel and forefoot (under big toe joint) to give the foot as much support as possible and to minimize pronation. (Don't build up under the big toe joint if you have a bunion there.)

Obvious Corrections. After you figure out what happened, be wiser about whatever caused the problem.

Prevention of Knee Injuries (Before They Occur). Now that you've hurt your knee (otherwise you wouldn't be reading this) you're naturally interested in keeping it from happening again. Nothing's worse than seeing your fellow runners cruise down the roads while you're grumpily hobbling around, counting the days. However, when you *do* recover (and you will, believe it or not!) you have the chance to build up the appropriate muscles that will support your weight better and take pressure off this critical area.

Running strengthens the back muscles of the leg: calves and hamstrings. The longer you run, the stronger and more powerful these muscles become. Strong quadriceps are necessary to keep the knee cap in alignment, support the knee, and check the driving strength of strong back leg muscles. Running itself doesn't do much for the quadriceps. Therefore the primary exercises for preventing knee injuries are designed to strengthen the quadriceps: the stiff leg lift (see p. 167), and cycling and exercycling (see pp. 203-4).

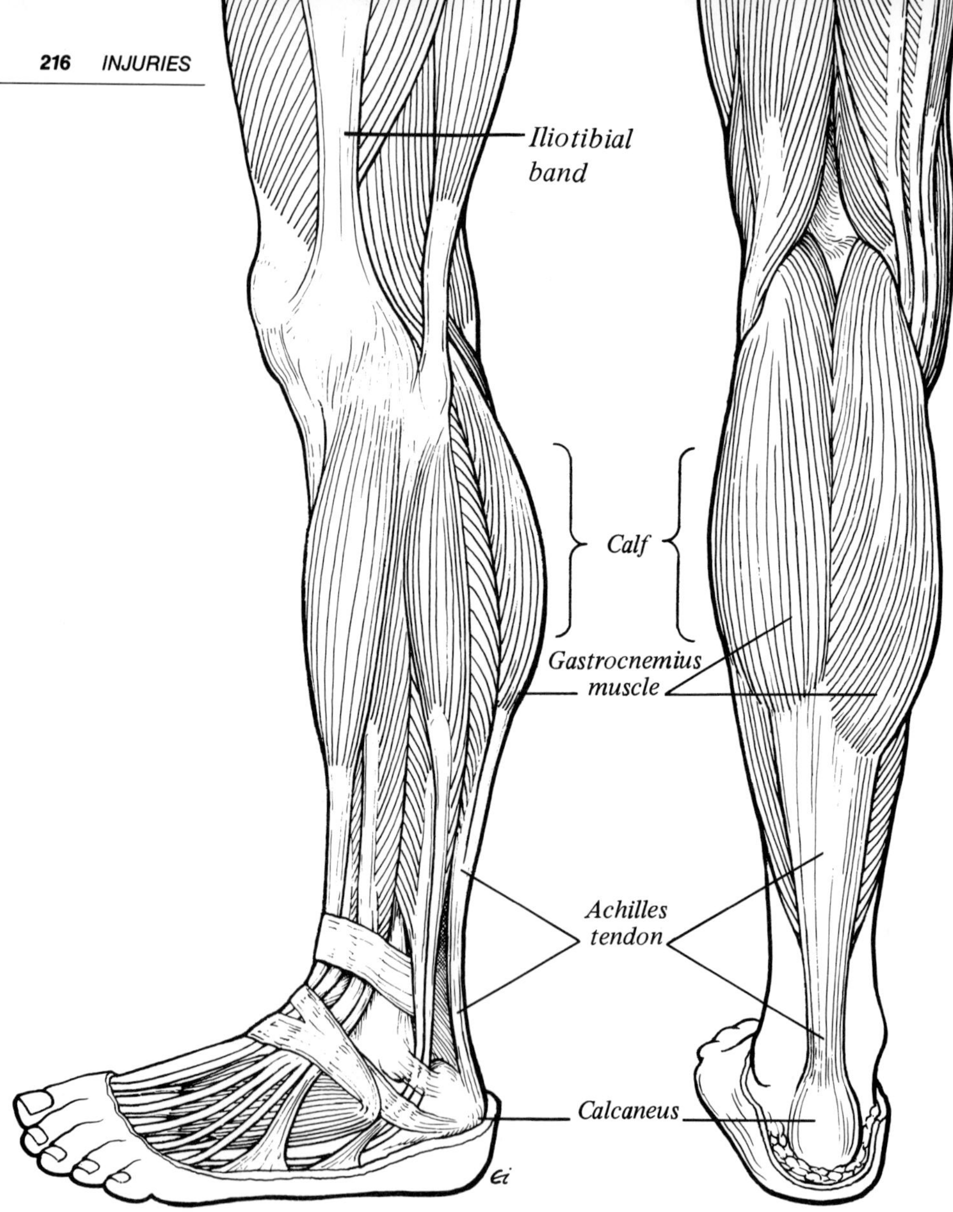

ACHILLES TENDON PROBLEMS

Achilles was one of the greatest warriors in Greek mythology. When he was a baby, his mother immersed him in the river Styx to make him invulnerable in battle. However, she held him by the heel and this remained his one vulnerable spot. He ultimately met his end when shot by a poisoned arrow in the heel.

Most of us were not immersed in the river Styx in this fashion, but are still vulnerable to Achilles problems. In a recent survey of running injuries, Achilles tendon problems ranked second in occurrence to knee injuries. They can occur in runners with both floppy and rigid foot types.

The Achilles tendon is the strongest tendon in the body. It attaches to the back of the heel bone, or *calcaneus*, rises and becomes thin behind the ankle, and then spreads out and attaches to the calf muscle group.

The Essence of Running. When the calf muscle contracts, the Achilles pulls the calcaneus strongly upward, lifting the rear part of the foot and preparing it for a strong "pushoff." Your power comes from this push. Other muscle groups, such as the hamstrings, are of course involved, but the calf and Achilles tendon are the workhorses.

Rigid-footed runners (or runners with a high arch) tend to push off powerfully, using their foot like a strong lever. This stresses the Achilles throughout.

Floppy-footed runners who pronate put most of the pressure on the inside part of the Achilles tendon. The torque of pronation may also stress other areas. Hills, speedwork and negative heel or low-heel shoes all put more pressure on the Achilles.

The Achilles tendon is covered by the *paratenon sheath.* The two are so closely attached that a problem with one is a problem with the other. Here we will consider them both as part of the same problem. The most common area of pain is in the narrowest part of the Achilles, about 1-1½" above the calcaneus. At this point the paratenon sheath wraps over the Achilles and attaches to the ankle bone on either side.

Problems usually take two forms: tendon inflammation and tendon tears.

Inflamed Achilles. With the normal stress of running, small micro-tears occur in the tissue of the Achilles tendon. Normally they heal quickly. However, if there is too much stress and too little rest, they won't heal, will collect in an area and produce inflammation.

Diagnosis. Inflammation is usually at the narrowest part of the tendon, at the paratenon sheath. The fluid between the tendon and the sheath expands. There is often a cracking noise when moving the tendon, and it may be sore. (This is rare.)

Achilles Tear. When the tendon is already weakened it can be partially torn by the additional stress of speedwork, hill running or simply stepping in a hole. A complete tear is a more serious and painful injury. This often requires surgery, but fortunately tendon tears occur in only about two percent of Achilles injuries.

Diagnosis: If you can't rise up on your toes while standing, you may have a tear. There is a lump in the lower calf area and a gap where the tendon is torn. You can feel this through the skin. If you suspect a tear try to find a specialist who has a good deal of experience with Achilles problems.

Treatment of Achilles Injuries

Inflamed Achilles

- Ice massage for 10 minutes at least twice a day. See p. 201 on icing.
- Use a heel lift—felt, cork, etc. (a Spenco is too soft)—in both running and street shoes—to reduce tension on tendon.
- Take aspirin (with meals or with milk) if okay with your stomach and your doctor. Be regular with it for a week or so to tell if it's effective. It reduces swelling.
- Consult with doctor about length of layoff.

Achilles Tear

- Ice massage and use heel lift as for inflamed Achilles (see above).
- Don't run for at least 4-6 weeks, (or length of time prescribed by doctor) to let swelling subside and healing process begin. If you stop at an early stage, your "vacation" may be only a few weeks, but if you push the tendon too far in this state you may be out for months. Consult with your doctor. When starting back, run every other day for another 4-6 weeks—or until things feel better and normal functioning has returned.

Note: Beware of injections of cortisone or other steroids, for they may weaken and/or dissolve the tendon. Get several opinions before getting such a shot; it could set you back months, years, or permanently.

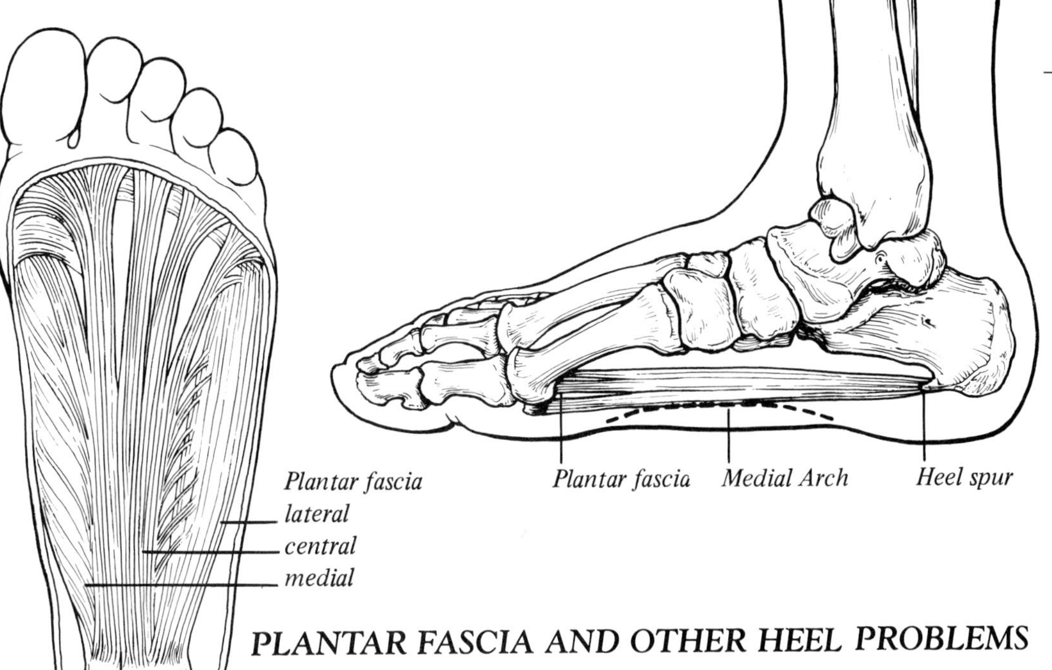

PLANTAR FASCIA AND OTHER HEEL PROBLEMS

Heel pain will often indicate a problem that may last for a long time. As with other injuries, be sensitive to the problem early and avoid a long-term layoff.

The plantar fascia (a connective tissue structure) stretches from the toes and ball of the foot, through the arch, and connects to the heel bone in three places: outside, center and inside. Normally it helps the foot spring as it rolls forward. It also provides support for the arch of the foot. The plantar fascia helps keep the foot on track, cutting down on oscillation.

When the foot over-pronates (rolls to the inside) the plantar fascia tries to stabilize it and prevent excessive roll. In time, the inside and sometimes center connections are overstressed and pull away from their attachments.

The first sign is usually heel pain as you rise in the morning. When you walk around, the pain may subside, only to return the next morning. Inflammation and increased soreness are the results of long-term neglect and continued abuse.

A heel bone spur may develop after a long period of injury when there is no support for the heel. The plantar fascia attaches to the heel bone with small fibers. When these become irritated they become inflamed with blood containing white blood cells. Within the white blood cells are osteoblasts which calcify to form bone spurs and calcium deposits. The body is trying to reduce stress on that area by building a bone in the direction of stress. Unfortunately, these foreign substances cause pain and further irritation in the surrounding soft tissue.

Long-term chronic pain in the heel may be due to nerve

entrapment of the calcaneal nerves which migrate through the enlarged muscle or medial arch, or by the heel spur. These nerves can be surgically cut to relieve pain. Be *very* cautious about consenting to surgery. It should be a last-resort treatment and at least two doctors should recommend it.

Types of Heel Problems

Plantar Fasciitis

Symptoms: Heel pain, usually on inside of forward part of heel. It's worst in the morning, eases as it gets warmed up.

Treatment:

- After pain starts, but before inflammation, *rest 4-5 days.*
- Ice massage 10 minutes, getting area quite cold. Let it "warm up" 20 minutes then ice again.
- Build up an arch support system in your shoes. Try to equalize the pressure of your body weight throughout your arch and away from the plantar area. Use a "cobra pad" or other device that supports the arch but releases pressure on the painful area. If homemade supports do not work, see a podiatrist about custom orthotics.

Heel Spur

Symptoms: Pain on forward inside or middle of heel, which unfortunately may last a long time. When massaging, you can locate the pain area and often a small lump. Bursitis is another common heel problem (often from repeated impact) that is treated the same as heel spur.

Treatment:

- Ice and use arch support as above. If you can localize the spur, cut a hole in a pad of felt and lay the hole over the spur. This supports the area around the spur and reduces pressure on it.
- Massage spur as above, 5-10 minutes a day. Start gently with thumb, gradually increase pressure until you're pushing hard directly on spur with knuckle or other firm object. Even if it hurts, it should help.

Plantar Fascia Tear (rare)

Symptoms: Sudden pain which usually keeps you from running and does *not* get better as day progresses. There is usually a bruise in the plantar area from bleeding and inflammation.

Treatment:

- Ice and use arch support, as above.
- See a doctor. Take 4-5 weeks off with his or her guidance.

Stress Fracture

Symptoms: Heel hurts all day long; pain often increases as you walk or run. More pain than with other heel problems. There is often swelling and there will be pain if you squeeze the heel from side to side.

Treatment:

- Ice and use arch support.
- Walk at first, then run lightly if there is no pain.

Nerve Entrapment (happens rarely)

Symptoms: Chronic pain that has lasted more than a year may be due to pain in the nerves that migrate through the enlarged muscle on the medial arch or by the heel spur. Pain is sharp and shooting, like electric shock sensations.

Treatment:

- Try ice, arch support, massage.
- If these fail, your doctor may recommend injection with a short-acting steroid or vitamin B-12, or surgical release of the nerve. Get a second opinion if this is the case.
- There are many dangers with injections, including the dissolving of tendon by the steroid and rupture of blood vessels or arteries by improper placement of the injection. Surgery has also been used for relief; releasing parts of the nerves or part of the stressed ligament connections can reduce pressure and pain. Be sure to get several opinions on either of these approaches and try to find a doctor who has handled this type of injury before.

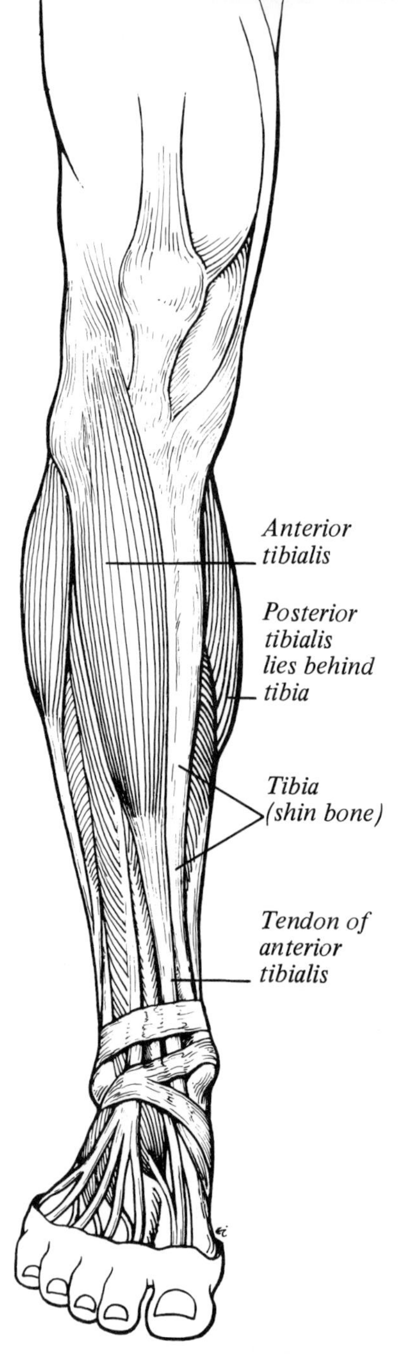

SHIN PROBLEMS

There are two types of shin problems. If you feel your lower front leg bone (*tibia*) you'll feel a flat boney area known as the shin. Just to the outside of this area is the *anterior tibialis* muscle. This muscle is used throughout the running cycle and because it receives a lot of shock, the membrane that attaches it to the bone is sometimes partially pulled away from the tibia and toothache-like pain in the area results. This most often happens when you've done too much, too soon, or changed either your shoes, the surface you've run on or your training schedule (e.g. fartlek, intervals, etc.) without enough time to adjust to the changes. Experienced runners often have this problem after running downhill.

More recently the term *shin splint* has been used to describe an injury to the *posterior tibialis* muscle. This muscle is on the inside of the flat shin bone. It is a deep muscle and is used to stabilize the foot during weight-bearing and to push off the ground. This muscle can be stretched and strengthened in conjunction with the other calf muscles, as described in the calf and Achilles stretch (see pp. 164-65).

Be careful to allow this muscle to heal. Cutting back on mileage is always required.

A floppy, over-pronated foot will roll inward, forcing the shin muscles into submission and stressing one or both of them. Runners with rigid feet tend to have interior shin problems.

Podiatrist Irving Miller of Atlanta recently told me he's seen an increase in pronation in older runners, which he feels is due to tightening of the muscles—particularly the calf muscles and those on the outside of the leg. This causes the feet to turn out and they are more likely to pronate during walking or running, causing shin problems. A gentle stretching program will help.

Five Shin Problems. The shin bone (*tibia*) is covered by a membrane called the *periosteum*. This is a tight band of soft tissue which includes nerves and blood supply. The muscles of the shin group attach to this membrane just below the knee and near the ankle by means of tendons. When the shin group is stressed, there are five places where problems can occur: in the muscle, in the tendon, on the periosteum, on the bone itself or in the muscle "compartments."

If you have any kind of shin problem, make sure you don't have any symptoms of the first two listed here—stress fracture or compartment syndrome—before you check out the other ones.

Bone Problems = Stress Fracture

Symptoms: Strong pulling at connection points, repeated impact or twisting stress will sometimes produce a crack or break in the surface or cortex of the tibia bone itself. This happens slowly and does not produce a sudden pain, although there is often throbbing pain. There may be inflammation. The best way to diagnose a stress fracture is by squeezing the heel from side to side, which produces pain. Stress fractures hurt more the farther you run. If pain remains after running, or there is numbness or tingling on the top of the foot, there is a serious medical problem.

Treatment: Stress fractures appear on X-rays about 4-6 weeks after occurrence and last about 6 weeks. See your doctor (usually an orthopedist), who may cast the leg to keep you from overstressing the area. Try to determine what caused the fracture and consider highly cushioned shoes (such as air soles) or orthotics.

Muscle Compression Syndrome = Compartment Syndrome

Symptoms: Of the four muscle bone compartments in the lower leg, most problems occur in the anterior (forward) group. The muscle has a tight band or fascia of tissue around it called a sheath. Normally the sheath expands as the muscle expands. However, when there is sudden swelling, and when the muscle is contained by bones or other muscles on two or more sides, the sheath may not be able to expand. The resulting pressure with no outlet may harm the nerve and/or blood vessels and arteries in the muscle. There may be pain or tingling in the muscle, sometimes traveling down the shin into the foot. The pain is general and usually increases dramatically as you run. The condition may come from sudden overuse, hill or speedwork, or from running too much on your toes.

Treatment: This problem can be quite serious and have permanent effects if you neglect it. If you feel numbness or pain in the top of your foot, don't run through it or numb it with medications (including aspirin). If it doesn't go away after two days, see your doctor.

Muscle Stress = Myositis

Symptoms: Muscle soreness, probably inflammation. In most cases, pain seems to come from inside of upper calf muscle and eases a little as you warm up in a run.

Treatment:

- Rest: Take 3-5 days off (*no running!*) to get healing started, then try walking. If this doesn't produce pain, try some light running. Try running every other day until the injury seems to be getting better. Talk to a doctor about it and stay below the pain threshold on each run.
- Ice if there is any swelling—10 minutes, at least once a day.
- If okay with your doctor and your stomach, take two aspirin with every meal.
- Do regular (and gentle) stretching for Achilles tendon and calf muscles. (See pp. 164-65.)
- Strengthen shin muscle group through exercise. (See p. 167.)
- Ask your podiatrist about a more stable shoe or orthotics.

Tendon Stress = Tendonitis

Symptoms: At the connection points, the tendons may be pulled away from the bone or otherwise injured. This usually localizes the problem at either the high or low connecting point in the leg and causes swelling. At the lower point, the problem is the posterior tibial tendon which you can see prominently when it's flexed—on the middle inside of the leg, right next to the tibia and just above the ankle bone. If that area is sore to touch, there may also be inflammation of the toe flexor tendons which lie immediately below this tendon. Here's how to isolate the muscle group and tell if the deep posterior tibial tendons are inflamed: Sit down. Hold your foot and lift it to the inside. If it hurts, it's your posterior tibial tendon. If it hurts when you hold your foot straight and try to "claw" with your toes, then the toe flexor tendons are inflamed.

Treatment: Same as for myositis, at left.

Stress on Membrane of Bone = Periostitis

Symptoms: The periosteum is the thin membrane (soft tissue) that covers the bone. Tendons attach to the periosteum rather than to the bone itself. With overstress, there can be irritation—normally at the upper and lower connection points. The pain is general in area, similar to a stress fracture, but there is no evidence of pain in a specific spot. Pain does not diminish and may even increase during a run. This may take 3-4 months to heal.

Treatment:

- Rest completely 2-4 weeks to get healing started. Confer with doctor to see when you can start running again. (See pp. 202-04 on alternative exercises to do during this period. Running in a swimming pool is best.)
- All other treatment same as for myositis, at left.

CROSS-TRAINING & BALANCING

Participation in one sport to the exclusion of others can produce muscular imbalance, and often leads to specific-sport injuries. In recent years, coaches and athletes have come to appreciate the value of engaging in several activities to achieve greater muscular balance. Where running primarily works the calf and hamstring muscles, cycling builds up the quadriceps, swimming exercises the upper body and cross-country skiing provides a superb overall body workout without the trauma of running. Here are some of the advantages of adding other sports to your training program:

Cardiovascular Training. You can increase your weekly cardiovascular training by adding other sports. If you spent the same total hours running, you'd be more likely to suffer injuries.

Variety. In the heat of the summer, swimming is an attractive alternative, as is cycling, with its built-in breeze. Exercycles, rowing machines and indoor pools offer similar relief from winter weather. Adding other sports to your running program helps overcome periods of low motivation, and you'll return to running stimulated and refreshed.

Burning Off Fat. Those who run to lose weight become excited as mileage increases and fat decreases. Unfortunately, further mileage increases often lead to injury. Again, adding other sports can keep the fat furnaces burning and the weight under control.

Triathlons. Where the Hawaii *Ironman* is for super athletes and/or those who can train six hours a day, the scaled-down versions are going to become increasingly popular in the '80s—especially those that can be finished in marathon time (3-4 hours) or less. If you've been running for a while, you're already trained for a third of the event. Here's a proposed schedule for starting triathlon training:

Monday:	Long cycle	***Friday:***	Speed swim/fun cycle
Tuesday:	Speed run	***Saturday:***	Rest
Wednesday:	Long swim	***Sunday:***	Long run
Thursday:	Speed cycle/fun run		

Each activity has a long day, a speed day and a fun day.

FOOD

20 NUTRITION

RUMORS ABOUND in the running underground about the eating habits of world-class athletes. Bill Rodgers supposedly puts mayonnaise on his pizza. I haven't personally verified this, although I've seen Bill consume some shocking food combinations which have influenced others. A few years ago I was circulating through a dining room of runners who were helping themselves to an abundant salad bar. One plate was devoid of everything, except for a mountain of black olive pits. Then-aspiring world-class marathoner Benji Durden explained his obsession concisely: "Bill eats them."

We're often tempted to imitate the eating habits of our running heroes, in hopes of finding that special fuel that will "light our fire." But in many cases runners excel *in spite of* their diets. Just because an occasional great runner seems to do fine on fast food, ice cream and soda pop doesn't mean you should follow suit. For one thing,

there are the long-range health aspects to consider: the differences between those who eat poorly and those who eat healthily may only show up 10-15 years down the line.

Further, "feeling good" and "surviving" are not enough. You may think you're feeling good while deterioration is slowly taking place inside. The Heart Association can tell you about heart attack victims who ate too much deadly animal fat for 30 years or more without any bad effects, until one day . . . clunk! The typical American diet can be downright dangerous.

Vegetarian History. We might get some clues to a good diet from considering what our ancient ancestors ate. Scientists tell us they were primarily vegetarians, and as proof point out the long winding digestive tract of human beings. Vegetables and grains don't give up their nutrients easily and it takes a long, sophisticated intestine to squeeze them out. This type of "processing plant" is necessary for herbivores. In contrast, the tract of a carnivore, like a tiger or dog, is straight and short.

Our ancestors wandered far and wide in search of nuts, fruits and roots. In the process they developed tremendous cardiovascular endurance and cunning. Only then did they become effective hunters. Since they lacked the speed of most quadripeds in hunting, they had to develop greater endurance, sometimes stalking animals for days and covering long distances. Thus the early hunters became the first human ultra-distance runners.

Many experienced runners today are primarily vegetarian, but supplement their diets with small quantities of meat (mostly chicken or fish). This is the diet I have followed for some years now, with good results. I arrived at this approach to food from considering not only the past, but also from recent nutritional findings and my own observations of how different foods and diets made me feel and affected my running.

In this chapter, we'll consider the six components of a healthy diet: protein, fat, carbohydrates, water, vitamins and minerals. This is not meant to be a scientific dissertation on the subject, but rather a brief look at these essential elements needed by everyone, with a special emphasis on what I believe to be the best combination for anyone engaged in vigorous physical activity.

Protein. It's been a common myth that athletes need vast quantities of protein. In fact, everyone needs protein, but many nutritionists today believe that runners need no more than anyone else and that the average American already consumes far more protein than necessary.

Protein is not used directly as fuel for exercise, but as building material for the cells, muscles and tissues of the body. A growing child needs three times the protein required by an adult, pound for pound.

We can get our protein, of course, from meat. We can also get it from non-meat products as well as dairy products and eggs. There are advantages to emphasizing the non-meat sources, especially today when we are likely to absorb the hormones, drugs and insecticides that grain-fed feedlot cattle have ingested. Also, the meat our nomadic ancestors *did* eat was from lean wild animals, whereas today's red meat has heavy amounts of saturated fat which can settle into human arteries and clog them. Its texture is so complex and hard to digest that it moves slowly through the digestive tract and may cause serious problems in the colon.

If you *do* opt for a vegetarian diet, you need to understand some basic principles of nutrition. By now you've probably heard that animal protein is "complete," while vegetable protein is not. The point here is that in animal products, all the amino acids (the basic constituents in protein) are present so that when you eat meat, you get all the basic elements of protein you need. These amino acids are used in different ways by the body; some are taken apart and put back together in other forms to meet particular needs. Excess amino acids are broken down into sugars and stored as fat.

A problem in getting your protein from non-meat sources like grains, seeds, dairy products and vegetables is that none of these contain all the amino acids. In fact, of the 22 amino acids the body uses, we can manufacture 13 from various constituents in the foods we eat. This leaves nine we must get directly. These are usually referred to as the "essential" amino acids. These nine are found together in meat, most milk products and soybeans. In any case, vegetarians must be sure to combine foods in their diets to provide these amino acids. This is not as difficult as it may sound, but you do need to understand a few basic principles.

Laurel's Kitchen is a book that describes this well. Some other good books (not strictly vegetarian) are *The Complete Book of Natural Foods* by Fred Rohe, *The Athlete's Kitchen* by Nancy Clark, and *The Pritikin Promise* by Nathan Pritikin. (The recipes in the latter are a great improvement over the earlier Pritikin books.)

Be careful about fad diets that aren't backed up by scientific evidence. At one point I tried an experimental vegetarian diet and found myself "running out of gas." Being used to 30-mile runs, I had trouble finishing 10 after about three weeks on this diet. I also had trouble with mental concentration. One source had told me that hazelnuts and carrot juice would give me the right combination of amino acids, so I ate them every day. Later, I calculated the amount of these ingredients I'd need and discovered I should have been making weekly trips to the grocery store for 50-pound sacks of each.

Fat. Presently the average American takes in 42% of his or her daily calories in fat. It turns out that this is one of the leading causes of heart disease in this country. As you've undoubtedly read, experts have lately recommended that we cut down on fat intake—although they disagree on how much. The Senate's Select Committee on Nutrition and Human Needs has suggested that 30% would be a reasonable amount of fat, while Nathan Pritikin recommends no more than 10%.

Having *enough* fat in one's diet seems no problem. So far the evidence suggests that a tablespoon of polyunsaturated vegetable oil per day is adequate for nutritional purposes. It would be hard not to get this minimum. How much beyond this minimum we take in depends on the kinds of foods we eat. Meat, cheese, nuts, grains and vegetables all contain varying amounts of "fatty acids," the chemicals we refer to as fats and oils.

The kind and quality of fatty acids varies among the different foods. Animal fats (found in meats, eggs, cheese and butter) contain a high percentage of cholesterol and saturated fats, the substances most implicated in heart disease. Red meat—beef, lamb or pork—is much higher in fat than chicken or fish. The fat content of dairy products is variable, from non-fat milk and low-fat cottage cheese or buttermilk at one end of the scale, to regular milk, cheddar cheese or sour cream at the other.

In general, it seems a good idea for long-term health to cut back on fatty foods. Since this is not a book on nutrition, I'd recommend you look at *Jane Brody's Nutrition Book,* a comprehensive guide on the subject that is easy to understand.

Carbohydrates. If we don't need that much protein, and we're already eating too much fat, what then are we supposed to eat? The answer is carbohydrates—foods rich in starch and natural sugars such as breads, grains, pasta, beans, potatoes and some vegetables. These starches are called "complex carbohydrates" because they are made up of a number of sugar molecules or "simple carbohydrates." After ingestion these complex carbohydrates are broken down into simple sugars and transported via the bloodstream to the liver, where they are converted to glucose. Some of this glucose is then converted to glycogen and stored in the muscles and liver. Carbohydrate is a "clean-burning" fuel in that it does not have the toxic by-products of fat and protein for your body to deal with.

Another advantage to a diet high in carbohydrates is that the foods they are found in provide not only the energy, vitamins and minerals we need, but dietary fiber as well. The fiber in vegetables is an aid in digestion, fills us up with fewer calories and plays an important role in moving food through the colon and preventing constipation. This is good news for runners and other people who want to keep their weight down.

However, when we consume too many carbohydrates, and take in more calories than we burn, the excess turns to fat. The same thing is true with fats and proteins. Our body burns sugar for energy and stores fuel in the form of fat.

Competitive runners, who—as you may know—will do just about anything to improve performance, have discovered the importance of carbohydrates as fuel for physical activity. (This is covered in more detail on pp. 236-37, *Carbohydrate Loading.*)

Water and Salt. The danger lies not in neglecting water entirely, but in failing to drink enough of it regularly. Your body may be anywhere from 60% to 70% water. Women have a slightly lower percentage than men, and athletes a little higher than non-athletes. These are minor differences, however. The basic fact is that we all need a surprising amount of water each day (about 2½ quarts), even when we're not exercising and the temperature is mild. When we're exercising just moderately in warm weather, this figure can easily double.

Water is essential for maintaining most of the vital processes of our body. Blood is mostly water. Water cools us in hot weather through perspiration and dilation of the capillaries on the surface of the skin.

Your body loses water gradually throughout the day, so it's best to take it in gradually. Small portions of 4-6 ounces will be assimilated more efficiently than larger ones. Since you're losing it every hour, try to replace it every hour. If you're drinking enough water, your urine should be light in color, like light beer. If your urine is dark, you need to drink more.

Athletes must keep in mind that thirst is not an adequate indicator of water loss. In competitive running, you must drink extra water before a race and, as most experienced runners can tell you, you must drink at the early water stops in a race, even when you're not thirsty.

Several days of dehydrating workouts can have serious effects. If you find you're losing too much weight after workouts, it's a sign of dehydration, not fat loss; that comes more slowly. This is an indication you need to drink more water. (Recommendations for drinking enough liquid for training and racing are on p. 100 and pp. 102-3.)

Should you be taking extra salt when you work out and sweat profusely? Most exercise scientists recommend that dietary salt is adequate and do not recommend supplements. People usually either salt their food or start craving salty foods if their salt level is too low.

Vitamins and Minerals. Vitamins are the catalysts which allow crucial bodily processes to occur. Where in years past many people thought that vitamin and mineral supplements were necessary for good nutrition, recently many nutritionists and sports physiologists have come to the conclusion that a balanced diet will generally supply what the body needs. This is especially true for people who are physically active, as they consume more food as fuel for their activities, and thus take in more vitamins and minerals.

Among the various minerals our bodies need, only a few are of real concern. Some, like sodium, are so plentiful in foods they're hard to avoid, while others, like selenium, we need in such small quantities it would be difficult not to get enough. Calcium, iron and zinc are three we should be aware of. Most women are probably already aware that their iron needs are greater until menopause. Only recently, however, has the importance of calcium been discovered. Researchers are beginning to connect a deficiency in calcium with osteoporosis and are raising the recommended dosages. (See p. 187.) This again seems to be of more concern to women than men. Zinc is also coming under closer scrutiny for its role in repairing tissues. By and large, nutritionists suggest that for these and other minerals we should eat whole grains, dark leafy greens and meat. (Good vegetarian sources of iron are beans, peas and raisins.) They also mention that liver is the best concentrated source of minerals; it's also high in fat, but a small portion (three ounces) supplies a high amount of iron, vitamin A, B vitamins, and minerals.

With vitamins, again, the best source is a well-balanced diet. If you do take supplements, it's important to be careful of possible overdoses of the fat-soluble vitamins A and D. These are stored in the body and if you take too much, there can be a toxic buildup.

Foods especially high in vitamins A and D are eggs, fortified milk (D) and yellow vegetables (A). Vitamin D is also manufactured by the body when the skin is exposed to sunlight. Good sources of vitamin E are whole grains, cereals and breads, beans, liver and green leafy vegetables. Vitamins E and K are fat-soluble and thus can be toxic, but this is extremely rare.

The water-soluble vitamins—the B complex and C—are not stored in the body and do need to be taken daily. These have a variety of functions and can be absent in a diet with a lot of highly processed food. C is found in citrus fruits, tomatoes, dark green vegetables and potatoes (baked but not fried). The B vitamins are available in whole grains and liver. Beans, peas and milk also provide certain of these. Of special importance to strict vegetarians (who eat *no* animal products, including milk, cheese or eggs) is vitamin B-12, which seems to be found only in animal products. Thus "vegans" should take a B-12 supplement.

In conclusion, a diet that combines a wide variety of fresh foods, whole grains, fruit, vegetables, dairy products and some meat should give you all the vitamins and minerals you need. If you're not getting all these, it's time to do a little research. What I've provided here is only a rudimentary introduction to the subject.

EATING FOR PERFORMANCE

I'D LIKE TO OFFER YOU an exclusive miracle diet that could propel you beyond your goals. There are rumors of such experimental approaches. In 1978, Dick Gregory prepared a special diet for one of Boston's better marathoners, Vinny Fleming. After following it for several weeks, he ran in the famous hometown marathon that year and took a special concoction at the 20-mile mark. Not only did he lower his time by several minutes, but he said he felt a great lift when he took the "brew" at 20 miles.

Dick won't release this formula, but I don't like hearing of things like this. They cloud the basic truth, which is that training does a lot more to improve performance than diet. It was Fleming's condition that allowed him to improve, not the drink. Given a certain level of conditioning, some diets will help a little, others will hinder a little. Diet matters more in the long run than in the short run.

Carbohydrate Loading. Research in the late '60s showed that rats stored greater amounts of glycogen when following a certain diet/exercise routine. It was surmised that runners could improve their performance by following the same carbohydrate depletion/loading program prior to a race. The routine is this: Seven days before the race, you run long and hard; this depletes the glycogen stored in the muscles and liver. The next three days you train normally and eat mostly fats and protein—this keeps the glycogen low. Then three days before the race you train lightly and load up on carbohydrates. This is supposed to stock you up with this clean-burning fuel.

I'm not a carbo-loading fan. I tried it in 1973 for the Boston marathon, when I was probably in the best condition of my life, and ran out of gas at the halfway mark. The only factor I'd changed in my routine was diet. Again in the 1974 Charleston Distance Run I followed it to the letter and cramped severely. This had never happened to me before and hasn't since.

I've naturally thought a lot about carbo-loading since these experiences and there are two good reasons why I don't recommend the depletion/loading program. First, a radical diet change like this can upset the body in many ways: lowering resistance to disease, upsetting emotions, body chemistry and rhythms. You certainly don't need this kind of disruption prior to a race. Second, fat, not glycogen, is the fuel you want to burn. Training teaches the muscles to use fat throughout the race and reduce the need for glycogen. Proper pacing will teach the body to use the limited glycogen stores to maximum advantage.

An alternative and a way to avoid these problems is to eat a balanced diet and merely add extra carbs the last three days. (Be reasonable and don't eat *too* much.) This way you can enjoy eating and avoid the unpleasant parts of the carbo-loading program. I've tried this with good results.

Fluids. The danger lies not in neglecting water entirely, but in failing to drink enough of it, regularly. Our body is mostly water; it's tucked away in various nooks and crannies. Glycogen cannot be stored without water, for example. Water cools us in hot weather through perspiration and dilation of the capillaries on the surface of the skin.

To replace the water you lose gradually throughout the day (even in cool weather), you should drink 4-6 ounces every waking hour, and include some dilute electrolyte beverages: orange, grapefruit or tomato juices or a commercial beverage such as ERG, which contains potassium and magnesium.

As race time nears, fluids should be more dilute. During the last two hours, I drink only water; this reduces the chance of getting an upset stomach. You can't drink enough during an event to replace what you're sweating away, so, like a good camel, have some in your stomach when you start. However, continue to drink small amounts. Do not drink a large amount at one time.

During the race. Dehydration is a formidable problem during the marathon, correspondingly less so in shorter races. On a warm day, a marathon racer can lose a quart or two of water an hour through sweating. Also lost are electrolytes (ions of magnesium, potassium,

sodium, calcium, etc.) that facilitate nerve transmission and other vital functions. Most runners I know tend to get upset stomachs from drinks with nutritive supplements taken during a long race. I know this is true in my case (although I like to take some ERG in the latter stages of a race). However, many others believe that at least some electrolyte fluids help.

Everyone is different and each runner's internal reaction to nutritive substances consumed during a race will be different. If you want to try out the electrolyte beverages, test them out on some of your long runs prior to the race.

24 Hours Before the Race and Counting... I begin my eating countdown the day before by cutting down on solid foods. Lunch is my last solid food meal. I'll eat some protein and try to leave satisfied, but not full. That afternoon and evening I'll take water and juices regularly. If I'm hungry I'll eat only easily digestible food, such as bread. I'll obviously avoid fried or greasy food or other foods that are hard to digest, like peanut butter or dairy products. I'll also stay away from high roughage items like salad, bran, etc.

The carbo-loading dinner before a race is great social fun. It's okay to eat a little, but don't load up, particularly if you want to run well. Too much food will be an extra burden on the system and may cause discomfort.

I like to wake up two hours before the race. During the first hour I'll take 500 mg of vitamin C and then drink 6 ounces of water every 20 minutes. I repeat this the last hour before the race as logistics permit. Hopefully I'll have some water with me at the start to sip, but primarily to dump on my head if the day is warm. It may look strange, but it works! (If you want to try this routine, test it out on your long runs first.)

Caffeine. There is now strong evidence that a cup of coffee an hour before a race will improve performance. This drug helps mobilize free fatty acids and triglycerides, making them available for energy utilization in the blood stream. It also helps you to wake up and get your sewage system cleaned out, avoiding the last minute lines at the "jiffy johns." Too much caffeine, however, can cause dehydration and may negatively influence your heart rhythm. Be careful and try it out on several trial runs before using it in races.

Pre-Race Dietary Countdown

24 hours and before: Normal balanced meals. Plenty of fluids all day long, especially electrolyte fluids. Before marathons you can eat extra carbohydrates.

18 hours before race: Start cutting back on solid foods. Keep drinking fluids. After lunch, cut out red meat, fried foods, dairy products, fats, nuts and roughage.

12 hours before race: Don't overeat. Only light, digestible foods like soup, crackers, toast in small quantity. Keep drinking water and electrolyte fluids.

4 hours and less: Water only, in small, regular amounts. Cold water is absorbed quicker. I recommend 6 oz. every 20 minutes, 8 oz. on hot days. If you want vitamin C, take it two hours or more before the race.

During race: Take a drink at every aid station—*especially the early ones.*

22 RUNNING OFF FAT

BY NOW JUST ABOUT EVERYONE knows that diets don't work. (At least not for long.) Haven't we all had friends who went on a diet, looked great for a while, and then slipped back to their old (or even greater) weight?

What *does* work, and it's becoming increasingly recognized, is exercise. And the exercise that's better than almost all the others for losing weight and keeping it off is—you guessed it—running.

Set Point. Research has shown that at any given time each of us has a built-in mechanism for maintaining our current level (or percentage) of fat—the so-called "set point." A complex computer in the brain accounts for activity, basic metabolism, food intake and then compares it to our current fat storage. If we are over-burning or under-eating our appetite is stimulated. Or if we have over-eaten or exercised too little our appetite is suppressed.

Running has helped me bring appetite, exercise and food into balance. When I started running at 13 I'd guess my body fat was about 11-13%. After two years of running it had dropped to about 9-10%. When I started training seriously for the Olympics in 1970 it dropped again to 5-7% and has remained in that range.

Running seems to keep my body and mind in touch. I'm much more sensitive now to over-eating or eating the wrong foods. My appetite shifts quickly when I increase or decrease my exercise—but this wasn't always the case. During my first 8-10 years of running, a decrease in running (due to injury) did not change my eating habits, and for a while I'd gain weight. Now, after over 25 years of regular running, my body is very sensitive and reacts quickly. If I run less, I eat less.

Because your brain is programmed for survival it will tend to add extra fat if there's any doubt. The normal lifetime pattern is to have the set point raised several times as the years pass. At each set point the body has what it believes to be the right percentage of fat. If you lower your fat percentage or deprive yourself of calories needed to maintain the current set point, you'll eventually catch up. That's why diets don't usually work.

Many runners, particularly veterans of a decade or more, have been able to lower the set point through exercise. This is usually done in a series of steps and is directly related to an increase in activity.

Lose Fat—Not (Necessarily) Weight. Endurance exercise is probably the best method of losing fat. Not only do you burn fat as you run, you build your running muscles into fat furnaces which consume the unwanted substance at a greater rate. Muscles feed on fat, so the higher your percentage of muscle, the more fat you'll burn all day long.

What do you want to lose? Most of us who step on the scales daily will say "weight." We *can* lose weight (and health) by eating a normal or even decadent diet and dehydrating ourselves, but the fat will remain. Alcoholics often lose weight by not exercising and letting their muscles wither away.

What you obviously want to lose is fat:

- Excess baggage weighing you down every step.
- Unwanted insulation keeping you hot.
- An unnecessary diversion of blood and oxygen (away from exercising muscles).
- Unsightly bulges.

Some people may not realize they have hidden stores of fat. Covert Bailey, author of *Fit or Fat?*, has measured thousands of people in his underwater tanks. Many are obese and don't realize it because the fat is marbled among the muscle cells. Only after most of the available fat storage spaces are filled inside the muscle tissue do these individuals begin to notice the formation of surface fat. Again, endurance activity is the best way to rid yourself of this unwanted burden and keep it off.

The scales shouldn't run or ruin your life. Muscle weighs more than fat. A weight gain when you begin an exercise program may be a *good* sign. You may be losing weight in fat as you gain muscle; without losing a pound, you'll probably lose inches.

Don't throw out the scales, however. They help you monitor dehydration. By weighing in every morning you can monitor your fluid balance. If there is a sudden two-pound drop or more, you can bet it's water and should start to replenish immediately. It takes about 25 miles of distance running to lose a pound of fat, so it's doubtful that any sudden weight loss will be fat.

Check the Fat. There are two ways of measuring. Calipers measure skin folds. They are quick and convenient. The other method is underwater weighing, which is generally considered to be more accurate. Here you are weighed first out of the water, and then again when submerged in a tank. You exhale as much air as possible while underwater, then the specialist takes a reading. The difference between the two weighings indicates your fat percentage, since fat floats, and lean muscle and bone sink.

Endurance Muscles Burn Fat During Exercise and Afterward. Running develops fat-burning muscles. As these muscles come into play, they gobble up fat during exercise and continue to do so for hours afterward—even during sitting and sleeping.

To effectively lower the body's fat stores, you must first mobilize them so they release their fatty acids and triglycerides into the blood stream. In this way they'll be taken into the exercising muscle cells and burned for fuel.

The 40-Minute Goal. When you begin to run you burn primarily carbohydrates and very little fat. After 5-10 minutes the percentage of fats burned rises while the percentage of carbohydrates drops. At about 30 minutes, you're burning fats as primary fuel. (See the chart on p. 45.) By that time there are abundant supplies of fatty acids in the blood stream. Hence the value of extending your exercise periods to 40 minutes or more. If running 40 continuous minutes tires you, take regular and frequent walks. To mobilize the fat, it's better to run 40-60 minutes, three times a week, than 20-30 minutes six times a week.

Distance, Not Speed, Burns Calories. A beginner is not strong enough to run for 40 continuous minutes and must burn carbohydrates. As muscles become stronger, the individual muscle cells increase their capacity both during exercise and afterward. Running burns about 100 calories per mile and it doesn't make much difference how fast you run. Stronger muscles will allow gradually longer runs and therefore burn more calories. So take it easy, go longer and burn 'em up!

The Afterburner. When you finish exercising, your body doesn't shut off. In a sense it keeps "running" and burning calories. When you exercise, the body is revved up. When you stop, it slowly tapers down over several hours to your base rate. (This fact isn't taken into account in the calories-per-mile charts or the miles-per-croissant charts.)

Burning Fat While You Sleep. Not only do you burn more calories than non-exercisers during and after exercise, but even while sitting and sleeping. With endurance-conditioned muscles, you will have a higher metabolism (transforming food into energy) rate at rest, and be warmer. Fit people tend to be warmer because their muscle furnaces are revved up, burning more calories day and night.

Sugar Burners Become Fat Burners. Endurance running can train your sugar-burning cells to become fat burners. This increases your fat-burning capacity and decreases your waistline. At birth your leg muscles are composed of a set amount of fast twitch and slow twitch muscles (further explained on p. 48). Fast twitchers fire quickly but not repeatedly and burn sugar. Slow twitchers burn fat and can work repeatedly, but don't work very fast. I have been measured by physiologist Dave Costill at 97% slow twitch. (I don't challenge anyone to a 100-yard dash!) Although slow-moving cells cannot ever work faster, the *fast twitch cells can be trained to perform as slow twitch.* Former sprinters, therefore, *are* capable of endurance running, although it may take many months for them to adapt.

Coffee. There is some preliminary evidence that drinking coffee before exercising may help reduce fat. Research on rats showed that ingestion of caffeine about an hour before endurance exercise resulted in a reduction of fat compared to rats who didn't take the drug. It is recommended that only one cup of coffee be taken about an hour before exercise.

Heavy Hands. Runners who carry weights on their hands have experienced accelerated fat reduction compared to those who cover the same distance without weights. The extra weight increases the total workload and nibbles away at body stores. It will, however, put extra pressure on joints, ligaments, tendons, etc., particularly if you overpronate. Leg weights put stress on the feet and are *not* recommended; going extra distance by *walking* is a better way to burn extra fat.

Caffeine and weights are minor additions to your fat-burning capacity. They may help take off a few pounds over several years, but the major reduction in fat comes from development of the massive fat-burning muscle power in your legs. You accomplish this by running regularly, and gradually increasing your distance.

Diets Only Work in Combination with Exercise. Most of the weight lost from diets is water. In fact, there is recent evidence that dieting without exercise will cause the dieter to actually gain weight in the long run.

Running Lean. Starvation diets are not necessary. Most runners find that their exercising allows them to eat just about what they want. The idea is to be moderate and not overeat. Calorie reduction can be a matter of taste. Gradually shift away from the fatty foods you like by acquiring a taste for similar foods with less fat.

Instead of:	***Try:***
Fried Foods	Foods marinated in herbs and broiled
Red meat	Fish or poultry
Peanut Butter	Just a taste of it on bread or crackers
Cheese	Low-fat cottage cheese
Whole milk	Non-fat milk
Salad dressing	Small amount of oil and add apple juice (and vinegar).
Potato chips, etc.	Cut vegetables (carrots, celery, etc.)

Complex carbohydrates such as whole grains and vegetables will satisfy your hunger and not give you big doses of calories. In fact, some physiologists say that fats "burn in a carbohydrate flame." You need enough carbohydrates to break down the fatty acids (the body's prime source of stored fuel) into energy. Beware of additives, however; salad is wonderful low-calorie food, but one tablespoon of oil in the dressing reverses the situation. Potatoes are great low-calorie filler-uppers—but watch that sour cream!

When to eat is very important. Try eating small snacks throughout the day to avoid being ravenous at meals, which leads to over-eating. When you wait a long time between meals you stimulate the fat-depositing enzymes; these little fellows take a big meal and store it in the way you want least. The longer you wait, the more enzymes are produced. Eating small amounts allows the body to burn it up as it comes in. It will also give you a steady flow of energy throughout the day—provided the snacks are not too concentrated in sugar or fat.

A slight, sensible reduction in calories, adapted gradually into your lifestyle, will allow your exercise to burn off even more calories. This sensible approach to your new healthy lifestyle can result in permanent changes: endurance exercise, a healthy diet, and a slimmer you.

The Pritikin Promise. For years, health expert Nathan Pritikin has advocated a low-fat, high-carbohydrate diet and daily exercise to lose weight and reduce cholesterol. Pritikin's first two books, *The Pritikin Program for Diet and Exercise,* and *The Pritikin Permanent Weight-loss Manual* were immensely popular, but many people seemed to find the recommendations and recipes too austere. Even when they tried the diet for a while, they would eventually slip back to their normal habits. Pritikin has changed this in his latest book, *The Pritikin Promise*, intended for "active and athletic people who consider themselves healthy." It's got excellent recipes and is full of ideas for taking the fat out while bringing the flavor in. You can learn how to make mock sour cream for your potatoes out of low-fat buttermilk, low-fat cottage cheese and vinegar. You can make waffles, pancakes or cornbread without egg yolks, oil or butter. You replace sugar, honey and maple syrup with apple juice concentrate. It's a great cookbook for the healthy runner's diet.

Don't Diet When Increasing Exercise. It's best not to diet and increase mileage at the same time. Both put great stress on the body and you should take them one at a time. Once you have stabilized at a higher mileage level and your body has adjusted, you can consider dieting. It's still best, however, to lose weight through increased exercise.

SHOES

23 SHOE SECRETS

INSIDE INFORMATION ON SHOE DESIGN

LIKE THE QUEST FOR THE HOLY GRAIL, runners search for the perfect shoe. We feel that somewhere there's a perfect pair that will cure foot problems, make us run faster and lead us bounding effortlessly into the sunset. We're persuaded by ads, influenced by magazine surveys and tempted by the shoes our friends wear.

Well, don't get your hopes too high. Although shoes have come a long way, I have yet to meet a runner who's found the perfect pair. Thirty years ago the standard was a canvas shoe made by one of the basketball companies. It was theoretically designed for indoor running, ping pong, volleyball or anything the salesman could talk you into. The black cloth absorbed perspiration and salt, which would frequently rub against your feet until they were blistered or raw. There was a hard gum rubber sole glued directly to the canvas . . . and that was it. Stability, cushioning, pronation control, and other things we now take for granted were in the realm of science fiction.

Some Running Shoe History. When I was in high school in 1960 my track coach talked about an exotic brand of shoes he'd discovered when stationed in Germany in the USAF: Adidas. My running friends and I were intrigued as we flipped through the black-and-white brochures. There were four or five shoes designed for training! It was difficult to convince our parents we needed $8 for running shoes instead of the usual $4, but we prevailed. The contrast in comfort provided by these new shoes was amazing. I was so proud I couldn't take them off. I wore them running, to class, to church, etc., much to the criticism, kidding and olfactory discomfort of my mother and classmates.

The rapid development and innovation in running shoes since those days has been largely due to the involvement of runners in the business. In the early '60s Phillip (Buck) Knight wanted to start a running shoe import company and brought some primitive Tiger brand models back from Japan to his coach, Bill Bowerman. Bill was a vocal critic of every shoe on the market and these foreign shoes stimulated his pioneer spirit and inventor's ingenuity. He tore them up and improvised, then tested them on the feet of his runners, such as Kenny Moore and Geoff Hollister.

Breakfast at Bowermans. When Barbara Bowerman left for church one Sunday morning, little did she know that husband Bill had plans for her waffle iron that did not include brunch. Having worked with the overall construction of shoes for several years, Bill was now trying to find the perfect sole material—one that would offer optimal traction, cushion and better wear. Looking around in the kitchen for ideas, he spotted the waffle iron, and running shoes have not been the same since. Neither has the taste of waffles around the Bowerman household.

The rubber waffles that came out of that iron became the soles for a new generation of Oregon distance runners who found them perfect for traction on the varied terrain of cross-country surfaces. Unexpectedly, they also found that the soles improved traction and cushion on hard surfaces. Traction was best where body weight pressed the hardest, and the waffle tips were distributed liberally enough to give traction on any part of the sole.

In the process, Bowerman brought in an orthopedic specialist, Stan James, in hopes of avoiding injuries by design. The result was the Nike shoe. Word spread quickly in the running underground that some crazy runners in Oregon had finally come up with something. By 1980, Nike Inc. was selling more running shoes in America than any other company.

Today you can find a running shoe for just about any shape foot, and devices to help avoid or minimize many of running's stresses. Each wave of research spawns a new generation of shoes, which makes the previous ones practically obsolete. With all the choices available it's important that the shoes fit your own particular anatomy and running style. If not, the shoes can *cause* problems. The wrong shoes, for ex-

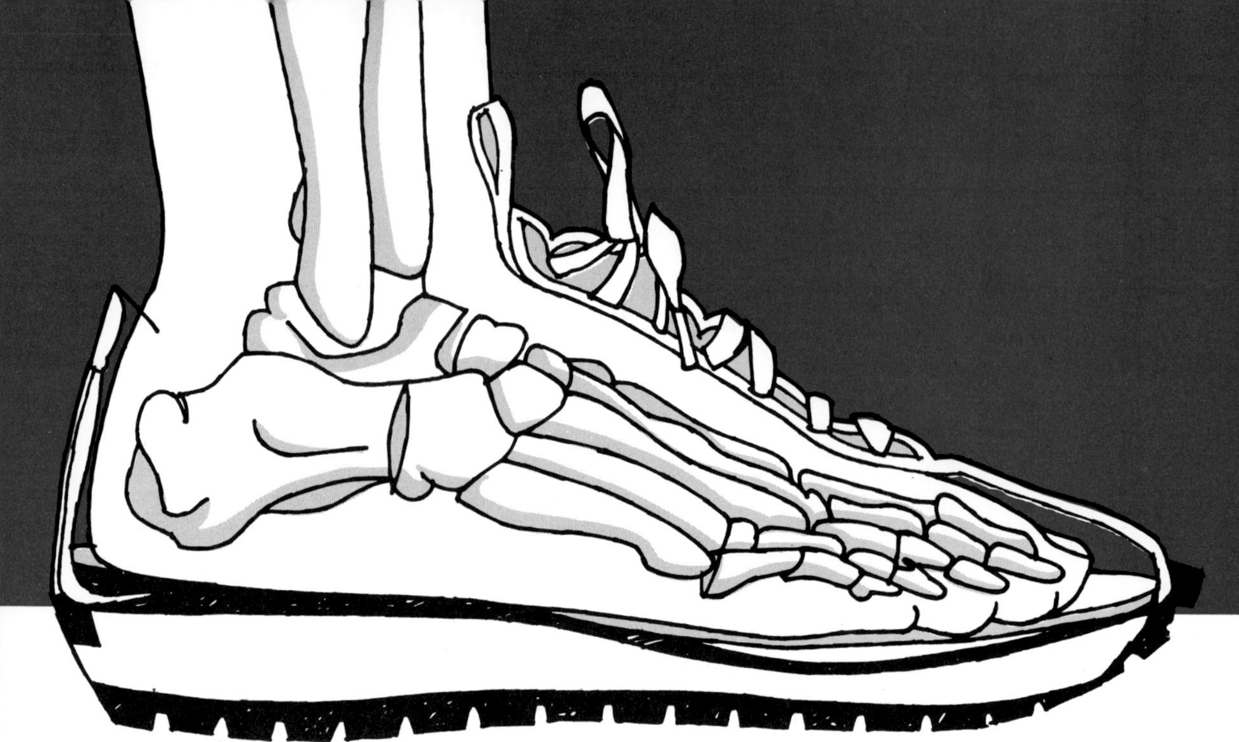

ample, might cause you to tilt your foot the wrong way and cause injury, or to waste money on expensive orthopedic devices you don't need.

Our experience in fitting shoes in the Phidippides stores has shown that salespeople who are also runners can give the best advice, and help lead you through the maze of new models. The problem in many areas, however, is finding such a person—one who knows running firsthand, is up-to-date on all the available shoes, has been trained in fitting techniques and can listen to your problems and help you make a sound decision.

You'll most likely have great trouble finding such a shoe expert. Most stores—even specialty stores—just hire people at minimum wages and give them no training. The running magazines try to fill the gap, but become too technical, and their attempts to simulate running in lab tests do not work. Moreover, the mass of facts overwhelms the reader. The magazines sometimes try to clarify things by setting up a point system and rating the shoes, but this doesn't provide enough information for the individual runner. Each person needs a unique combination of features. A ranking will usually list the best shoes for a mythical "average" runner.

In this chapter I'll give you a list of important factors to consider in choosing shoes. You can then apply this information to your own running style, weight, tendencies and aims—to find the best combination for you.

Board Last or Slip Last. It's helpful to be familiar with two basic types of shoe construction.

Board (or cement) last construction is where a piece of fiber-board material is placed between the foot and the midsole material. This provides extra support for the foot and usually reduces flexibility.

Slip last construction is where the sole and midsole material are cemented directly to the cloth upper, with no insole board. Shoes built this way tend to provide less stability, but are more flexible.

Definitions of Foot Movements. Before we begin a discussion of foot types, we'll define the basic types of foot movements:

Pronation is a normal shock-absorbing mechanism. Most runners land on the heel, then the foot rolls forward and inward with body weight on the center of the forefoot. This provides cushioning.

Over-pronation is when the runner rolls excessively to the *inside,* particularly in the forefoot. The knees and inside of the shins are stressed. This is indicated by wear on the inside of the heel, but particularly by wear on the inside of the forefoot (even when heel wear is on the outside).

Excessive supination is rolling excessively to the *outside* of the foot so that the ligaments, tendons and bones on that side are sore and strained. This is indicated by excessive wear on the outside of the sole and little wear elsewhere.

What Type Foot Do You Have? The single most important factor in proper shoe selection is your type foot: *rigid* or *floppy*. The human foot is designed to be both a (rigid) lever and a (floppy) platform. This enables us to propel ourselves forward, yet at the same time adapt to varying surfaces. Many feet, because of bone structure and muscular attachments, can be described as being "hinged" predominantly one way or another: either forward and back (rigid) or side to side (floppy), with some feet having a degree of both characteristics.

The Rigid Foot

Characteristics. The rigid foot moves predominantly forward and back, with a strong push-off. Like a horse's hoof, it's an efficient lever for speed. The runner may land on the heel, but the rigid foot rolls quickly forward and gets a strong push from the forefoot. Excessive supination, often seen with the rigid foot, results when feet yield too much on the outside. This may put too much stress on the bones, tendons and ligaments on the outside of the foot.

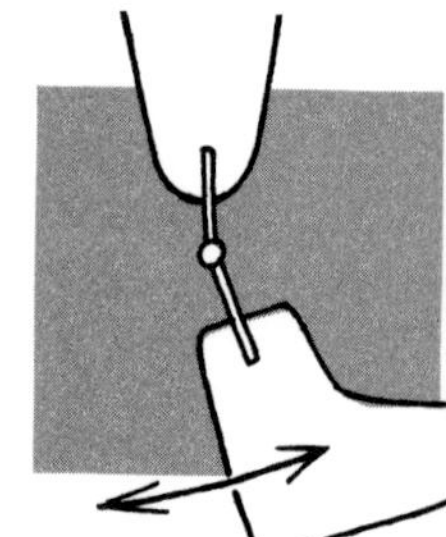
Rigid foot

Shoe wear. The wear pattern of a rigid foot is along the outside of the shoe, particularly on the outside and middle of the forefoot.

Shoe type needed. A rigid foot needs good flexibility and good forefront and rearfoot cushion. There is not as much need for stability as there is with a floppy foot.

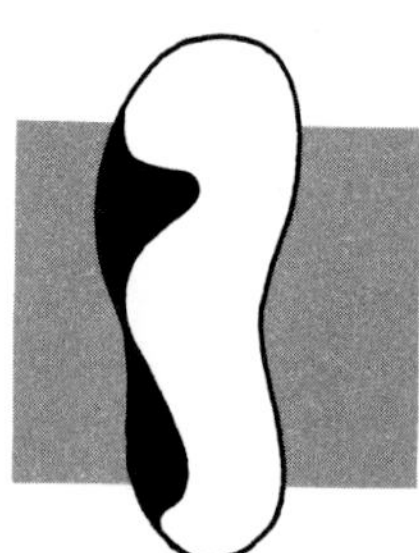
Shoe wear rigid foot

The Floppy Foot

Characteristics. The floppy foot acts as if hinged from side to side. The first strike is usually on the outside (sometimes the inside) of the heel, but then it rolls to the inside of the forefoot. Rolling inward in this fashion can result in over-pronation and cause knee or shin problems.

Shoe wear. The wear pattern of a floppy foot is a series of spots where the foot pushes. The empty space between may show little or no wear. Of particular concern is a wear pattern on the inside of the heel or the inside of the forefoot which denotes over-pronation. Here the foot is rolling too far. The foot, knee and hip are no longer in alignment and the knee and shin areas usually take too much stress.

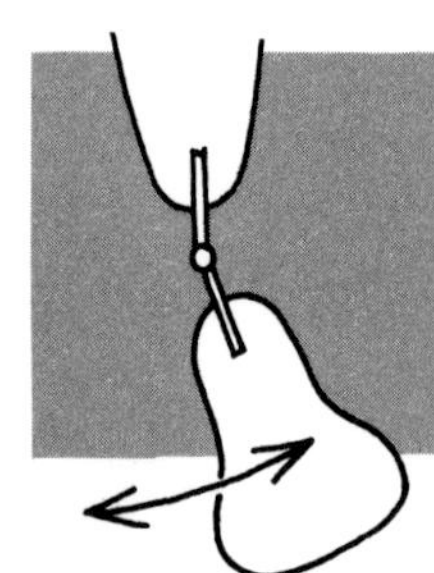
Floppy foot

Shoe type needed. A floppy foot needs support. The rear foot and especially the forefoot must have a stable platform. Shoes with a board last tend to be more stable. Some runners need only a board last and a strong arch support. Others will need a custom orthotic to correct excess motion. If you're having problems, consult a podiatrist. Too much cushion can compromise the stability of even a well-made shoe, and any orthopedic devices which are designed to control pronation. *It's best to sacrifice cushion for stability*—there's usually a direct trade-off.

A word on pronation. Don't assume that pronation means trouble. If you aren't having problems you'll probably get them by installing devices in your shoes. If you are a pronator and having knee or shin pain, you may benefit from correction, but get good advice first. I've seen severe pronators who don't seem to have any problems—they must have compensation mechanisms somewhere in their legs or feet.

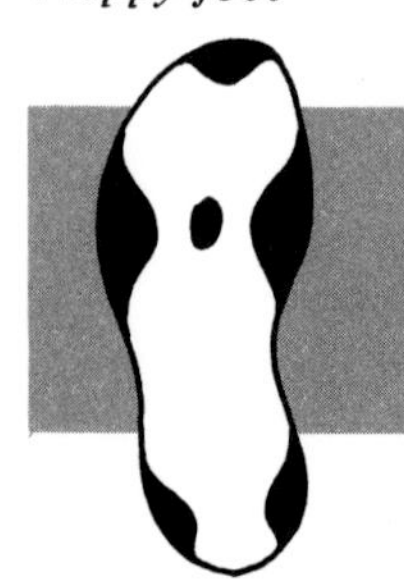
Shoe wear floppy foot

Shoe Shape. There are two basic shoe shapes: straight and curved. Try on shoes of both types to see which is best for your foot. A straight shoe looks about the same as its mate on the bottom. A curved shoe, however, will look radically different from its partner. If your foot is curved, a straight shoe will put pressure on your big toe and toe joint. If your foot is straight, a curved shoe will put pressure on the outside and you'll probably have extra room on the inside of the forefoot. The "modified straight last" is a compromise between the two.

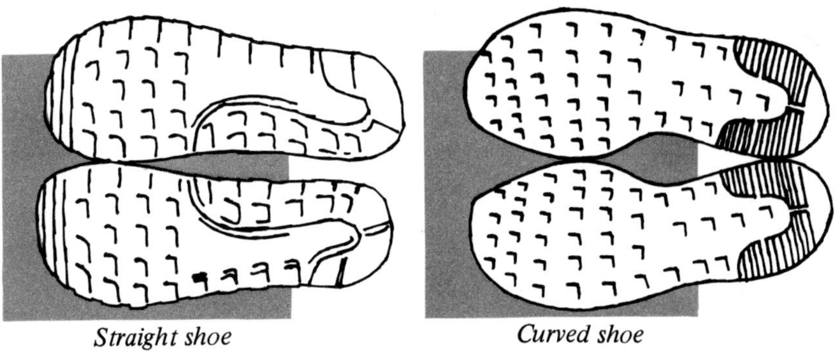

Straight shoe *Curved shoe*

Generally, the shape of the shoe should correspond to the shape of your foot. Be sure there are no areas of pressure or pain, or any feeling of binding when you flex your foot.

Shoe Fit

Expansion/contraction. Your foot will swell as you run, more so during the summer. Fit your shoes with this in mind. It's best to try shoes on in the afternoon, since feet swell during the day. You don't want your foot to slip around inside, but you don't want too much pressure on it either.

Toe room. When you run, your foot is like a pendulum. With each swing, more blood is pumped into the feet, especially the toe region, causing the toes to swell. Lack of toe room is the primary cause of toe blisters and black toenails. Generally, *½" of toe room* is sufficient to avoid problems. Since one foot is usually larger than the other, fit the larger one. If you've had toe problems, look for a shoe with a rounded rather than pointed toe box.

As long as the shoe fits snugly across the middle of your

foot, don't worry about 1" of extra room at the toe. Toes want freedom like everyone else!

Heel fit. Your heel should fit snugly but not be confined. Ideally there should be a very *slight give* at the heel, but not enough so you feel anxiety. *The shoe should feel like an extension of your foot,* not separate from it. Also, there should be no heel roll from side to side within the shoe.

Socks. Use socks of the same thickness as those you'll be running in when you try shoes on.

Take a Test Ride. Be sure to walk around in the shoes as much as possible. This tells you how the shoe responds to your feet in motion. Some stores do not let you run in the shoes—but you really should. This is the only way to tell how the shoe fits and works. Look around for a store that allows this.

Cushion. If you run on a golf course all the time, you'd need very little cushion in your shoes. Most of us, however, have to deal with the shock from pavement every step of the way—at least in many of our runs and races. If our shoes don't absorb the shock, it gets passed up the line—to feet, knees, hips and to crucial muscles and tendons. Remember the two foot types, and their differing requirements:

- *The rigid foot* needs cushion and flexibility, especially in the forefoot.
- *The floppy foot* needs stability, and only enough cushion to take the edge off road shock. Too much cushion can allow excessive pronation.

Over-pronators. Beware of soft shoes. Too much cushion will allow your foot to keep on rolling as it pronates. This problem increases with the vertical layers of midsole material in the shoe. You want adequate shock absorption until the foot reaches a flat, stable resistance. Then the foot will either get a little push from the shoe, or at least be able to make its own force as it pushes off.

Too much cushion causes instability. In addition to magnifying pronation problems, it causes you to waste energy with each step. If you run in the shoes before buying them you'll feel the cushion in action.

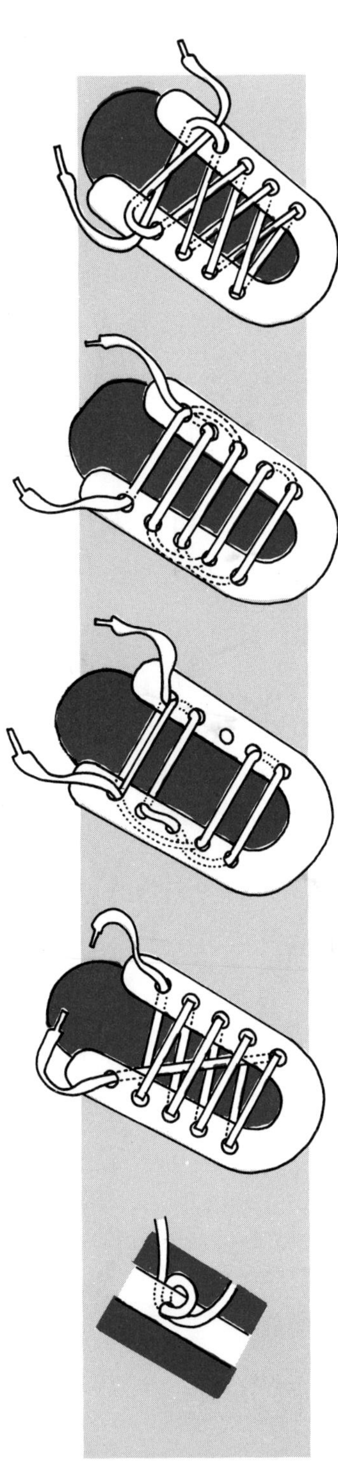

Creative Lacing

Cutting heel slippage:

You can get a tighter heel fit by tightening the top laces. To avoid pinching the foot, use the stirrup lace method. This distributes pressure over four, rather than two holes.

Relieving lace pressure:

Popularized by Arthur Lydiard, this eliminates pressure on the top of the foot from laces crossing under the border. It takes a while to learn, but is a secure, comfortable system.

Releasing spot pressure:

If you have spots on the top of your foot that are under pressure, just skip the eyelets that go across that area. This relieves pressure there and allows you to tighten other areas.

More toe room:

This lacing system, suggested by Harry Hlavac, D.P.M., makes your toe area more of a "tent." By pulling tightly on the short (straight) lace, you'll increase the amount of toe room and reduce pressure on the toes.

Isolating individual laces:

If one area of your foot needs to be loosely laced while others remain tight, just loop lace around lace hole.

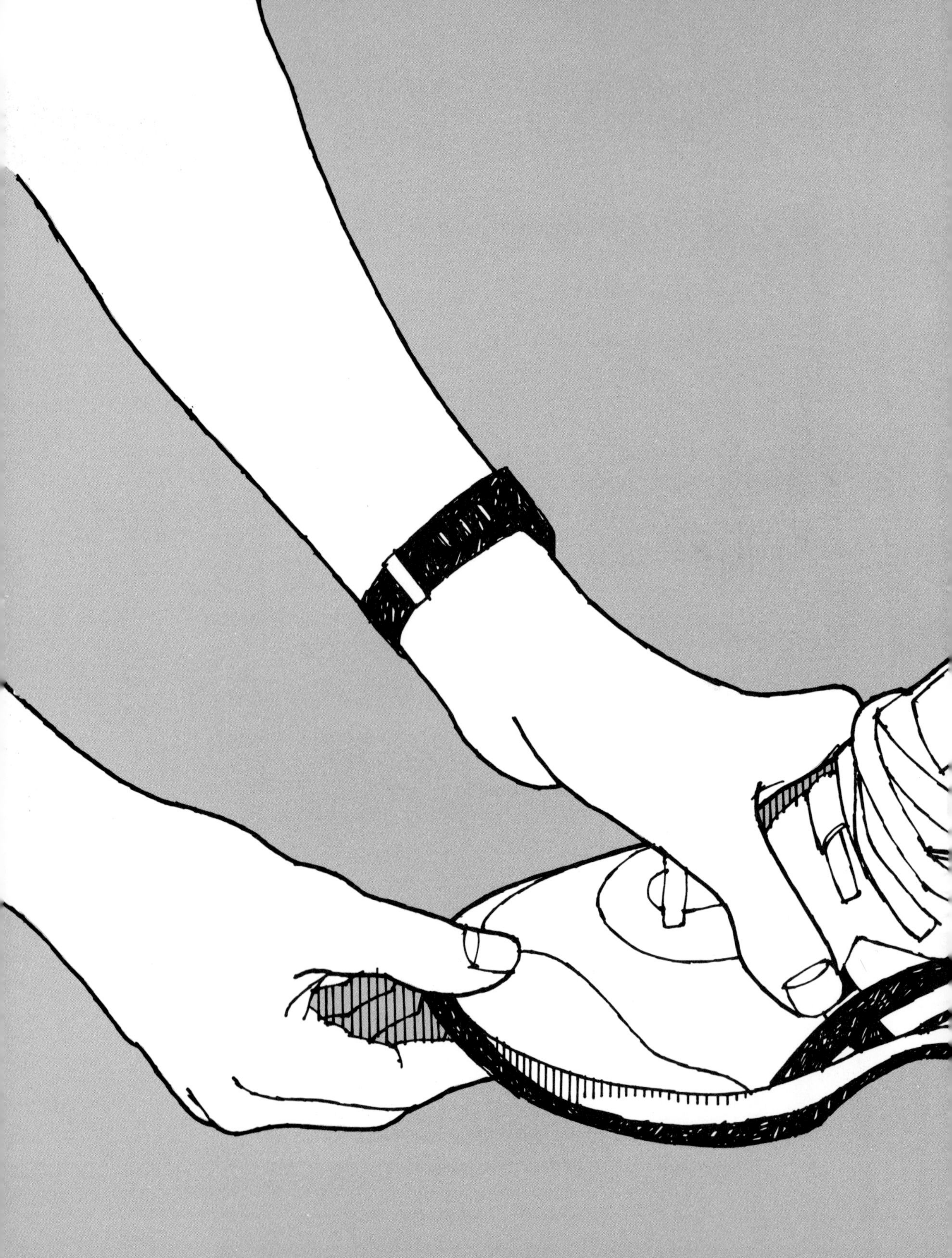

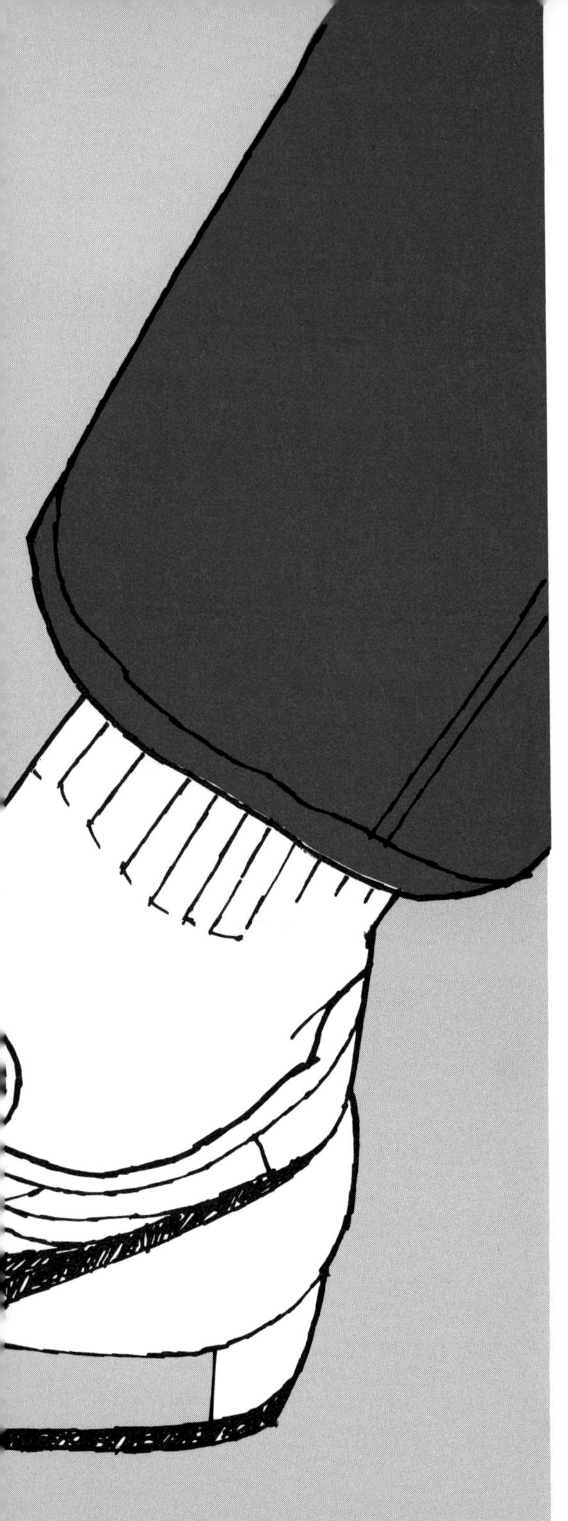

24 SHOE SHOPPING

SOME SHOE COMPANIES invest millions in research while others opt for big advertising budgets. This makes it difficult to tell the help from the hype. How do you sift through the gleam of new designs, the claims for spectacular features, the hundreds of shoes in running stores?

It helps to find a store staffed by runners who are trained in fitting. The ideal advisor will listen to you and then try to find a shoe that fits your needs and problems. However, *you're* the one who has to make the final decision; even the best salesperson can't get inside the shoe with you and feel how it fits. Also—unfortunately—a lot of stores either don't have good advisors or may try to sell you any shoe—whether it's right or not—just to make the sale.

SHOE SELECTION CHECKLIST

Here are some key questions to consider in making the right shoe choice. Copy this and take it into the store with you.

How Many Miles a Week Do You Run?

☐ *Under 20:* Practically any of the better brand shoes—Adidas, Brooks, Etonic, Nike, Saucony, Tiger, etc.—will do. These shoes shouldn't break down for a long time. Unless you have some diagnosed foot problems, you don't need an expensive pair.

☐ *20–50:* Most running shoes are designed for people in this group. As your mileage increases, look for better quality.

☐ *Over 50:* You need a sturdy shoe, designed for the way you run and for your foot type.

On What Surfaces Do You Run?

☐ *Grass or dirt:* You don't need much cushion, but should look for traction, stability and protection from rocks.

☐ *Pavement:* Adequate cushion. Remember, when you gain cushion, you lose stability. If you pronate excessively, you must strike a balance, but should choose on the side of stability.

Is Your Foot Floppy or Rigid? (To determine which type you are see pp. 251-52.)

☐ *Floppy:* Stable platform, less cushion, sometimes pronation control devices (often built into shoes). Look for a shoe with a board last. (See p. 252.)

☐ *Rigid:* Flexible, cushioned shoe. Look for a slip-lasted shoe. (See p. 251.)

Is Your Foot Straight or Curved? (See p. 253.)

☐ *Straight:* If a curved shoe puts pressure on the outside of your foot and there's extra room on the inside, you have a straight foot.

☐ *Curved:* If a straight shoe causes pressure on your toe and joint, you have a curved foot.

INJURIES THAT INFLUENCE SHOE CHOICE

If you've had shoe-related injuries, it's best to get medical advice. The trouble is, things keep changing so fast in the shoe market that podiatrists and orthopedists can't possibly test out all the new shoes and haven't the time to follow up on how the old shoes hold up over time. So it pays to know some basic principles yourself about what to look for.

Through the years I've found that some problems can be helped by certain types of shoes. In the Phidippides stores we've helped thousands of runners select their shoes.

The following is offered, not as medical advice, but from one runner to another:

Knee Problems or Shin Problems

- *Rigid foot:* More cushion and flexibility. If your ankle turns or twists frequently, look for a shoe that's stable and strong on the outside throughout.
- *Floppy foot:* Strong platform, board last construction with little or moderate cushion. Strong heel construction.

Achilles Problems. Higher heel lift, heel counter that fits your heel well, but does not pull on the tendon when shoe flexes. For this reason, flexibility is also needed. Shoe should have excellent rear-foot stability.

Plantar Fasciitis (Heel Pain). More stability through board last. Heel counter must be secured to midsole very well and should fit your heel with no room to roll.

Shin Splints. Board last, moderate cushion, stable shoe.

OTHER SHOE TIPS

Breaking in Shoes. I'm amazed at how many people go out and run 10-12 miles the first day in a new pair of shoes and then complain about blisters. Walk around the first day or two. Wear the shoes during your normal daily activities if you can, so they will begin conforming to your feet. At first, run only a mile or two, then gradually increase. After about seven days they should be broken in.

Breaking Down Shoes. Several areas of the shoe will break down simultaneously. Each step destroys the individual separation of air bubbles and breaks down the midsole, causing it to flatten. As it compresses, you lose cushion and support. This happens so gradually you may not notice it until you compare it to a new shoe.

The upper part of the shoe stretches and weakens at stress points. As this happens, the foot loses its support laterally. This is particularly a problem for pronators. With less support there is more likelihood of injury. As the materials fatigue, the foot is allowed to roll more and more. Monitor this slow breakdown by trying out new shoes and comparing the cushion and support at periodic intervals.

Alternating Shoes. Shoes last longer if you let them rest and dry out between runs. Thus it's good to have two pairs. When one pair has been used for half of its "life," get a new pair and start alternating. However, it's not good to alternate between a brand new pair and a worn-out pair, as this can cause injuries.

Ned Frederick, physiologist and director of research at Nike, recommends that when you find a shoe that works well, buy two pairs. This ensures that you'll have another pair of the same model (before it's superseded by a newer and different design). It also gives you a reference point: you keep one pair in the closet and run in them only once every few weeks. By directly comparing these to the other everyday pair you'll know how much cushion and support you've lost.

What's That Smell? Three friends were traveling in Greece and, after checking into their hotel, took a run. After dinner later that night, when they opened the door to their room, they were met with such a horrendous odor they quickly shut it and called the management. The proprietor was apologetic and called the fumigators. All were convinced that an animal must have crawled into the room and died. After several minutes inside, one of the fumigators emerged, holding at arm's length a well-seasoned pair of running shoes belonging to the Americans.

Shoes have materials and glue that react differently to perspiration. Wash with soap and water and a stiff brush. A light soaking in baking soda will help the inner odor, but board-lasted shoes will often buckle after soaking. After washing, lightly squeeze the water out and put them to dry in a warm place, with paper inside them. Saddle soap will keep the leather parts soft.

START TO FINISH

25 SHOULD KIDS RUN?

The Benefits. The earlier a child starts running, the better the cardiovascular foundation for later years. Such a development gives the child a head start in long-term health benefits and in competition, should it follow. At each stage, the heart, lungs and circulatory system are strengthened and the effects are multiplied through the growing years. However, the most important ingredients are fun and success. If a child feels good about running he or she is likely to continue.

The Dangers. I'm not qualified to comment on any possible damage that endurance running might do to joints, bones or vital parts of a growing body. I've never seen evidence of sensible training in children leading to any such problems, but if you are in doubt you should contact your pediatrician or family physician.

But one of the real dangers for young runners is psychological burnout. Most child running stars or top high school athletes never reach their running potential because of the "too far, too fast, too soon" syndrome. Well-meaning but over-zealous parents or coaches naturally want to get children involved in healthy activity and may influence them to train too hard, and race too often. Without the sense of pace and restraint bestowed by maturity they are driven until they become bored, disillusioned or discouraged.

The Real Goals. I became addicted to running at age 13, probably because my goals were relaxation and the good feelings from exercise. If kids can appreciate these internal rewards, they will probably be on the road to a lifetime fitness program. There's also a lot of fun in low-key competition, trips and running friendships. It's important that the main goals of running be the psychological and health benefits and that victories, times and trophies not become ends in themselves.

If you "hold 'em back," they'll want to continue. When kids are restrained slightly, their desire builds inside. Carefully monitor your child's program and hold back slightly on a regular basis—not letting youthful enthusiasm run unchecked.

Racing. Informal competition is beneficial, but I feel that children's racing teams, with intense speedwork and regimented competition are not right in early years. An occasional road race, fun run or school field day can provide informal competition without great pressure. Marathon training and racing are also too intense and likely to produce early burnout. Marathons can be run throughout one's life, so there's no need to rush into them.

A Recommended Program

One through five years: Encourage running and all types of vigorous activity. Take the child to an occasional race, say things like "Someday when you grow up, you may want to run in a race like this..." Talk about some of the health benefits.

5-11 years: If the child shows an interest in running, you can provide encouragement. Run along with him or her and talk about the health benefits. Never force, push or extend the run too far; at the same time, don't let the child push too hard; save that desire for the next time. Use road races or fun runs as rewards for regular exercising.

11-12 years: If there is a junior high running program and your child wants to participate, monitor it. Two to three workouts a week and three to four races a season are reasonable. Avoid intense interval work and high mileage. Running in local races could be based on practicing three times per week.

13-18 years: Encourage other activities along with running–studies, music, dating, work on the school newspaper, etc. Now the young runner can start training seriously as long as it doesn't get out of control. Avoid high mileage (above 40-50 miles a week), intense speedwork and races every weekend. At 15, a physically mature and talented runner could try national competition–if ready. (I don't believe in national competition for kids under age 15. Let it be a mystery how they stack up against their age group peers. A few local races for kids this age are plenty.)

18 and older: You are now an advisor. He or she can decide when to run a marathon, how hard to train, whether to enter national competition, etc. The rules of sensible training, adequate rest, planning, etc., as outlined earlier in the book, now apply.

26 RUNNING AFTER 40

WE HAVE NO CONTROL over time. Like stars speeding through space, we head certainly toward the end of life as if it were a mysterious black hole, not knowing when or where we might enter it. Running is one of those significant distractions that can make our passage more interesting and stimulating.

Although we can't predict exactly how long we'll live, there's growing evidence we can affect the aging process. Through healthy living habits, we not only have a better chance of living longer, we can significantly improve the quality of our lives while we're here.

Runners notice the aging process: a little slower starting in the morning, a few more aches and pains now and then, slower healing of injuries. Right now I'm 39, poised at the boundary of the 40-year "wall." A few individuals have inspired me to pass through this wall without the usual forebodings. These folks have shown me that there is abundant life beyond 40, and that, as you grow older, your body can give you better running service if it's well cared for.

Slower Recovery Time. Harold Tinsley, president of the Road Runners Club of America, is one of a small group of runners who arrived at the masters category (40+) without the extended "break" most adults take after high school or college. Not only was Harold a lone pioneer runner in the '60s and '70s, but he promoted races in those years to get others running in his hometown of Huntsville, Alabama. He was also an early entrant in the field of computer engineering and now designs high-tech processing systems for outer space (and for races–in his basement Harold has developed the best system for processing race results I've seen).

As the effects of aging have gradually set in, he's found that recovery from a hard workout doesn't come as quickly as before. The times of his speed repetitions at 45+ are not much slower than the times of his teenage years, but *he* is slower for several days afterward.

Harold says one benefit of maturity is increased concentration. We're able to push ourselves harder in every area of our lives. Goal oriented, we push our bodies through distractions and further into fatigue. We've learned to get more out of our bodies and—on the down side—we push them toward injury more efficiently. We're more tired when we break down and it takes longer to recover. Also, there's generally more stress in our lives (work, family, etc.) that adds to the difficulties of running, and the recovery time.

Harold suggests we schedule more easy days after hard days as the years pass. He also believes that overeating or heavy consumption of fatty foods leads to decreased performances. The advantages of taking more rest and eating lightly are even more important as the years pass.

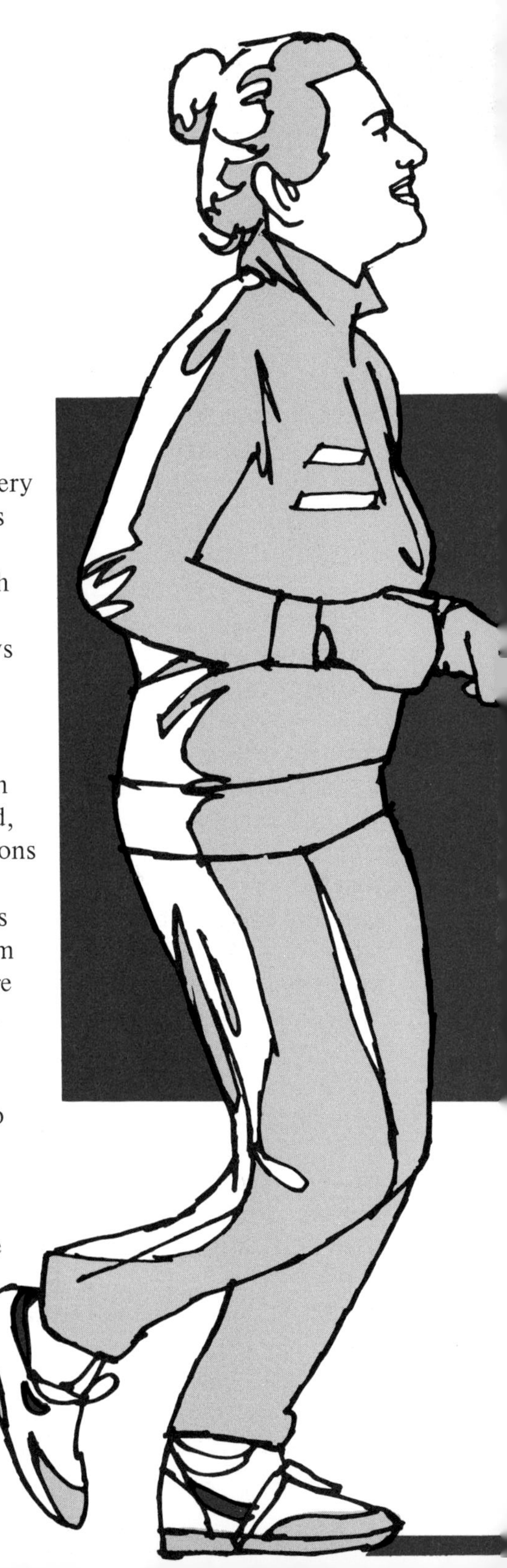

A Mid-life U-Turn. Tom Conklin had been an average athlete in high school football, basketball and track. As he became a successful Chicago attorney he gradually succumbed to the sinfully delicious temptations of the successful adult world. Three packs of cigarettes a day, caffeine and sugar helped him through a harried life which included two divorces. A 1980 physical showed a very high risk of heart disease and a strong indication of an impending heart attack. Tom—an admitted "type-A" personality (hard-driving, compulsive overachiever)—was obviously depressed with the diagnosis. After thinking about it for a few weeks, Tom realized he was dying. Shortly thereafter, he decided to live.

Through friends, he found a professional fitness consultant who started him on a basic program of calisthenics, stretching, racquetball and jogging. At first, he felt glued to the ground as he ran his 20 yards, then walked 100 yards. After two months he was able to run 400 yards, but the arthritis in his knee was so painful he thought he'd have to quit running. He was taking 12 aspirin a day to control inflammation.

Then some friendly competition got his type-A adrenalin flowing. Other lawyers in his firm started to run 10K's. He found that having the race distance as a goal gave the daily workouts a purpose, and he started to make real progress. Gradually the joint pains went away and by fall he was running two miles and making bold and irresponsible statements like, "I'm going to run a marathon in one year," hedged with the attorney's disclaimer, "God willing."

He credits lessons in the Alexander Technique (a method of moving the body with balance and coordination) and Arthur Lydiard's training schedule with helping him to his goal. His weight dropped from 235 to 170 pounds, and to date he's run seven marathons. When I met Tom at our Tahoe Trails running camp, his 2½ years of running had left him addicted and training for his next marathon.

Tom thinks you have to watch out for the supposedly mature over-40 ego and not let it gain control. Rather let progress come as it will and don't force it. He also feels that diet was a big factor in his turn-around. He feels markedly better since giving up sugar and red meat and eating lots of whole grains and vegetables.

Running Every Other Day. Several years ago Dr. George Sheehan changed his "running week" from seven days to three. Many of us figured that the good doctor was losing interest—until, at 62, George ran his fastest marathon ever. George now runs ten miles every other day, and feels that this maintains his condition better than running 5-6 miles *every* day. He adds long runs when he wants to run a marathon.

Jack Foster, who took up running at 33 and ran a 2:11 marathon at age 41, celebrated his 50th birthday in 1982 by running just over 2:20 in the marathon. This was incredible in itself, but even more so when you consider that he has also shifted to a three-day running week.

To maintain his competitive edge, Jack runs accelerations once a week. He runs a 1000-meter course in a nearby park at about a 5-minute mile pace and jogs 600 meters to recover. Usually, he does two of these repetitions, but increases the number when a crucial race approaches. He does two weekly runs: two at 15 miles, one at 20. (He used to run about 10 miles every day.) On Saturdays Jack rides his bicycle over the roads in his New Zealand neighborhood. The former competitive cyclist also finds that younger instincts prevail, making this a hard 3-4 hour cardiovascular workout without putting so much mechanical stress on his joints.

You won't run as fast as Foster (he's the best in the world for his age), but the same principles apply to all runners as they pass the master's checkpoint. Scientists have known for years that the longer runs are better for the system. You might consider running longer three days per week and resting more in between. This allows time for other adult (or childish) pursuits.

Running After 60. Mavis Lindgren grew up in rural Canada and had a series of childhood illnesses. Her parents moved west to British Columbia to be near hospitals which might be necessary to save their little girl's life. In her teens she contracted tuberculosis; after a struggle she defeated it, but it left her weak and sickly for most of her adult life. In her 50s she caught a series of infections which led to a three-year lung infection. Doctors then told her—this was 20 years ago—that this sickness would be her last. How right they were!

Instead of dying, Mavis held on to life for another few years and was barely able to join her husband Carl as he began a walking program. Although doctors had told her to avoid exercise all her life, she started to jog along with Carl; at first she could only go 2-3 yards. She kept at it, and suprisingly, a year later was jogging about a mile.

Now past 75, Mavis not only runs marathons, but is setting records for her age group. She's lively and energetic, and the woman that couldn't resist infection for over 50 years now hasn't had a cold in ten years. Talking to her is an inspiration. In her earlier years she was afraid to talk in front of people. "Now," she says, "it's hard to stop me from lecturing about running and the good health it's brought me."

All in the Family. I've watched a young boy without much obvious talent work his way to become one of the nation's top collegiate distance runners. I've seen housewives become world-class marathoners and old friend Frank Shorter, Olympic champion. But the person who has inspired me the most isn't an Olympian, a world recordholder or a national champion. Instead it's a man who started to run when he was 52.

At that age, Elliott realized that over half of his high school football teammates had died of degenerative diseases. At 200 pounds, he was a heavy fat eater and non-exerciser whose doctor had told him he had to exercise if he was to survive. This former high school all-state football player just *knew* that 30 years of inactivity shouldn't prevent him from running circles around the slow joggers he saw in the park outside his office. Reality, however, was harsh; when he began his exercise program, he couldn't make it to the first telephone pole.

Each day Elliott pushed himself to that next telephone pole. After 4-5 months, he could run a mile or so. Running helped the weight come off and as it melted, running became easier and less painful. At first, walking was rough on his ego, but he found that interspersing the running with walks helped increase his endurance with reduced stress. He had to leave his competitive days behind and learn that running could be fun.

Elliott kept up with his telephone pole course and soon found he could run a 5K, then a 10K. He wasn't interested in form at first, but as it improved he found he could go farther. As he learned to run efficiently he realized that his 8-minute miles felt similar to the 5-minute miles of his college track days. He had made the transition by listening to his body.

Slowly his body remembered how to run. In 1978 he qualified for the Boston Marathon, 45 pounds lighter than when he'd started. Then a few days before his 59th birthday, Elliott ran the Callaway Gardens (Georgia) Marathon in 2:59!

This is an exciting story for me, for Elliott Galloway is my dad. What's inspired me most is the daily discipline and positive health style which has made Dad younger than he was 20 years ago. None of us has firm control over the thin thread of life from which we're suspended. The odds are, however, that my dad will continue to inspire me as he runs into the next century. In the process, *my* son can get to know him, and better know himself.

As we watch the seconds tick off on the great clock of our lifetimes, we can choose either to accept the deterioration that comes from neglect, or take control of our health and lives. There are thousands of stories like my dad's, each a significant act of courage. Each person that's done it now has a psychological edge in the battle of passing years. You don't have to just sit there and let things get worse as you get older. The choice is yours.

APPENDIX

PREDICTING RACE PERFORMANCE

This chart will help you predict a future race performance based upon a past race at another distance. The figures are reprinted from *Computerized Running Training Programs* by James B. Gardner and J. Gerry Purdy (see p. 276) and are based upon what the authors call a *normal performance curve*, which enables one to "... predict a performance at one distance based on a performance at another distance.... It does not predict an exact competitive performance, since there are many tactical, psychological and environmental factors which affect each performance...."

One of the questions that arises in considering such a chart is, "Doesn't each runner tend to excel at a certain distance?" Your best distance may be a 10K and therefore your marathon time shown on the chart will not be up to the "equivalent" time shown on the same line. Or your best race may be a marathon... etc. Gardner and Purdy continue: "It should be noted that a performance in an event that is not the runner's specialty will typically be at a lower performance level than his performances in his own event. Yet the normal performance curve still applies...." They also point out that the athlete must be trained for the event in which he is competing in order to score at a near equal level to his other events.

From a shorter distance to a longer one: If you predict your marathon time from a shorter race and fall short, you have the speed, but not the endurance for the longer race. To remedy this, alter your program so you run longer (and possibly less frequently) and increase the number of repetitions in your speed sessions to 13.

From a longer distance to a shorter one: If your 10K time is not as good as predicted by your marathon or half marathon time, you have the endurance, but not the speed. See Chapter 8, *Speed,* and Chapter 12, *The Advanced Competitive Runner.*

Note: In altering your progam, do so carefully and *gradually.* Be sensitive to how your body feels if you deviate from the 10K or marathon charts.

5Km	8Km	10Km	15Km	20Km	25Km	30Km	Marathon	50Km
12:58	21:23	27:09	41:50	56:50	1:12:05	1:27:32	2:06:18	2:31:43
13:02	21:30	27:17	42:05	57:09	1:12:29	1:28:02	2:07:02	2:32:35
13:06	21:38	27:27	42:20	57:29	1:12:54	1:28:32	2:07:45	2:33:28
13:11	21:45	27:36	42:30	57:49	1:13:19	1:29:30	2:08:30	2:34:21
13:15	21:52	27:45	42:45	58:08	1:13:44	1:29:54	2:09:14	2:35:15
13:20	22:00	27:55	43:00	58:29	1:14:10	1:30:05	2:10:00	2:36:10
13:24	22:08	28:04	43:20	58:29	1:14:36	1:30:36	2:10:46	2:37:05
13:29	22:15	28:14	43:30	59:09	1:15:02	1:31:08	2:11:32	2:38:01

Continued next page

PREDICTING RACE PERFORMANCE

Continued from previous page

5Km	8Km	10Km	15Km	20Km	25Km	30Km	Marathon	50Km
13:33	22:22	28:24	43:45	59:30	1:15:28	1:31:41	2:12:19	2:38:58
13:38	22:30	28:34	44:00	59:51	1:15:55	1:32:13	2:13:06	2:39:55
13:43	22:38	28:44	44:20	1:00:13	1:16:22	1:32:46	2:13:54	2:40:53
13:48	22:45	28:54	44:35	1:00:34	1:16:50	1:33:20	2:14:43	2:41:51
13:52	22:52	29:04	44:50	1:00:56	1:17:18	1:33:54	2:15:32	2:42:51
13:57	23:02	29:15	45:05	1:01:18	1:17:46	1:34:28	2:16:22	2:43:51
14:02	23:10	29:25	45:20	1:01:41	1:18:14	1:35:03	2:17:12	2:44:52
14:07	23:20	29:36	45:40	1:02:03	1:18:43	1:35:38	2:18:04	2:45:53
14:12	23:28	29:47	45:56	1:02:26	1:19:12	1:36:14	2:18:55	2:46:56
14:17	23:35	29:57	46:13	1:02:49	1:19:42	1:36:50	2:19:48	2:47:59
14:23	23:45	30:08	46:30	1:03:13	1:20:12	1:37:26	2:20:41	2:49:03
14:28	23:53	30:20	46:47	1:03:37	1:20:42	1:38:03	2:21:34	2:50:08
14:33	24:00	30:31	47:05	1:04:01	1:21:13	1:38:40	2:22:29	2:51:13
14:39	24:10	30:42	47:23	1:04:25	1:21:44	1:39:28	2:23:24	2:52:20
14:44	24:20	30:54	47:41	1:04:50	1:22:15	1:39:57	2:24:20	2:53:27
14:50	24:30	31:06	47:59	1:05:15	1:22:47	1:40:36	2:25:10	2:54:35
14:55	24:40	31:18	48:18	1:05:40	1:23:20	1:41:15	2:26:13	2:55:44
15:01	24:48	31:30	48:36	1:06:06	1:23:52	1:41:55	2:27:11	2:56:54
15:07	24:58	31:43	48:55	1:06:32	1:24:25	1:42:35	2:28:10	2:58:05
15:12	25:08	31:55	49:15	1:06:58	1:24:59	1:43:16	2:29:10	2:59:17
15:18	25:17	32:07	49:34	1:07:25	1:25:33	1:43:58	2:30:10	3:00:30
15:24	25:27	32:20	49:54	1:07:52	1:26:08	1:44:40	2:31:11	3:01:44
15:30	25:37	32:33	50:14	1:08:19	1:26:42	1:45:22	2:32:13	3:02:59
15:36	25:48	32:46	50:34	1:08:47	1:27:18	1:46:06	2:33:16	3:04:15
15:43	25:58	32:59	50:55	1:09:15	1:27:54	1:46:50	2:34:20	3:05:32
15:49	26:09	33:12	51:16	1:09:44	1:28:30	1:47:34	2:35:25	3:06:50
15:55	26:19	33:26	51:37	1:10:13	1:29:07	1:48:19	2:36:30	3:08:09
16:02	26:30	33:40	51:58	1:10:42	1:29:45	1:49:05	2:37:37	3:09:29
16:08	26:41	33:54	52:20	1:11:12	1:30:23	1:49:51	2:38:44	3:10:51
16:15	26:52	34:08	52:42	1:11:42	1:31:01	1:50:38	2:39:53	3:12:13
16:22	27:03	34:23	53:05	1:12:13	1:31:40	1:51:26	2:41:02	3:13:37
16:28	27:15	34:37	53:27	1:12:44	1:32:20	1:52:14	2:42:13	3:15:02
16:35	27:26	34:52	53:50	1:13:15	1:33:00	1:53:03	2:43:24	3:16:28
16:42	27:38	35:07	54:14	1:13:47	1:33:41	1:53:53	2:44:37	3:17:56
16:49	27:50	35:22	54:37	1:14:20	1:34:22	1:54:43	2:45:50	3:19:25
16:57	28:02	35:37	55:01	1:14:53	1:35:04	1:55:35	2:47:05	3:20:55
17:04	28:14	35:53	55:26	1:15:26	1:35:47	1:56:27	2:48:21	3:22:27
17:11	28:27	36:01	55:51	1:16:00	1:36:30	1:57:19	2:49:38	3:24:00
17:19	28:39	36:25	56:16	1:16:35	1:37:14	1:58:13	2:50:56	3:25:34
17:27	28:52	36:41	56:41	1:17:10	1:37:59	1:59:08	2:52:15	3:27:10
17:34	29:05	36:58	57:07	1:17:45	1:38:44	2:00:03	2:53:36	3:28:48
17:42	29:18	37:14	57:33	1:18:21	1:39:30	2:00:59	2:54:58	3:30:27
17:50	29:32	37:31	58:00	1:18:58	1:40:17	2:01:56	2:56:21	3:32:01
17:58	29:45	37:49	58:27	1:19:35	1:41:04	2:02:54	2:57:45	3:33:49
18:07	29:59	38:06	58:55	1:20:13	1:41:52	2:03:53	2:59:11	3:35:33
18:15	30:13	38:24	59:21	1:20:51	1:42:41	2:04:53	3:00:39	3:37:19
18:23	30:27	38:43	59:51	1:21:30	1:43:31	2:05:53	3:02:07	3:39:06

5Km	8Km	10Km	15Km	20Km	25Km	30Km	Marathon	50Km
18:32	30:42	39:01	1:00:20	1:22:10	1:44:22	2:06:55	3:03:37	3:40:55
18:41	30:56	39:20	1:00:49	1:22:50	1:45:13	2:07:58	3:05:09	3:42:46
18:50	31:11	39:39	1:01:19	1:23:31	1:46:05	2:09:02	3:06:42	3:44:38
18:59	31:26	39:58	1:01:50	1:24:12	1:46:58	2:10:07	3:08:17	3:46:33
19:08	31:42	40:18	1:02:20	1:24:55	1:47:52	2:11:13	3:09:53	3:48:30
19:17	31:57	40:38	1:02:52	1:25:38	1:48:47	2:12:20	3:11:32	3:50:28
19:27	32:13	40:58	1:03:24	1:26:21	1:49:43	2:13:28	3:13:11	3:52:29
19:36	32:30	41:19	1:03:56	1:27:06	1:50:40	2:14:38	3:14:53	3:54:32
19:46	32:46	41:40	1:04:29	1:27:51	1:51:38	2:15:48	3:16:36	3:56:37
19:56	33:03	42:02	1:05:03	1:28:37	1:52:37	2:17:00	3:18:21	3:58:44
20:06	33:20	42:23	1:05:37	1:29:24	1:53:37	2:18:14	3:20:08	4:00:53
20:17	33:37	42:46	1:06:11	1:30:12	1:54:38	2:19:28	3:21:57	4:03:05
20:27	33:55	43:08	1:06:47	1:31:00	1:55:40	2:20:44	3:23:48	4:05:19
20:38	34:13	43:31	1:07:23	1:31:50	1:56:43	2:22:01	3:25:41	4:07:36
20:49	34:31	43:55	1:07:59	1:32:40	1:57:47	2:23:20	3:27:36	4:09:56
21:00	34:50	44:18	1:08:37	1:33:31	1:58:53	2:24:40	3:29:34	4:12:18
21:11	35:08	44:43	1:09:15	1:34:24	2:00:00	2:26:02	3:31:33	4:14:42
21:22	35:28	45:07	1:09:53	1:35:17	2:01:08	2:27:25	3:33:35	4:17:10
21:34	35:47	45:32	1:10:33	1:36:11	2:02:17	2:28:50	3:35:39	4:19:40
21:46	36:07	45:58	1:11:13	1:37:06	2:03:28	2:30:16	3:37:46	4:22:14
21:58	36:28	46:24	1:11:54	1:38:02	2:04:40	2:31:44	3:39:55	4:24:50
22:10	36:48	46:51	1:12:36	1:39:00	2:05:53	2:33:14	3:42:06	4:27:30
22:23	37:10	47:18	1:13:18	1:39:58	2:07:08	2:34:46	3:44:21	4:30:12
22:36	37:31	47:46	1:14:02	1:40:58	2:08:25	2:36:20	3:46:38	4:32:59
22:49	37:53	48:14	1:14:46	1:41:59	2:09:43	2:37:55	3:48:58	4:35:48
23:02	38:16	48:42	1:15:31	1:43:01	2:11:02	2:39:32	3:51:21	4:38:41
23:15	38:38	49:12	1:16:17	1:44:05	2:12:23	2:41:12	3:53:46	4:41:38
23:29	39:02	49:42	1:17:04	1:45:09	2:13:46	2:42:53	3:56:15	4:44:39
23:43	39:26	50:12	1:17:52	1:46:15	2:15:11	2:44:37	3:58:47	4:47:43
23:58	39:50	50:43	1:18:41	1:47:23	2:16:37	2:46:23	4:01:23	4:50:51
24:12	40:15	51:15	1:19:31	1:48:32	2:18:06	2:48:11	4:04:02	4:54:04
24:27	40:40	51:48	1:20:22	1:49:42	2:19:36	2:50:02	4:06:44	4:57:21
24:43	41:06	52:21	1:21:15	1:50:54	2:21:08	2:51:55	4:09:30	5:00:42
24:58	41:32	52:55	1:22:08	1:52:08	2:22:42	2:53:50	4:12:20	5:04:08
25:14	41:59	53:29	1:23:02	1:53:23	2:24:19	2:55:48	4:15:13	5:07:39
25:30	42:27	54:05	1:23:58	1:54:40	2:25:58	2:57:49	4:18:11	5:11:15
25:47	42:55	56:41	1:24:55	1:55:59	2:27:38	2:59:53	4:21:13	5:14:56
26:04	43:24	55:18	1:25:54	1:57:19	2:29:22	3:02:00	4:24:19	5:18:42
26:21	43:53	55:56	1:26:53	1:58:41	2:31:07	3:04:09	4:27:29	5:22:33
26:39	44:23	56:35	1:27:54	2:00:06	2:32:55	3:06:22	4:30:45	5:26:30
26:57	44:54	57:14	1:28:57	2:01:32	2:34:46	3:08:38	4:34:05	5:30:33
27:16	45:26	57:55	1:30:01	2:03:00	2:36:40	3:10:57	4:37:30	5:34:43
27:35	45:58	58:36	1:31:06	2:04:31	2:38:36	3:13:20	4:41:00	5:38:58
27:54	46:31	59:19	1:32:14	2:06:04	2:40:35	3:15:46	4:44:36	5:43:20
28:14	47:05	1:00:02	1:33:23	2:07:39	2:42:38	3:18:16	4:48:17	5:47:49

RACE PACE CHART

This chart will help you plan your race by giving you key check points along the way. During a race it gets increasingly difficult to do the mental arithmetic needed to tell if you're on pace at each mile marker. If you write these check-point times on your hand or arm in indelible ink, it should help you to stay on pace. This chart can also be used after a race to tell your actual pace. *Note:* mi= miles, km= kilometers.

Minutes per mile	Times for the following distances: 2mi	3mi	5km	4mi	5mi	6mi	10km	7mi	8mi	9mi	15km
4:50	9:40	14:30	15:01	19:20	24:10	29:00	30:02	33:50	38:40	43:30	45:03
5:00	10:00	15:00	15:32	20:00	25:00	30:00	31:04	35:00	40:00	45:00	46:36
5:10	10:20	15:30	16:03	20:40	25:50	31:00	32:06	36:10	41:20	46:30	48:09
5:20	10:40	16:00	16:34	21:20	26:40	32:00	33:08	37:20	42:40	48:00	49:42
5:30	11:00	16:30	17:05	22:00	27:30	33:00	34:10	38:30	44:00	49:30	51:15
5:40	11:20	17:00	17:36	22:40	28:20	34:00	35:12	39:40	45:20	51:00	52:48
5:50	11:40	17:30	18:07	23:20	29:10	35:00	36:14	40:50	46:40	52:30	54:21
6:00	12:00	18:00	18:39	24:00	30:00	36:00	37:17	42:00	48:00	54:00	55:56
6:10	12:20	18:30	19:10	24:40	30:50	37:00	38:19	43:10	49:20	55:30	57:29
6:20	12:40	19:00	19:41	25:20	31:40	38:00	39:22	44:20	50:40	57:00	59:03
6:30	13:00	19:30	20:12	26:00	32:30	39:00	40:24	45:30	52:00	58:30	1:00:36
6:40	13:20	20:00	20:43	26:40	33:20	40:00	41:26	46:40	53:20	1:00:00	1:02:09
6:50	13:40	20:30	21:14	27:20	34:10	41:00	42:28	47:50	54:40	1:01:30	1:03:42
7:00	14:00	21:00	21:45	28:00	35:00	42:00	43:30	49:00	56:00	1:03:00	1:05:15
7:10	14:20	21:30	22:16	28:40	35:50	43:00	44:32	50:10	57:20	1:04:30	1:06:48
7:20	14:40	22:00	22:47	29:20	36:40	44:00	45:34	51:20	58:40	1:06:00	1:08:21
7:30	15:00	22:30	23:18	30:00	37:30	45:00	46:36	52:30	60:00	1:07:30	1:09:54
7:40	15:20	23:00	23:49	30:40	38:20	46:00	47:38	53:40	61:20	1:09:00	1:11:27
7:50	15:40	23:30	24:20	31:20	39:10	47:00	48:40	54:50	62:40	1:10:30	1:13:00
8:00	16:00	24:00	24:51	32:00	40:00	48:00	49:42	56:00	1:04:00	1:12:00	1:14:33
8:10	16:20	24:30	25:22	32:40	40:50	49:00	50:44	57:10	1:05:20	1:13:30	1:16:06
8:20	16:40	25:00	25:53	33:20	41:40	50:00	51:46	58:20	1:06:40	1:15:00	1:17:39
8:30	17:00	25:30	26:24	34:00	42:30	51:00	52:48	59:30	1:08:00	1:16:30	1:19:12
8:40	17:20	26:00	26:55	34:40	43:20	52:00	53:50	1:00:40	1:09:20	1:18:00	1:20:45
8:50	17:40	26:30	27:26	35:20	44:10	53:00	54:52	1:01:50	1:10:40	1:19:30	1:22:18
9:00	18:00	27:00	27:57	36:00	45:00	54:00	55:54	1:03:00	1:12:00	1:21:00	1:23:51
9:10	18:20	27:30	28:28	36:40	45:50	55:00	56:56	1:04:10	1:13:20	1:22:30	1:25:24
9:20	18:40	28:00	28:59	37:20	46:40	56:00	57:58	1:05:20	1:14:40	1:24:00	1:26:57
9:30	19:00	28:30	29:30	38:00	47:30	57:00	59:00	1:06:30	1:16:00	1:25:30	1:28:30
9:40	19:20	29:00	30:01	38:40	48:20	58:00	1:00:02	1:07:40	1:17:20	1:27:00	1:30:03
9:50	19:40	29:30	30:32	39:20	49:10	59:00	1:01:04	1:08:50	1:18:40	1:28:30	1:31:36
10:00	20:00	30:00	31:04	40:00	50:00	60:00	1:02:08	1:10:00	1:20:00	1:30:00	1:33:12

Distance equivalents:

1 kilometer = .6214 miles
10K = 6.21 miles
15K = 9.32 miles
20K = 12.43 miles
25K = 15.54 miles
30K = 18.64 miles
Half marathon = 13.1 miles (21.1 km)
Marathon = 26 miles, 385 yards

Minutes per mile	10mi	20km	½ Marathon	15mi	25km	30km	20mi	Marathon	50km
4:50	48:20	1:00:04	1:03:52	1:12:30	1:15:05	1:30:06	1:36:40	2:07:44	2:30:10
5:00	50:00	1:02:08	1:05:33	1:15:00	1:17:40	1:33:12	1:40:00	2:11:06	2:35:20
5:10	51:40	1:04:12	1:07:58	1:17:30	1:20:15	1:36:18	1:43:20	2:15:28	2:40:30
5:20	53:20	1:06:16	1:08:55	1:20:00	1:22:50	1:39:24	1:46:40	2:19:50	2:45:30
5:30	55:00	1:08:20	1:12:06	1:22:30	1:25:25	1:42:30	1:50:00	2:24:12	2:50:50
5:40	56:40	1:10:24	1:14:17	1:25:00	1:28:00	1:45:36	1:53:20	2:28:34	2:56:00
5:50	58:20	1:12:28	1:16:28	1:27:30	1:30:35	1:48:42	1:56:40	2:32:56	3:00:17
6:00	1:00:00	1:14:33	1:18:39	1:30:00	1:33:10	1:51:48	2:00:00	2:37:19	3:06:20
6:10	1:01:40	1:16:38	1:20:50	1:32:30	1:35:45	1:54:54	2:03:20	2:41:41	3:11:30
6:20	1:03:20	1:18:43	1:23:01	1:35:00	1:38:20	1:58:00	2:06:40	2:46:03	3:16:40
6:30	1:05:00	1:20:47	1:25:13	1:37:30	1:40:55	2:01:06	2:10:00	2:50:25	3:21:50
6:40	1:06:40	1:22:52	1:27:23	1:40:00	1:43:30	2:04:12	2:13:20	2:54:47	3:17:00
6:50	1:08:20	1:24:56	1:29:34	1:42:30	1:46:05	2:07:24	2:16:40	2:59:09	3:22:10
7:00	1:10:00	1:27:00	1:31:32	1:45:00	1:48:40	2:10:30	2:20:00	3:03:03	3:37:20
7:10	1:11:40	1:29:04	1:33:57	1:47:30	1:51:15	2:13:36	2:23:20	3:07:55	3:42:30
7:20	1:13:20	1:31:08	1:36:08	1:50:00	1:53:50	2:16:42	2:26:40	3:12:17	3:47:40
7:30	1:15:00	1:33:12	1:38:20	1:52:30	1:56:25	2:19:48	2:30:00	3:16:39	3:52:50
7:40	1:16:40	1:35:16	1:40:30	1:55:00	1:59:00	2:22:54	2:33:20	3:21:01	3:58:00
7:50	1:18:20	1:37:20	1:42:42	1:57:30	2:01:35	2:26:00	2:36:40	3:25:23	4:03:10
8:00	1:20:00	1:39:24	1:44:52	2:00:00	2:04:10	2:29:06	2:40:00	3:29:45	4:08:20
8:10	1:21:40	1:41:28	1:47:02	2:02:30	2:06:45	2:32:12	2:43:20	3:34:07	4:13:30
8:20	1:23:20	1:43:32	1:49:15	2:05:00	2:09:20	2:35:18	2:46:40	3:38:29	4:18:40
8:30	1:25:00	1:45:36	1:51:25	2:07:30	2:11:55	2:38:24	2:50:00	3:42:51	4:23:50
8:40	1:26:40	1:47:40	1:53:07	2:10:00	2:14:30	2:41:30	2:53:20	3:47:13	4:29:00
8:50	1:28:20	1:49:44	1:55:18	2:12:30	2:17:05	2:44:36	2:56:40	3:51:35	4:34:10
9:00	1:30:00	1:51:48	1:58:00	2:15:00	2:19:40	2:47:42	3:00:00	3:56:00	4:39:20
9:10	1:31:40	1:53:52	2:00:11	2:17:30	2:22:15	2:50:48	3:03:20	4:00:19	4:44:30
9:20	1:33:20	1:55:56	2:02:22	2:20:00	2:24:50	2:53:54	3:06:40	4:04:41	4:49:00
9:30	1:35:00	1:58:00	2:04:33	2:22:30	2:27:25	2:57:00	3:10:00	4:09:03	4:54:50
9:40	1:36:40	2:00:04	2:06:44	2:25:00	2:30:00	3:00:06	3:13:20	4:13:25	5:00:00
9:50	1:38:20	2:02:08	2:08:55	2:27:30	2:32:35	3:03:12	3:16:40	4:17:50	5:05:10
10:00	1:40:00	2:04:16	2:11:07	2:30:00	2:35:20	3:06:24	3:20:00	4:22:12	5:10:40

SELECTED READING LIST

The Aerobics Program for Total Well-Being
by Dr. Kenneth Cooper.
M. Evans and Co., Inc.
216 E. 49th St.
New York, NY 10017.
1982, 320 pp., $16.95.

Dr. Cooper wrote the original "how-to" book on increasing exercise and improving cardiovascular conditioning. Now, 10 years after his landmark *Aerobics,* he has put his most recent discoveries and some surprising conclusions together in this book. Cooper's approach is particularly good for those who are satisfied by quantifying things. The program explains exactly how much exercise is needed for various levels of fitness and gives point values for many sports and activities.

The Athlete's Kitchen
by Nancy Clark.
C.B.I.
51 Sleeper St.
Boston, MA 02210.
1981, 322 pp., $9.95.

If you were in the living room you might expect preaching, but from this kitchen you receive suggestions and direction. She addresses real-life problems: how to live with caffeine, fast foods and still give the body what it needs. Particularly interesting are her healthy recipes such as Zero Calorie Dressing, and Quick One-Pot Chicken Dinner.

The Complete Book of Running
by James F. Fixx.
Random House, Inc.
201 E. 50th St.
New York, NY 10022.
1977, 336 pp., $12.95.

Jim is a master writer who spent years researching and producing this book. It reads well, has good practical information, and has helped hundreds of thousands get off their rears and on to the roads. Jim loves running and it comes out in his stories and informative accounts.

Computerized Running Training Programs
by James B. Gardner and J. Gerry Purdy.
Tafnews Press: Book Division of *Track & Field News*
Box 296
Los Altos, CA 94022.
1970, 258 pp., $9.00 postpaid.

I first knew Purdy as a laid-back high school javelin thrower. Now he runs marathons, designs computer systems across the country and finds time for one interesting project after another. His computer tables, published in 1970, have no equal, to my knowledge. You can equate performances, find pace by effort level, and set up interval workouts according to your present level and goals.

The Foot Book
by Harry Hlavac.
World Publications, Inc.
Box 366
Mountain View, CA 94042.
1979, 400 pp., $14.95.

When I get a pain, I limp to the bookshelf and grab this well worn volume. Harry not only helps you find the problem, but tells you what to do about it. The explanations and illustrations tell you what is going on (or is not, unfortunately). He gives you two tests to distinguish "runners knee" from similar ailments. There are step-by-step diagams for wrapping, taping and supporting your foot. I believe that Hlavac is one of the top analysts of running problems anywhere, and this book is a chance to listen to his advice.

Improving Your Running
by Bill Squires.
The Stephen Greene Press
Fessenden Rd.
Brattleboro, VT 05301.
1982, 224 pp., $7.95.

The coach of Boston's best runners explains his ideas. This book is particularly valuable for serious competitive runners.

Jog, Run, Race
by Joe Henderson.
World Publications, Inc.
Box 366
Mountain View, CA 94042.
1977, 224 pp., $5.95

If I listed all of Joe's books that I recommend, there wouldn't be room for many others in this section. Joe is a great running advisor and conveys this beautifully in his books. I particularly like *Jog, Run, Race* because of the blend of practical advice and Joe's philosophy. As you read it, you will see how Joe's gentle leadership, as editor of *Runner's World* magazine, was so influential in the running revolution.

The Marathon Footrace
by David Martin and Roger Gynn.
C.C. Thomas
2600 So. First St.
Springfield, IL 62717.
1979, 504 pp., $35.50.

This is as accurate a resource as one can find on the subject. These two meticulous experts tear marathoning history apart from the ancient Greeks to 1978. There are extensive tables of results and interesting stories. It is reported, for example, that the first Boston marathon did not follow any portion of Paul Revere's famous ride, that it started at Metcalf's mill and was 250 meters shorter than the first Olympic marathon one year earlier. Here are the facts!

Physiology of Fitness
by Brian Sharkey.
Human Kinetics
P.O. Box 5076
Champaign, IL 61820.
1979, 430 pp., $10.95.

Don't let the graphs, definitions and technical sound of the title turn you off. This easy-to-read book will introduce you to the world of physiology thoroughly and pleasantly. If you want to know what goes on inside muscles, etc., you can turn to this book for information with illustrations.

Positive Addiction
by William Glasser.
Harper and Row Publishers, Inc.
10 E. 53 St.
New York, NY 10022.
1976, 176 pp., $12.45.

This book gives the best explanation (I've seen) of why we get so attached to strenuous activity. Glasser gets into the function of the brain and how certain activities allow us to shift to the right hemisphere (the creative, intuitive side). When this part of us is in operation we relax, use more of our mental capacity and feel more "whole."

The Pritikin Promise
by Nathan Pritikin.
Simon and Schuster, Inc.
1230 Ave. of the Americas
New York, NY 10020.
1983, 432 pp., $19.95.

Of the thousands of diets which promise everything, this is about the only one I've seen that will both help you lose weight and become more healthy. I think this will be the diet of the future, for it cuts down on fat and sugar and offers good-tasting combinations of healthy food. There are even tasty junk food alternatives with healthy corn chip recipes and low fat (but high-flavor) dips.

Running Free
by Joan Ullyot.
G.P. Putnam's Sons
200 Madison Ave.
New York, NY 10016.
1982, 288 pp., $5.95.

Joan has become the leading expert in women's running. This book gives inspiration from a former "cream puff" and offers much practical advice about women's running problems. As an M.D., she tackles medical problems with inside information, such as why runners have high levels of HDL cholesterol and why this is beneficial. Joan writes as she speaks, in a direct, conversational style, with good stories and complete information.

Running the Lydiard Way
by Arthur Lydiard and Garth Gilmour.
World Publications, Inc.
Box 366
Mountain View, CA 94042.
1978, 256 pp., $12.95.

Arthur Lydiard put together the training program that is now used by virtually every world-class distance runner in the world. This book shows how these concepts can be used by everyday runners. I learned a great deal from him and this book will bring his ideas and training schedules directly to you.

Runners and Other Ghosts on the Trail
by John L. Parker.
Cedarwinds
Drawer A
Cedar Mountain, NC 28718.
1979, $3.95.

This is a collection of interesting people who will become your friends by the short time it takes you to reach the back cover. He tells us the little things such as Benji Durden playing electronic games on his watch during a serious talk by the top official in organized running, Adrian Paulen. The runner who showed that there was running life after college, Jack Bacheler, is shown leading a new generation of runners in North Carolina. If you like running stories, you'll love this one.

Stay Young at Heart
by John D. Cantwell.
Nelson-Hall Publishers
111 N. Canal St.
Chicago, IL 60606.
1975, 212 pp., $16.95.

John is a cardiologist in Atlanta who is known world-wide for his work. He's also a runner and former college athlete who knows about runners' problems first-hand. This interesting volume tells when you have a heart problem and when you don't. John writes of the wonderful things exercise does for us, but he also shows in case histories how it's not a cure-all. This is an interesting, well written and well researched book.

Stretching
by Bob Anderson.
Shelter Publications, Inc.
P.O. Box 279
Bolinas, CA 94924.
1980, 190 pp., $8.95

I don't know of anyone who gives of himself like Bob does. When he does a clinic, he not only gets down on the floor and makes sure you are doing the stretch correctly, he massages your feet! Bob knows his subject because he lives it and believes in it with a contagious energy. You'll find stretches for every part of the body, illustrated and described. There are several alternatives, stretching routines and key stretches for just about every activity you can dream of (including his first love, running). This is *the* book on stretching.

Ultramarathoning
by Tom Osler and Ed Todd.
World Publications, Inc.
Box 366
Mountain View, CA 94042.
1979, 299 pp., out of print.

These two pioneers passed through road racing in the dark (underground) ages, and marathoning when it was so off-beat that *Track and Field News* magazine didn't cover it. They have some colorful history of professional running in the early part of this century–6-day races, transcontinental foot races, indoor ultramarathons, etc. There is also solid advice about training and racing these monster events from these experienced ultra veterans. From these guys, I learned the concept of taking walking breaks during long runs.

ABOUT THE AUTHOR

JEFF GALLOWAY has been running since 1958. Born in Raleigh, North Carolina, Jeff started running in high school and was state champion in the 2-mile. He attended Wesleyan University and was All-American in cross-country and track. After three years in the U.S. Navy, he attended graduate school at Florida State University and received a master's degree in social studies.

In Florida Jeff started training with Frank Shorter and Jack Bacheler. In preparing for the 1972 Olympics, the three runners spent two months training in the mountains at Vail, Colorado, and all three made the Olympic team that year. Jeff, according to runner/writer Joe Henderson "... should have been an Olympic marathoner, but instead made the team in the 10,000 and then helped friend Jack Bacheler make it in the longer distance."

In 1973 Jeff set an American record in the 10-mile and represented the U.S. as a member of the U.S. National Track and Field team in Europe, Russia and Africa. In the mid-'70s Jeff began to follow a training program that emphasized more rest and less weekly mileage, coupled with a long run every other week and at age 35 ran the Houston-Tenneco Marathon in 2:16.

Jeff Galloway's Competitive Career

High school: 1 mile: 4:28; 2-mile: 9:48
College: 1-mile: 4:12; 2-mile: 9:06; 3-mile: 14:10
Other times: 6-mile: 27:21
10K: 28:29
10-mile: 47:49 (U.S. record, 1973)
Marathon: 2:16:35

He was the first winner of Atlanta's Peachtree Road Race in 1970 and later became a key organizer in the event. He put together the world-class field of Bill Rodgers, Frank Shorter, Don Kardong and Lasse Viren in 1977, which gave international recognition to the race and in three years, entries climbed from 1200 to 12,000. As co-founder of the Avon International Women's Marathon in 1978, he promoted the cause that resulted in a women's Olympic marathon. He is also co-director of the Manufacturers Hanover Corporate Challenge.

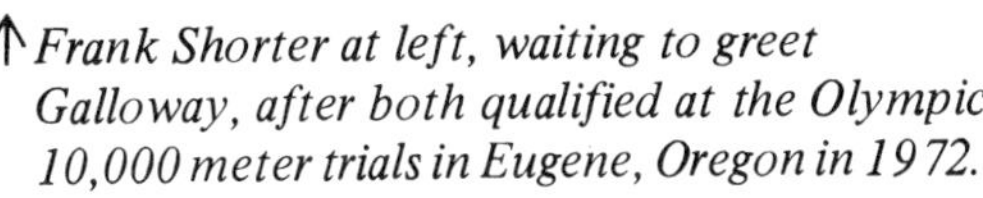
↑ *Frank Shorter at left, waiting to greet Galloway, after both qualified at the Olympic 10,000 meter trials in Eugene, Oregon in 1972.*

← *Shorter and Galloway running the 6-mile in the Florida Relays at Gainesville, Florida in 1973.*

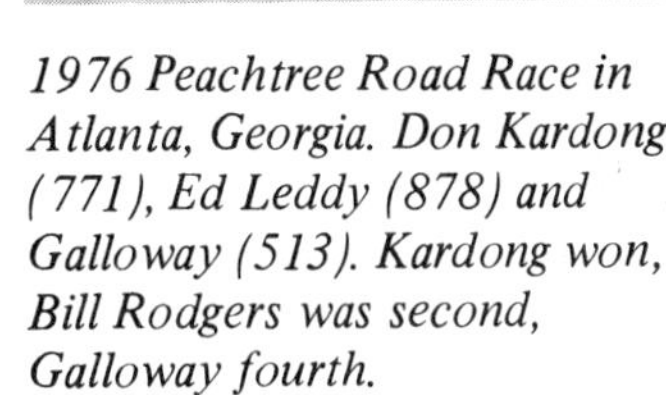
1976 Peachtree Road Race in Atlanta, Georgia. Don Kardong (771), Ed Leddy (878) and Galloway (513). Kardong won, Bill Rodgers was second, Galloway fourth.

In 1973 Galloway founded Phidippides, now a nationally franchised network of 35 running stores. In 1975 he started his first vacation fitness camp and there are now three in operation each summer in California, Colorado and British Columbia. Coaches and lecturers at the camps include Bob Anderson, Covert Bailey, David Costill, Joe Henderson, Harry Hlavac, D.P.M., Arthur Lydiard, John Pagliano, D.P.M., and Joan Ullyot, M.D.

Jeff met his wife Barbara at a track meet in Florida—Barbara was on the Florida State women's track team. They were married in 1976. Barbara runs practically every day and has competed in over 30 marathons. Her best 10K time is 41:50 and marathon time, 3:18.

Jeff now conducts over 60 running clinics a year and makes 80-100 apppearances at running stores, YMCAs, and fitness clubs. For years he has listened to the problems of everyday runners and tried to work out creative solutions to their varying problems—particularly those that have a limited amount of time to train.

Jeff and Barbara live with their sons Brennan and Westin in Atlanta, Georgia.

REFERENCES

Drawings by Edna Indritz, pp. 41, 46, 49, 211, 212, 216, 219, 222.

The following books were used as reference:

Benjamin, Ben E., Ph.D. *Listen to Your Pain*. Penguin Books, 1984.

Edwards, Linden F. *Concise Anatomy.* Blakiston Publications, 1950.

Figge, Frank H.J., ed. *Sobotta-Figge Atlas of Human Anatomy.* Hafner, 1968.

Grant, J.C. Boileau. *An Atlas of Anatomy.* 2nd ed. Williams and Wilkins, 1947.

Grollman, Sigmund. *The Human Body.* Macmillan Publishing Co., Inc., 1964.

Hlavac, Harry F., D.P.M. *The Foot Book.* World Publications, 1977.

Kessel, Richard G., and Randy H. Kardon. *Tissues and Organs: A Text-Atlas of Scanning Electron Microscopy.* W.H. Freeman & Co., 1979.

Maximow, Alexander, and William Bloom. *A Textbook of Histology.* 7th ed. W.B. Saunders Company, 1957.

McMinn, R.M.H. and R.T. Hutchings. *Color Atlas of Human Anatomy.* Year Book Medical Publishers, 1977.

Netter, Frank. *The Ciba Collection of Medical Illustrations.* V.5: Heart, 1969.

Pernkopf, Eduard. *Atlas of Topographical and Applied Human Anatomy.* Urband and Schwarzenburg (Baltimore-Munich) and W.B. Saunders Co., Ltd., 1980.

Toldt, Carl. *An Atlas of Human Anatomy for Students and Physicians.* Macmillan Publishing Co., Inc., 1928.

Chapter 4–Physiology

Page 45, chart. Subjects were given a two-hour treadmill test at 65% maximum oxygen uptake (the runner's ability to consume oxygen), during which the respiratory exchange of oxygen and carbon dioxide were measured. From this measurement the scientists estimated the amounts of fats and carbohydrates burned. *A Scientific Approach to Distance Running* by David L. Costill. Track & Field News, Los Altos, California, 1979.

Chapter 7–Mileage Programs

Page 73, chart. This is based on several studies of maximum oxygen uptake (the ability of the body and particularly the exercising muscles to utilize oxygen) as related to the number of training days per week. *Exercise in Health and Disease* by Michael L. Pollock, Ph.D., Jack H. Wilmore, Ph.D. and Samuel M. Fox III, M.D. W.B. Saunders Company, 1984.

Chapters 20, 21, 22–Nutrition, Fuel and Running Off Fat.

Brody, Jane. *Jane Brody's Nutrition Book.* W.W. Norton & Company, 1981.

Pritikin, Nathan. *The Pritikin Promise.* Simon and Schuster, 1983.

Smith, Nathan J., M.D. *Food for Sport.* Bull Publishing Company, 1976.

Chapters 23, 24–Shoe Secrets* and *Shoe Shopping

Cavanagh, Peter R., Ph.D. *The Running Shoe Book.* Anderson World, Inc., 1980.

Hlavac, Harry F., D.P.M. *The Foot Book.* World Publications, 1977.

INDEX

Achilles, 216
Achilles tendon injuries, 216-18, 259
addiction, 33, 35, 143-44, 194, 199
Adidas, 248
aerobics, 19
  definition, 42
  during pregnancy, 191
  training, 55, 82
Aerobics Program for Total Well-Being, The, 19
Aerobics Research Institute, 33
Alexander Technique, 266
altitude, 74-75
amino acids, 231
anaerobic running
  definition, 43
  during pregnancy, 191, 192
Anderson, Bob, 162
animal fats, 232
ankle efficiency, 151
anterior tibialis muscle, 222
armswing, 150
arthroscopy, 210
Ashenfelter, Horace, 20
aspirin, 202, 218
Athens, 14
Athlete's Kitchen, The, 231
Avon 15K, 89

Bacheler, Jack, 101
back, lower, injuries, 160
Bailey, Covert, 242
base training, 55, 80, 82, 108, 123
Bay to Breakers, 20, 26
"bear," the, 93
Benjamin, Ben E., 201
beta endorphin hormones, 33
blood, 33, 43, 233
  chemistry, 47
  flow, 48, 55
boredom
  creative distractions, 104
  fighting during runs, 88
Boston Marathon, 20, 21, 51, 95, 179, 236, 268
Bowerman, Bill, 16, 21, 67, 71, 249
Boyer, Steve, 74
Braxton-Hicks contractions, 192
breathing, 152
Brown, Doug, 177
Burfoot, Amby, 16, 21
burnout, 143-44
bursitis, 220

Caesarean mothers, 195
caffeine, 239, 244
calcaneus, 217, 220
calcium, 201, 234
carbohydrates, 43, 44, 47, 232-33
  complex, 245
  -loading, 233, 236-37, 239
cars, 115
Charleston Distance Race, 237
children running, 262-63
chondromalacia, 214
CHP Rule, 152-53
Cimons, Marlene, 51
Clark, Nancy, 231
Clark, Rae, 75
Clarke, Ron, 20, 105
clothes, 76-78, 106, 115
cold weather, 76-77
compartment syndrome, 224
competition, 26, 28, 262-63
Complete Book of Natural Foods, The, 231
Computerized Running Training Programs, 271
Conklin, Tom, 266
Cooper, Dr. Kenneth, 16, 21
Corporate Challenge, 26
cortisone injections, 218
cramping, 122
cross-country skiing, 202, 204
cycling, 202, 203-04, 226

Daily runs, 55, 56
Dakar, 10
Dale, Dr. Edwin, 185-87, 189
Davis, Bill, 75
De Castella, Rob, 47
dehydration, 65, 76, 242
  and cooling, 102-03
  as cause of injury, 207
  during marathon, 237
  during pregnancy, 194
Dellenger, Bill, 18
di-saccharides, 43
Dixon, Rod, 103
dogs, 115
Durden, Benji, 228

Electrolytes, 78, 237
endurance, 83, 135
  improving for the marathon, 121
  muscles, 243
ERG, 237, 238
Essential Exercises For the Child-Bearing Year, 194
estrogen, 186
exercises and drills
  Bent-Knee Curl-ups, 193
  Bent Knee Extension, 169
  Bounding, 175
  Chair Hurdle, 169
  Hill Springs, 174
  "Kegel" exercises, 193
  Kick Outs, 173
  "Kicking Skip," 173
  Plow, 169
  postpartum exercise program, 195
  Quick Knee Lifters, 172
  Running Tall, 175

Fartlek, 58, 73
  advanced, 136
  definition, 84
  variations, 84
  vs. interval training, 86, 91
fat (in diet), 43-44, 47, 231-32, 237
fatty acids, 232, 239
Fit or Fat? 242
femur, 212
Fleming, Vinny, 236
floppy-footed runners, 213, 217, 251-52
fluids, 237
Foot Book, The, 201
form work, 56, 64, 108, 123, 146-157
  hill running form, 155-56
Foster, Jack, 72, 267
  "Foster's Rule," 73, 122
Frederick, Dr. E.C., 35, 162, 260
Furstenberg, Karl, 147

Galloway, Barbara, 182-195
Galloway, Elliott, 268-69
Gammoudi, Mohamed, 20, 105
Gardner, James B., 271
glycogen, 43, 44, 103, 236-37
goals
  after age 40, 265
  defining, 52
  for advanced competitor, 135

for kids, 262
for marathon, 121
40-minute goal, 243
planning for, 62
setting race goals, 26, 53, 55, 56,
setting realistic, 82
84, 94, 98
Greeks, ancient, 14
Gregory, Dick, 177, 236

Halberg, Murray, 17
Harris, Dr. Waldo, 18
heart
calculating maximum heart rate, 33-34
strengthening, 33, 55
heart disease, 19
factor in airplane crashes, 19
history of, 33
rate of, 19
heel injuries, 219-221, 259
Henderson, Joe, 88
high blood pressure, 33
Hillary, Sir Edmund, 35
hill training, 57, 80, 82, 108, 123, 170
as alternative to interval workouts, 91
for advanced runners, 135
hills
during races, 95
running form for, 155-56
Hlavac, Harry D.P.M., 201, 255
Hollister, Geoff, 71, 249
Honolulu Marathon, 162
hot weather, 77-78, 94-95, 101
adjusting race pace for, 95, 102
hurting
during race, 103-04
see also injuries
hypothalamus, 186

Ice for injuries, 201, 214, 218, 220, 224
iliotibial band, 212, 213
inflammation, 201, 202, 214, 217, 219, 220-21, 223-25
injuries, 27, 69, 199-225
Achilles tendon, 216-18, 259
alternative exercises during, 202-04
analyzing, 207
and shoe choice, 259
common mistakes that lead to, 39, 118-19, 134
defining, 199-200
early warning signs, 144, 157, 200, 219
for advanced competitors, 134
guidelines for treating, 200-02
healing process, 205-06
ice, use of, 201, 214, 218, 220, 224
heel, 159, 219-221
knee, 160, 166, 211-15, 259
loss of conditioning due to, 205
lower back, 160
most frequent causes of speed injuries, 90
remaining injury-free, 68, 210, 215
shin, 160, 167, 222, 259
interval training, 58, 73
advanced, 137
basic principles, 86-87
definition, 86
iron, 234
Ironman Triathlon, 47, 226

James, Stan, 249
Jane Brody's Nutrition Book, 232
jogging, 17, 35
as warmup for races, 100, 107
in America, 17
running slow to run fast, 52
the jogger, 25
to recover, 87

Kelley, John J., 20
"kick," the, 141-43
kids running, 262-63
knee injuries, 160, 166, 211-15, 259
Knight, Phillip (Buck), 249

Lactic acid, 44, 70-71, 104
Laurel's Kitchen, 231
Leerman, Monica, 89
Lindgren, Jerry, 105
Lindgren, Mavis, 267
Listen To Your Pain, 201
liver, 234
long run, the, 51, 119-120
"crashing" during, 51
how long?, 55
increasing, 83
individual response to, 72
preparing for, 120
program, 119
Los Angeles Times, 51
lungs, 33, 48-49
exposure during cold weather, 76
Lydiard, Arthur, 16-17, 21, 51-52, 57, 148, 170, 173, 255, 266

Magee, Barry, 17
marathon
training charts, 124-131
training for, 51, 84, 116-131
recovery from, 122
Maternal and Child Health Center, 192
menstruation, effect of
irregularities, 186, 189
normalizing, 186
metabolism, 241
mileage
and shoes, 258
as cause of injuries, 213, 223
cutting, 42, 52
daily mileage program, 71-73, 119
during pregnancy, 191
increases, 27, 39, 246
weekly mileage program, 74-76
Minsk, Russia, 10
mitochondria, 40, 41, 70, 71, 104
Molina, Scott, 47
mono-saccharides, 43
"monster," the, 177
Moore, Kenny, 20, 67, 72, 249
Morocco, 10
Mt. Everest, 35
Mt. Hood 40-miler, 74
muscle, 47, 48
muscle compression syndrome, 224
muscles, 40, 43, 45
cell changes, 74, 77
fast/slow twitch, 48, 142, 244
fat among, 242
lactic acid and, 93
performance, 104
relaxing before race, 106
myofibrils, 40
myositis, 224

New York City Marathon, 75, 103
Nike, 11, 249
Noble, Elizabeth, 192
Norgay, Tensing, 35
nutrition
after age 40, 265

caffeine, 239, 244
calcium, 201, 234
carbohydrates, 232-33, 239, 245
eating and drinking before the race, 100, 238-39
fat, 231-32, 241
food-into-energy cycle, 43, 47
protein, 230, 238
reducing calories, 245-46
salt, 233
to prevent osteoporosis, 187
vegetarianism, 229-230, 231
vitamins and minerals, 234-35
vitamin C supplements, 77, 201, 239
water, 233
when to eat, 245

Olympics, the, 14, 16, 17, 20, 21, 67, 101, 105, 140, 177, 241
Oregon, University of, 17, 67
orthopedists, 200, 209-210, 223
osteoporosis, 187
oxygen, 33, 43, 77, 103

Pace
definition, 88
during long runs, 120, 121
easy day pacing, 90
for races, 93-95, 102, 237
"pace-wise," 85
patella, 212
Peachtree Road Race, 26
peaking
definition, 98
formulas, 99
for veteran, 139
principles, 99
periosteum, 223, 225
periostitis, 225
Perkins, John, 75
Phidippides, 11, 14
planning, 29, 32, 51-53, 62
plantar fascia injuries, 219 21
plantar fasciitis, 168, 219, 259
plateaus, 82, 139
Plica syndrome, 214
podiatrists, 200, 209-210
posterior tibialis muscle, 222
posture, 149, 155
Prefontaine, Steve, 140
pregnancy
contractions while running, 192
getting back in shape after, 193-95
nursing, 195
precautionary measures, 190-93
running during, 188-193
Pritikin diet, 47, 231
Pritikin, Nathan, 231, 232, 246
Pritikin Permanent Weight-Loss Manual, The, 246
Pritikin Program for Diet and Exercise, 246
Pritikin Promise, The, 231
problem-solving, 179-81
pronation, 213, 214, 215, 219, 251-252, 254
protein, 230, 238
pulse rate, 33, 34, 65, 134, 144
Purdy, J. Gerry, 271

Race pace chart, 274-75
race performance, predicting, 271-73
race walking, 202, 204
racing
after race, 107
art of, 97-114
before race, 100, 106-07
eating and drinking before, 100
final mile, 142-43
for kids, 262
need for fluids during, 237, 238-39
over 40, 263-69
strategy for advanced competitor, 140
reactive hyperemia, 42
repetitions, 86, 88, 137
reproduction
and men, 76
effect of running on fertility, 186, 188
rest, 27, 32, 39
after age 40, 265
after races, 72-73, 107, 122
during, after pregnancy, 190-93
easy day rule, 72, 135
easy week rule, 39, 74, 119, 133
intervals during speedwork, 58, 87
strategic rest, 52, 68-69
stress and rest, 39, 40, 42, 70, 134
with injuries, 200, 224
rigid-footed runners, 213, 217, 251-52
Road Runners Club of America, 264
Rodgers, Bill, 16, 21, 228
Rohé, Fred, 231
rowing, 202, 204
"runner's knee," 213
Runner's World, 89
Running Body, The, 35
Running Experience, The, 18
Running Free, 188, 193
running log, 61-65
Ryun, Jim, 141, 177

Salazar, Alberto, 103
salt, 233
sarcolemma, 40
scar tissue, 205
Schul, Bob, 20
Schuster, Dr. Richard, 200
Scott, Dave, 47
selenium, 234
set point, 241
Sheehan, Dr. George, 72, 266-67
shin injuries, 160, 167, 222-25, 259
shin splints, 222
shoes, 248-61
alternating, 261
arch supports in, 215, 220-21
as cause of injury, 210
barefoot running, 138-39
board last, 249
breaking in, 259
cushions in, 223, 254
fit, 253
lacing, 255
low-heeled, 217
shapes, 253
shopping for, 257-261
slip last, 249
smell, 260
to correct rigid or floppy feet, 215
Shorter, Frank, 21, 101, 141, 268
sickness, 68-69
skiing, 19
slump, 68-69
Smith, Geoff, 103
Snell, Peter, 17, 170
Sparta, 14
speedwork, 58-59, 81-91, 108, 123, 136
alternatives to, 89
as cause of injury, 90
history of, 84
rest after speed, 73
sprinting, 90
steeplechase, 20, 71
steroids, 218, 221

strengthening
 ankles, 173
 butt muscles, 172
 feet, 168, 174
 hip flexors, 170, 172, 174
 perineal muscles, 193
 quadriceps, 166, 170, 172, 175, 215
 shin muscles, 167, 170, 172
 stomach, 168
stress fracture, 221, 223
stretching, 159-165
 after injury, 224
 calf and Achilles, 164
 hamstrings, 164-65
 lower back, 165
stride length, 151
sugars, 43
 glucose as fuel, 103
supination, 251
surgery, 220, 221
sweat, 77
swimming
 as substitute for running, 192, 203
 running in swimming pool, 203

Tarahumara Indians, 14
tendonitis, 214, 225
 patella, 214
10K
 peaking formula for, 99
 training charts, 109-114
 training for, 75, 83-84
Thomas, Frank, 75
tibia, 212, 222-23
Tinley, Scott, 47
Tinsley, Harold, 264
training, 27, 38-45, 52-53
 advanced program, 135-39
 pyramid, 53-59, 64, 83-84
triathlon training, 226
triglycerides, 239
"twilight zone," the, 104

Uhrhammer, Jerry, 18
Ullyot, Joan, M.D., 188, 193
University of California
 Medical School, 187

Vacation Fitness Camps, 11,
 170, 266
vegetarianism, 229-230, 231
Viren, Lasse, 140
vitamin supplements, 77, 201,
 234, 239
vitamins and minerals,
 234-35

Walking
 after pregnancy, 193
 during interval training, 86-88
 during marathon training, 119-120
 during pregnancy, 190, 191, 192,
 193, 195
"wall," the, 44, 116-18, 140
warming down, 87, 90
warming up, 87, 90
 for race, 100-01, 106-07
wastes, 48, 55, 71, 77, 103
water
 during races, 106, 122
 for nutrition, 232, 233-34, 237,
 in the heat, 78, 103, 237
 239
weight
 loss, 16, 17, 32, 184-85, 242
 maintenance, 134
 monitoring, 65
weight training, 141, 244
Wesleyan University, 147
Western States 100, 75
will power, 180-81
women's running
 body fat, 184-85, 195
 breast support, 187, 195
 female organs, 187-88
 feminine image, 187
 muscles, 184
 percentage of water in body, 233
 stress incontinence, 188, 193
 structural differences in, 184
Wottle, Dave, 177

Zinc, 234

CREDITS

Editor
Lloyd Kahn, Jr.

Art Director
David Wills

Contributing Editor
Gary T. Moran, Ph.D.

Consulting Editor
Charlotte Leon Mayerson

Professional Consultants
Harry Hlavac, D.P.M. (Injuries)
Paul T. Hohe, M.D. (Women's Running)
Elizabeth Noble, R.P.T. (Women's Running)
Joan Lamb Ullyot, M.D. (Women's Running)

Copyediting
David Cole
Lesley Creed
Jeff Creque
Marianne Orina
Daniel Rogoff

Typesetting
Trudy Renggli
Barrie Stebbings

Assistant to the Art Director
Patricia Maloney

Production Art & Pasteup
Patricia Maloney
Susan Sanders
Belinda Zell

Proofreading
Marianne Orina

Photostats
Marinstat, Mill Valley, Calif.

Photo Printing
General Graphic Services,
San Francisco, Calif.

Illustrations

Drawings by Richard Golueke appear on pages 14-15, 22, 23, 34, 37, 66-67, 79, 80-81, 92, 96, 132, 145, 146-47, 155, 158, 163, 164, 165, 167, 168-69, 171-75, 183, 197, 198, 208, 227-29, 238, 240, 247, 256, 265, 269, 270.

Drawings by Edna Indritz appear on pages 41, 46, 49, 211, 212, 216, 219, 222.

Drawings by David Wills appear on pages 5, 50, 54, 69, 76, 77, 105, 116-17, 151, 248-49, 262-63.

Photographs used as reference for drawings were taken by:

Tony Duffy, Duomo, p. 155.

Tracey Frankel, p. 238.

Lloyd Kahn, Jr., pp. 13, 22, 151, 158, 164, 171-75, 198, 227-29.

David Madison, p. 79.

Jane Sobel, Janeart Ltd., p. 197.

Dave Stock, pp. 37, 96, 146-47, 176, 240.

Steven E. Sutton, Duomo, pp. 80-81.

Presse Sports, p. 132.

David Wills, pp. 14-15, 34, 66-7, 69, 92, 116-17, 145, 163, 165, 167, 168-69, 250, 256.

Belinda Zell, pp. 262-63.

We are grateful to Rich O'Brien of *The Runner* and Andrea Chomyn of *Runner's World* for helping us locate some of the above photographers.

Models for stretching, exercise & drill instructions:
Gary Baxell
Kelly Blackwell
Greg Sheats

Typesetting and Printing

Type for body of book was set on an IBM Electronic Selectric Composer run by a Pilara 2000 Word Processor.

Type face for text is Press Roman.

Headline type is Letraset L.C.D.; sub-heads are Goudy Bold Italic.

Type for 10K and marathon training programs and racing charts set by Barlow Printing, Petaluma, Calif.

Book paper is 60 lb. Bookbinders Matte.

Printed by the Murray Printing Company, Westford, Mass.

Acknowledgements

Thanks to the following who, in one way or another, helped make this book possible:

Bob & Jean Anderson/Don Baxter, M.D./
Debbie Beckman/Rich Benyo/David Berta/
Elaine Bowen/Richard Calmes/
John Cantwell, M.D./Tom Conklin/
David L. Costill, Ph.D./Dennis Curley/
Ed Fox/E.C. Frederick, Ph.D./
Barbara Worral Galloway/Patty Harris/
Kim Heinzerling/Joe Henderson/
Jack Howell/Sarah Hunt/Gary Langley/
Arthur Lydiard/Dan Manza/
Allan McDonald, M.D./
Irving Miller, D.P.M./
Stanley Newell, D.P.M./Donna Orford/
John Pagliano, D.P.M./
Michael L. Pollock, Ph.D./Gerry Purdy/
Richard Quiñones/Laura Riley/
Kirk Rosenbach/Greg Sheats/
George Sheehan, M.D./Tracy Stone/
Dianne Taylor/Don Weiner.